Baklava to Tarte Tatin

Recipe Making and Travel Photographs: Bernard Laurance
www.cookingwithbernard.com
Edited by Sébastien Cauchon
Recipe Photography: Amélie Roche
Food Styling: Audrey Cosson

English-language edition
Editorial Director: Kate Mascaro
Editor: Helen Adedotun
Translated from the French by Carmella Abramowitz Moreau
Design: Delphine Delastre
Copyediting: Luisa Weiss
Layout Adaptation and Typesetting: Thierry Renard
Proofreading: Nicole Foster
Indexing: Cambridge Publishing Management Ltd
Color Separation: IGS-CP, L'Isle d'Espagnac, France
Printed in China by Toppan Leefung

Originally published in French as *Les Desserts de Bernard:*
Mon tour du monde en plus de 110 recettes
© Flammarion, S.A., Paris, 2014

English-language edition
© Flammarion, S.A., Paris, 2015

editions.flammarion.com

15 16 17   3 2 1

ISBN: 978-2-08-020215-4

Dépôt légal: 09/2015

Bernard Laurance

Baklava to Tarte Tatin

A World Tour in 110 Dessert Recipes

Recipe photography by Amélie Roche

Flammarion

Contents

North Africa and the Middle East

Asia and Oceania

Introduction

Recipe Magic

Since my very early childhood, I've been fascinated by the question of culinary proportions and how seemingly tiny changes in a recipe can considerably modify the results. As a young boy, I would pretend to be a sorcerer. I would combine the most unlikely ingredients in order to concoct potions that would give me magical powers. As I grew up, I instinctively understood that with the right quantities and the appropriate techniques, one could achieve extraordinary results. I still find the culinary arts downright bewitching today.

When it comes to cooking, I've always been somewhat obsessive, particularly in my quests for The Ultimate Recipe; a generations-old specialty with infinite variations; a recipe said to be a closely guarded secret; a recipe created by a pastry chef who has accomplished the feat of combining ingredients to create a must-eat, must-make cake; a recipe stored in a bank safe that everyone would like to get their hands on. I simply can't help myself: I have to take off in pursuit of the elusive key elements. No sooner have I enjoyed a good dish or dessert, one that's delicious or has a story behind it—during my travels, at a restaurant, or with friends—than I rush to my kitchen-cum-laboratory to commence my experiments. Being told that a recipe cannot be made at home only strengthens my determination.

Like a mad scientist, I focus on testing and combining ingredients to the exclusion of all else. I add a pinch of this and a dash of that; I modify cooking times; I try baking, grilling, steaming. I taste. And taste again. "Stubborn as a mule" may be a cliché, but it's one that describes me well. This idiosyncratic, totally empirical way of working means that along the way, there are innumerable—and only too predictable—bungles. There's a good deal of exasperation too. But when the long-awaited moment comes, the moment when my eyes and palate confirm that the object of my experiments and the hoped-for result are one—well, that's worth all the gold in the world. I believe that piercing the enigmas of the recipes we fall in love with is the holy grail of all amateur and professional cooks.

I was about seven years old when I began testing the recipes my mother taught me: cakes, cut-out cookies, even savory dishes like artichoke bottoms filled with poached eggs and smoked salmon. At about thirteen, I developed a fascination for fresh yeast and all its possibilities. Intrigued by its mysterious smell and how it transforms dough, I began trying to reproduce the yeasted recipes I liked best. With my Breton roots, I began, perhaps unsurprisingly, with *kouign amann* (yeasted Breton butter cake), a sugary, buttery pastry that comes from the Finistère department of Brittany, on the western coast of France, where my family used to holiday. At the time, there were practically no recipes available for the general public that explained the folding techniques required for *kouign amann*— or none that I managed to find. The cake was as much of a mystery as it was a joy to eat. I date my obsession for accuracy and precision in recipes to that time.

I set to work to make *kouign amann*. Every week over a period of several months, I tested a different recipe, starting repeatedly from scratch. I tried all possible techniques and modified the proportions of the ingredients until I produced a cake that looked and tasted like those sold in bakeries— the ones I had long been fantasizing about (a habit I still have). This is the very recipe that I share with you in this book (see page 77).

I applied the very same method to all the experiments I subsequently undertook. I baked, and baked again, until the result was exactly what I was seeking. A recipe remains secret only as long as its DNA has not been deciphered. You need the proportions of the ingredients and the method to put them together. Once you have these two elements, you can make anything at home. It's something of a treasure hunt, involving tracking down clues, understanding the underlying rationale, and mastering the skills and the sleights of hand. Apply all these fundamentals and you can clone the cake you've admired in a pastry shop window or tasted at a tea salon. My childhood fascination now drives me to find and decode the components of all the dishes I've loved, even if this involves an inordinate amount of time, tiring myself out, and, occasionally, setting aside certain recipes only to return to them later with a fresh approach.

During my teenage years, I carefully kept notes in a small blue binder of all the recipes I loved. My dream was to publish a cookbook one day. Since I'd never wanted to open a restaurant—the profession of restaurateur is one to be admired, but very tough—I was never forced to give up my dream, even when I began working. Late in 2009, when I was reassessing the path my career was taking, I realized it was time for my dream to become reality. I began a blog in which I shared my culinary discoveries and in the process tidied up my recipes. It didn't take long for me to realize how much pleasure I derived from sharing my craft with others and I soon started giving cooking classes. Carried away by this all-consuming passion and the desire to recreate everything I tasted in my tiny kitchen, and encouraged by the warm response to my blog, I now had an excuse to cook obsessively and non-stop.

For me and my readers, I have reinvented myself as a recipe sleuth. As soon as I taste a dish, I feel compelled to identify its ingredients. It makes no difference whether it is savory or sweet, but it's even more important for sweet dishes, where the outcome is a matter of proportions that cannot be modified once it's in the oven. Just think what you can do with flour, sugar, butter, and eggs—the simplest of ingredients. It's almost magical: modify the quantities and the way they are put together and the possibilities are endless. I like to make the comparison with the notes of a piano, whose harmonies are infinite.

Hunting down a magic formula is fascinating, but it can also be exasperating at times. I spent more than six months and made over thirty-five attempts in my quest to achieve a custard cream filling for the Portuguese *pastéis de nata*. And I'll spare you my first disastrous tries to make Spanish *turrón de Alicante*. But my guiding principle remains that with the staples in one's kitchen, just about anything can be made at home. All you need to know is how to combine them.

So, my pastime is hunting out recipes that are said to be secret and then, once I've gathered as many clues as possible, shutting myself in my kitchen. When I begin decoding, I do nothing else. I start again as many times as necessary; the recipe occupies my mind day and night as I work on the solution. My kitchen is filled with bowls and notes on the different combinations already attempted. I rarely move on to the next recipe before solving the mystery at hand.

For years, I have been traveling the world. Everywhere I go, I return with samples of what I enjoyed tasting there. I'm fascinated not only by dishes, but also by the techniques specific to each part of the world. I have great admiration for culinary knowledge transmitted over the generations and try to pass it on with due respect for age-old traditions.

After applying my method for working out the intricacies of recipes to those I've brought back from afar, I found myself with a collection from around the world. I've published some on my blog, but saved many for the book you are now holding.

In this book, I give you a careful selection of my favorite recipes collected over the years, recipes tried and tested to come as close as possible to the originals I ate, and recipes in accordance with traditional methods of preparation. From the *canelés* of Bordeaux to Turkish delight, from enormous New York cookies to Japanese *daifuku mochi*, I have endeavored to make each one as authentic as possible. I can't in all honesty tell you that they're all easy, but there are no insurmountable difficulties and the recipes can be trusted.

Today, my dream has come true. My book has been written and published. I opted to focus on desserts here because it was through them that I acquired my love of cooking; it is here that the slightest variations have the greatest effect. So stock up your kitchen cupboards and your refrigerator, don't neglect your friends and family (I've sometimes given up all social life and I don't recommend you take a leaf from my book in this respect), and put your trust in me. With this collection of recipes explained in detail and illustrated by mouthwatering photos, you'll be able to take a deliciously sweet trip around the world without having to leave your kitchen.

Europe

Flourless Almond Cake
Amandier

In certain regions of France, this cake is called *gâteau de Visan*, from the name of the Provençal village where it originated, or *suprême des volcans* (marvel of the volcanoes). With its delicious flavor of almonds and butter, it is irresistible and entirely flourless to boot. I use a combination of confectioners' sugar and granulated sugar to achieve the texture I like best. The confectioners' sugar gives the top crust a sheen, while the granulated sugar adds a lovely caramel color to the cake as it bakes. The recipe below, with vanilla extract, is the one I make most often at home. Feel free to vary the recipe with lemon or lime zest in place of the vanilla or even a tablespoon of orange flower water instead. I like to eat thin slices of this cake with a cup of tea in the afternoon.

Makes one 6-inch (15-cm) cake
Preparation time: 15 minutes
Cooking time: 35 minutes

INGREDIENTS
1 cup plus 3 tablespoons (3 ½ oz./100 g) ground almonds (almond flour), sifted
1 pinch salt
⅓ cup (2 oz./50 g) confectioners' sugar
¼ cup (2 oz./50 g) granulated sugar
2 ¾ tablespoons (1 ½ oz./40–45 g) beaten egg
4 tablespoons (2 oz./60 g) unsalted butter, melted and cooled
½ teaspoon vanilla extract

Preheat the oven to 320°F (160°C). Line the base of the cake pan with a disc of parchment paper and grease the sides.

In a large mixing bowl, combine the ground almonds, salt, confectioners' sugar, and granulated sugar.

Add the beaten egg, melted butter, and vanilla extract to the dry ingredients. Mix until smooth. Scrape the batter into the prepared cake pan and smooth the top.

Bake for 35 minutes, until the cake is golden brown and a cake tester inserted into the center comes out clean.

Carefully turn the cake out of the pan and allow to cool completely on a rack.

Wrap in plastic wrap until serving. The almond cake will keep in an airtight container, or well wrapped in plastic wrap, for several days, though it's unlikely that anyone will resist for that long.

Praline, Pistachio, and Hazelnut Pastes

Here are three pastry basics that will allow you to make any number of recipes, such as Paris-Brest (see page 25), Sesame Nougatines (see page 228), or Strawberry-Pistachio Layer Cake (see page 144). With a sturdy stand mixer, the pastes are easy to make. They can be stored in a jar at room temperature for a couple months.

For **praline paste**, place the sugar, ground vanilla, and water in a large heavy saucepan over medium-high heat. Bring to a boil. When the syrup begins to thicken, stir in all the nuts with a wooden spoon. After a while, the syrup will bubble and eventually crystallize. It is then transformed into a coarse powder. This is quite normal and exactly what we're trying to achieve.

Continue to stir well so that all the nuts are coated with sugar. Use the spoon to separate any that stick together. At this stage, the nuts will begin to make a noise, because they'll be roasting. Lower the heat if they are roasting too fast.

After 4 to 5 minutes, the sugar will start to melt again and transform into caramel. Again, check that the heat is not too high: it might burn the caramel, giving it a bitter taste.

When all the sugar has melted, pour the mixture onto an oiled marble pastry slab, a silicone baking mat, or heat-resistant parchment paper and allow to cool completely.

Break the caramel into large chunks and place, in batches if necessary, in the bowl of a food processor. Begin processing. Within a few seconds, you'll have a powdered praline that you can sprinkle over ice creams. If you continue to process, the powder will be transformed into a praline paste. The more the mixture is processed, the more liquid it will become.

Keep in mind that professionally made praline paste is made with stone rollers that give the paste a very silky texture. Homemade praline paste will be a little more grainy. However, this doesn't detract from the taste at all; in fact it adds a delightfully crunchy texture.

PRALINE PASTE
DAIRY, EGG, AND GLUTEN FREE
Makes 1 ¼ lb. (500 g) praline paste
Preparation time: 20 minutes
Cooking time: 10 minutes

INGREDIENTS
1 cup (7 oz./200 g) sugar
1 small pinch ground vanilla bean
2 tablespoons (30 ml) water
1 scant cup (5 ¼ oz./150 g) unpeeled almonds
1 scant cup (5 ¼ oz./150g) unpeeled hazelnuts

PISTACHIO PASTE
DAIRY, EGG, AND GLUTEN FREE
Makes 1 ¼ lb. (500 g) pistachio paste
Preparation time: 20 minutes
Cooking time: 10 minutes

INGREDIENTS
1 ¼ cups (9 oz./250 g) sugar
2 tablespoons (30 ml) water
1 ⅔ cups (9 oz./250 g) shelled unsalted pistachios

1 Pour the nuts into the syrup.

2 Mix well when the sugar becomes grainy to ensure that all the nuts are coated.

3 Pour the caramel onto a heatproof surface and allow to cool.

4 Place chunks of caramel into a food processor and process.

5 After a few seconds, it will be reduced to powder.

6 After a few more minutes, it will be transformed into a paste.

For **pistachio paste**, follow the procedure for the praline paste until the syrup crystallizes. Here, my method diverges with the previous method. I find that if the crystallized sugar dissolves into caramel, the pistachio paste takes on a taste that is too strong.

To avoid this, as soon as the syrup becomes grainy, stir the pistachios just to coat them, taking care to keep them separate. If you see that the sugar begins to melt again, leave just a light coating of caramelized sugar on the pistachios and remove from the heat.

Before all the sugar melts again, pour the mixture onto a silicone baking sheet, an oiled marble pastry slab, or heat-resistant parchment paper. Instead of a caramel block, you will have sugar-coated pistachios. Allow to cool completely.

Working in batches if necessary, process the pistachios and crystallized sugar (some will remain, so include it) in the bowl of a food processor until the mixture forms a paste. It may take some time, but rest assured, a paste will form—you just need to be patient.

(continued on page 20)

HAZELNUT PASTE
DAIRY AND EGG FREE
Makes 1 ¼ lb. (500 g) hazelnut paste
Preparation time: 20 minutes
Cooking time: 10 to 12 minutes

INGREDIENTS
1 ½ cups (9 oz./250 g) shelled hazelnuts,
  peeled or unpeeled
1 cup plus 1 scant cup (250 g) confectioners'
  sugar

• • • • • • • • • • • • • •

For **hazelnut paste**, preheat the oven to 350°F (180°C).

Place the hazelnuts on a baking sheet and roast for 5 minutes. Remove from the oven, stir well, and return to the oven for another 5 to 7 minutes, until lightly browned.

Allow the hazelnuts to cool. If your nuts weren't peeled, rub them with a clean cloth: the skin will come off. Don't worry about any skin remnants, because once the nuts are transformed into a paste, there won't be any trace of skin left.

Place the hazelnuts in the bowl of a food processor and add the confectioners' sugar. Begin processing, in batches if necessary: the mixture will soon be reduced to a fine powder. Continue mixing until a paste forms.

Praline Paste (top),
Hazelnut Paste (center), and
Pistachio Paste (bottom)

Swedish Oatmeal and Chocolate Cookies

Havreflarns

Makes about 50 sandwich cookies
(or 100 single cookies)
Preparation time: 10 minutes plus 2 hours
resting time
Cooking time: 8 to 9 minutes per batch

INGREDIENTS

1 cup minus 1 tablespoon (6 ⅓ oz./180 g)
margarine
2 ½ cups (7 oz./200 g) oats, regular
or quick-cooking
1 ½ cups (10 ½ oz./300 g) sugar
½ cup plus 1 tablespoon (2 ½ oz./70 g)
all-purpose flour
1 generous pinch salt
1 extra large (US) or large (UK) egg
1 or 2 drops vanilla extract
¼ teaspoon baking powder
¼ teaspoon baking soda
9 oz. (350 g) bittersweet or milk chocolate

These cookies have become widely known ever since a certain international chain of Swedish furniture stores started selling them in their grocery section. The oatmeal cookies, sandwiched together with bittersweet or milk chocolate, are totally irresistible. They are also available without chocolate. If you make them yourself, you can choose which cookie you prefer, and go for the best quality chocolate. To reproduce the cookies in my kitchen, I don't use butter (much as I love it), but rather margarine. You can opt for an all-butter version (using the same amount of butter as indicated in the list of ingredients), but be aware that the result will not be quite the same as those store-bought cookies. The margarine brings out the flavors of the oatmeal and the chocolate without overpowering them.

When you prepare your ingredients, measure the baking powder and soda with particular care. It may seem paradoxical, but if your cookies rise too much, it means that not enough baking powder was used. A few readers of my blog wrote to me about the problems they'd had: the cookies had risen but were hollow. They are meant to be very flat. I returned to my experiments and realized that a lack or absence of raising agents resulted in a less attractive cookie. The two raising agents cause the cookies to rise and spread considerably, until they drop back, seemingly exhausted by their efforts, to their standard height. Without raising agents, it's the eggs that cause the cookies to rise, but they won't spread. It's therefore important to respect the quantities of baking powder and soda, and to incorporate them only when the dough has cooled somewhat so as not to activate them before it's necessary.

Melt the margarine in a saucepan over low heat. You can also melt it in the microwave, but to avoid splatters, put the margarine in a bowl covered with plastic wrap with a few holes poked in it. Once melted, allow the margarine to cool for a few minutes.

Combine the oats, sugar, flour, and salt in a mixing bowl.

Stir the melted, cooled margarine into the dry ingredients. Stir in the egg and vanilla extract.

(continued on page 24)

Add the baking powder and baking soda and mix until thoroughly combined.

Cover the dough with plastic wrap and chill for at least 2 hours.

Preheat the oven to 350°F (180°C). Line a baking sheet with parchment paper.

After the dough has rested, scoop out spoonfuls of dough and roll into balls. It's best to weigh the balls of dough so you're sure to have identical cookies to sandwich together. The size I find best weighs ⅓ oz. (8 g).

Place the balls of dough on the prepared baking sheet, leaving 2 inches (5 cm) between them.

Bake for 8 to 9 minutes. The cookies should be golden around the edges with a lightly colored center.

Using a spatula, transfer the cookies to a rack and allow to cool completely. Repeat with the remaining dough. As soon as the cookies have cooled, place them in an airtight container—they can't take any humidity at all!

To make chocolate-sandwich *havreflarns*, melt the chocolate over a hot water bath or in 20-second bursts in the microwave oven, stirring after each time.

If you wish, you can temper the chocolate, but for this you'll need couverture chocolate, which you can find online or at specialized stores. Follow the tempering curves indicated on the packaging. The addition of cacao butter will allow you to temper the chocolate without following the temperature curves. But there's no need to complicate this step unduly: you can also use ordinary chocolate. The only risk is seeing a few white streaks when the chocolate sets.

Using a dipping fork, dip the bottom of each cookie in the melted chocolate, just enough to coat the rim; only the bottom and rim of the cookie should be coated in chocolate. Keeping the cookie on the fork, transfer it to a cooling rack, turning it upside down so that the chocolate side is on top. Take a second cookie and place it on top of the chocolate filling. Repeat this step with the remaining cookies.

Allow the chocolate to set and return the sandwich cookies to the airtight container. Well protected from humidity and air, these cookies keep for up to 1 month.

Praline Cream–Filled Choux Pastries

Paris-Brest

Makes 9 individual pastries
Preparation time: 1 hour 30 minutes to
  2 hours
Cooking time: 30 minutes plus 20 to
  30 minutes for baking

Special equipment: a candy thermometer

INGREDIENTS

FOR THE CHOUX PASTRY
½ cup (125 ml) milk
½ cup (125 ml) water
1 ¼ teaspoons (5 g) sugar
1 teaspoon (5 g) salt
7 tablespoons (3 ½ oz./100 g) butter
1 cup plus 1 tablespoon (5 oz./140 g)
  all-purpose flour
1 cup (250 ml) eggs, lightly beaten
  (about 5 eggs)
Peeled and chopped almonds or hazelnuts
  for sprinkling

FOR THE PASTRY CREAM
2 vanilla beans
Generous ⅓ cup (3 ½ oz./100 g) egg yolks
⅓ cup (1 ¾ oz./50 g) cornstarch
⅔ cup (4 ½ oz./125 g) sugar, divided
2 cups (500 ml) low-fat milk
3 tablespoons (2 oz./50 g) unsalted butter

FOR THE CUSTARD-BASED BUTTERCREAM
Scant ⅓ cup (3 oz./80 g) egg yolks
½ cup (3 ½ oz./100 g) sugar, divided
Scant ½ cup (100 ml) whole milk
3 ¾ sticks (15 oz./420 g) butter,
  room temperature
1 lb. (450 g) praline paste (page 18)

Confectioners' sugar for dusting

I spent months hunting for *the* recipe for this classic French dessert. And by "*the*" recipe, I mean one I really like! Because in France there are as many types of Paris-Brest as there are pastry chefs who prepare it. I tried several recipes, to no avail. I made a martyr of myself, tasting a wide range of Paris-Brest cakes, until I understood exactly what I was looking for. All that remained was to draw up the recipe that corresponded. I did it all instinctively, jotting down the proportions and quantities as I worked. The result of my labors is a rich and unctuous Paris-Brest cream filling. It is, in fact, a mousseline cream (a buttercream to which pastry cream has been added), but with modified proportions of ingredients. For the base, I use a vanilla custard but add no Italian meringue, as is traditionally done. This creates a wonderful cream with a fine texture that holds so well you can even have fun piping out patterns.

It's important to prepare the rounds of choux pastry a day ahead so that they can firm up a little before being filled; they'll be easier to cut in half. You can also prepare the pastry cream and praline filling a day ahead and assemble the cakes just before serving.

Preheat the oven to 400°F (200°C).

Pour the milk and water into a heavy saucepan over low heat and stir in the sugar and salt. Add the butter. Bring to a boil and remove from the heat.

Pour in all the flour and mix energetically with a wooden spoon to combine. Return to low heat briefly, stirring constantly, to dry the batter out. Continue until the batter pulls away from the bottom of the saucepan.

Transfer the batter to a mixing bowl or the bowl of a stand mixer fitted with the flat beater attachment. Gradually add the eggs, beating well after each addition. Continue to beat until the mixture is smooth and holds soft peaks.

Draw 3 to 3 ½ inch (7 to 8 cm) diameter circles on 2 sheets of parchment paper. Place the sheets, drawing side down, on 2 baking sheets. Spoon the choux batter into a piping bag fitted with a ½-inch (16-mm) plain or star tip. Pipe circles of batter into the traced circles and sprinkle the tops with the chopped nuts.

(continued on page 26)

1 Stir the batter for 1 minute over low heat to dry it out.

2 When the batter forms a ribbon and holds soft peaks, it's ready.

3 Pipe out circles of choux batter.

4 When the custard is whisked to cool it, it becomes foamy.

5 Combine the components of the cream: custard, butter, praline, and pastry cream.

6 Fill the choux pastries with praline buttercream.

Bake for 20 to 30 minutes, keeping a careful eye on the choux. They must be golden, nicely puffed up, and firm to the touch. If you remove them too soon, they will deflate.

Place the baked choux rounds on a cooling rack and leave for 12 hours or overnight.

To make the pastry cream, slit the vanilla beans lengthwise with a small knife and scrape the seeds into a mixing bowl. (You'll need the pods for the next step.) Add the egg yolks, cornstarch, and half the sugar, and whisk together until the sugar has dissolved.

In a heavy saucepan over low heat, bring the milk to a boil with the remaining sugar, butter, and the empty vanilla bean pods.

Slowly pour the boiling milk over the egg yolk mixture, stirring well, and then return the mixture to the saucepan. Stirring constantly, bring to a boil and simmer for 2 minutes.

Pour the pastry cream into a heatproof dish or bowl, press a piece of plastic wrap directly on the surface to prevent a skin from forming, and allow to cool to room temperature. Place in the refrigerator until the next day.

(continued on page 28)

Following the recipe on page 18, prepare the praline paste, setting aside about 50 whole caramelized almonds for garnish. Store them in an airtight container.

For the custard-based buttercream, whisk the egg yolks and half the sugar until pale and thick.

In a heavy saucepan over low heat, bring the milk to a boil with the remaining sugar. Pour it gradually over the egg yolk-sugar mixture, stirring constantly.

Return the liquid to the saucepan over low heat. Whisking constantly, heat the custard to 187°F (86°C).

Pour the custard into the bowl of a stand mixer fitted with the whisk attachment. Whisk at medium speed until the custard has cooled completely. If you don't have a stand mixer, you can use an electric beater or whisk by hand. Transfer the custard to another mixing bowl. It should be the same temperature as the butter when you combine the two.

Clean the bowl you have just used and place the butter in it. Whisk at high speed for 5 minutes, until the butter is light and fluffy.

Pour the custard over the butter, and whisk until completely combined.

Now add the praline paste and whisk for 1 or 2 minutes further, until combined. Chill the cream for 1 hour.

Whisk the chilled praline buttercream to aerate it again.

Remove the vanilla beans from the chilled pastry cream and weigh out 1 ¼ lb. (500 g). Whisk it briefly to ensure that it is smooth again. Transfer it to the bowl of the stand mixer with the whisked praline buttercream and beat together until completely combined.

To assemble, cut the rounds of choux pastry in half horizontally.

Spoon the filling into a piping bag fitted with a tip of your choice (plain or star tip), and pipe out a first circle of cream over the lower halves of the choux pastry. Add more cream, filling generously. Place 5 or 6 caramelized almonds evenly on the cream. Set the top half of the choux pastry over the cream and chill for at least 3 hours before serving.

Dust lightly with confectioners' sugar before serving.

Bordeaux Tea Cakes
Canelés

• • • • • • • • • • • •

Makes 22 *canelés*
Preparation time: 15 minutes
Chilling time: 24 to 48 hours
Cooking time: 50 minutes to 1 hour

Special equipment: 2 ½-inch (5-cm)
   canelé molds

INGREDIENTS
2 vanilla beans
2 cups plus scant ½ cup (1 lb. 1 oz./475 g)
   sugar
2 eggs plus 4 yolks
4 cups (1 liter) whole milk
Scant ½ cup (100 ml) dark rum
2 tablespoons vanilla extract
3 tablespoons (2 oz./50 g) unsalted butter
2 ¼ cups (10 oz./280 g) all-purpose flour

• • • • • • • • • • • • • •

Canelés (and not *cannelés*) come from the city of Bordeaux and are made in fluted molds (*moules à cannelures*). They may well have originated as *canaules*—a type of bread made with egg yolks that went out of fashion in the nineteenth century and was revived early in the twentieth century by a pastry chef who added rum and vanilla to the batter.

The recipe I give you here is one that I've been keeping to myself for years. Long ago, I spent several weeks doing nothing but making *canelés* to try to uncover their mystery. I tried everything: heating the milk, then pouring it boiling, lukewarm, and cold over the sugar-egg mixture, which I sometimes beat till pale and thick and sometimes not. I tried every possible resting time and all lengths and types of baking. I even baked the same dough at different times using all manner of molds. And I came to several conclusions: the only molds to use are copper molds; and to turn the *canelés* out of their molds, the optimal solution is a non-stick cooking spray with release agents (with just butter and flour, *canelés* won't budge from their molds). Avoid silicone molds, which never give the same results as copper molds. Your *canelés* will undoubtedly taste good, but they'll have neither the trademark crisp crust, nor the moist interior. Copper molds are expensive, but you can buy them in batches of six. And keep in mind that they'll last a lifetime. There is one other alternative: aluminum molds with a non-stick lining. The result won't be as good as with copper, but it will be better than silicone. But never use butter to grease the molds. It does not prevent the batter from sticking when the *canelés* are baked and they are a nightmare to turn out.

The chilling time is all-important and must be respected; this is why it's preferable to prepare the batter one or two days ahead. This stage is essential if you want excellent results for your *canelés*. I tried every possible permutation of the different stages; one—when I was staying with a friend in Rabat who asked me to bake some *canelés*—was particularly memorable. We left our batter to chill for one hour and . . . disaster, with almost all of the *canelés* overflowing from the molds in the oven. The next afternoon, with the same baking conditions and the same molds, but after a long resting period, the *canelés* were perfect.

Lastly, the *canelés* should be baked in two stages. And you'll need to find the right baking time for your oven! The time I indicate here works to perfection with my oven, but of course all ovens have their own quirks.

Despite my dissecting all the intricacies of this little cake, there is still something mysterious about them, even if you'll now be able to make marvelous ones at home.

Slit the vanilla beans lengthwise and scrape the seeds into a large mixing bowl. Reserve the vanilla pods. Add the sugar, eggs, and egg yolks to the vanilla seeds and whisk just until the eggs and sugar are well-combined—no need to whisk until pale and thick.

In a large heavy pot over low heat, place the milk, rum, vanilla extract, butter, and vanilla pods. Cook just until the butter melts, then pour a little of the warm liquid over the egg-sugar mixture.

Whisk in one-third of the flour. Whisk in more of the hot milk mixture. Continue, adding the flour in two more batches, alternating milk and flour. This will ensure that you don't have any lumps to contend with.

Chill the batter for at least 24 hours and up to 48 hours.

Remove the batter from the refrigerator 30 minutes before you begin baking. Whisk it briefly to ensure that the batter is smooth—the fatty substances will have risen to the surface.

Preheat the oven to 520°F (275°C). Spray the insides of the molds with baking spray and turn them upside down to rest on paper towel so the excess can drip off. *Canelés* must be baked in two stages. An initial period in a very hot oven will set the batter in the mold. A lowered temperature will finish cooking the *canelés*. If your oven doesn't reach this temperature (but it should attain at least 480°F/250°C), extend the first baking time a little. The most difficult aspect of this recipe is to find baking times that work with your oven, so my advice is to bake just 5 or 6 *canelés* at first, until you find the right temperature.

Remove the vanilla pods from the batter. Fill the greased molds almost to the top, to a tiny fraction of an inch from the rim.

Place all the molds on a baking sheet and set on a rack in the middle of the oven. Bake for 10 minutes at 520°F (275°C), or for 13 minutes at 480°F (250°C) if that's the hottest temperature your oven reaches. Lower the temperature to 400°F (200°C) and bake for an additional 35 minutes to reach the right degree of doneness for the interior (the color of the top will barely change).

(continued on page 32)

As soon as you remove the baking sheet from the oven, tip the *canelés* out of their molds and place them upside down on a cooling rack for at least 2 hours. They are most delicious between 2 and 6 hours after baking. At their best, *canelés* are airy, like a sponge. Of course, you can crisp them up by placing them in a 400°F (200°C) oven for 5 to 7 minutes and then allowing them to cool to lukewarm for 10 minutes.

Store in an airtight container for up to 1 week.

In a moment of complicity,
who knows, one day
as we sip our tea, I might share with you
the secret of my Bordeaux canelé.
Camila Nicácio

Death-by-Chocolate Cake
L'assassin

Makes one 6-inch (15-cm) cake,
 to serve 4 to 6
Preparation time: 25 minutes
Cooking time: 45 minutes
Chilling time: 12 hours or overnight

INGREDIENTS

¾ cup (6 ⅓ oz./180 g) beaten eggs
 (about 3 eggs)
1 tablespoon (⅓ oz./10 g) all-purpose flour
1 ¼ cups (9 oz./250 g) sugar
3–3 ½ tablespoons (50 ml) water
1 ¼ sticks. (5 oz./150 g) salted butter,
 room temperature, diced
4 oz. (125 g) bittersweet chocolate,
 at least 60 percent cacao

To my mind, this is the ultimate in chocolate cakes. The secret of its molten core, despite the lengthy baking time, lies in the proportions I've devised for this scrumptious and indulgent cake. Its originality lies in the way I sweeten the cake, namely with a salted butter caramel instead of plain sugar.

The idea for the cake came to me while I was dozing one day. The brainwave sent me immediately to the kitchen to see how to put it into practice. The result exceeded my hopes and for once, I got it right on my first attempt.

Here is my *assassin*, crisp on the outside and rich, dense, and creamy on the inside.

Preheat the oven to 295°F (145°C). Line the base and sides of a 6-inch (15-cm) springform pan with parchment paper. (Cut out a disc the size of the base, and a strip the length of the circumference and the width of the rim.)

With an electric beater, whisk the eggs and flour for 5 minutes, until very foamy. Transfer the mixture to the bowl of a stand mixer fitted with a whisk attachment, where you'll need it to combine with the caramel a little later.

Place the sugar in a heavy saucepan over medium heat with just enough water to soak it, about 3 to 3 ½ tablespoons (50 ml). Ensure that there is no sugar on the sides of the saucepan, because this might cause all the caramel to crystallize again. Do not stir or move the pan until the syrup boils.

Cook until the caramel is a rich amber color. Remove from the heat.

Very gradually add the diced butter and mix to incorporate. With each addition, the caramel cools a little and absorbs the water contained in the butter. What we want is for the water to evaporate. Initially, the caramel will sizzle with each addition, but this soon subsides.

As soon as all the butter has been incorporated, set the stand mixer to minimum speed and drizzle in the salted butter caramel until well combined.

Melt the chocolate over a hot water bath or in short bursts in the microwave oven, stirring after each burst. Pour it into the caramel mixture and whisk briefly until combined.

(continued on page 34)

Scrape the batter into the pan and smooth the top. Bake for 45 minutes—it rises astonishingly high. To test for doneness, gently move the pan back and forth to see how the batter reacts. It should wobble a little in the center, without appearing liquid, like a jam that is setting. As it cools, it will return to its original depth.

Put the pan on a rack and let cool to room temperature. Then refrigerate the cake for 12 hours or overnight before turning it out. Bring it to room temperature for at least 20 minutes before serving in thin slices.

If you want to make a larger cake, refer to the coefficients below. Simply multiply each ingredient by the coefficient that corresponds to the pan. For example, for a 7-inch pan, multiply each ingredient by 1.36. Of course, round up or down to the easiest figure to weigh. However, you'll need to increase the baking time, which depends partly on your oven. Do not remove until the cake has risen well and a crust has formed.

DIAMETER OF MOLD	COEFFICIENT
7 in.	1.36
8 in.	1.78
9 in.	2.25
10 in.	2.78
16 cm	1.14
18 cm	1.44
20 cm	1.77
22 cm	2.15
24 cm	2.56

Macarons

Practically nothing has been left unsaid about French *macarons*. When I began making *macarons*—just like everyone else—my problems started. I realized that my baking results varied from one day to the next. I vowed to do everything possible to find a recipe that never failed. I spent literally weeks working on the project, testing different methods and recipes, and reading all the books I could find on the subject. I kept changing the basic recipe and became skeptical about much of the advice I read.

After all this experimentation, I finally mastered the art of making *macarons*. Which all goes to show that it just takes practice. For a few years now, I have been giving cooking workshops and every month, I give one or two lessons on how to make *macarons*. I explain everything I know and I'm always thrilled to see the faces of the participants light up as they see the little collar at the base of each cookie forming in the oven as the *macarons* bake. No, I don't use egg whites from eggs cracked open a day or two earlier. No, I don't bake several batches at once. No, I never leave the oven door open just a hairbreadth and, lastly, no, I don't pour any water at all under the parchment paper when I remove my *macarons* from the oven. Yet my method works very well indeed. The *macarons* I make are smooth, shiny, and don't crack, even though I don't leave them to form a crust.

You must be asking what I have changed in the essential recipe. I've modified the proportions of confectioners' sugar in relation to the ground almonds (or other nuts). After several experiments with more ground almonds, I realized that I was making *macarons* that were a little flat and dull. By changing the recipe and using a little more confectioners' sugar in relation to the amount of ground almonds, the *macarons* became more resistant, forming a sort of glaze that protected them in the oven. This gave them a sheen and almost instantaneously helped them form a crust.

As far as the egg whites are concerned, I crack my eggs open the day I use them. So if you are suddenly inspired to make *macarons*, go ahead. There's no need to use day-old egg whites. However, to help them whip up, I use cream of tartar, a trick many professionals use. It contains an acidifying powder that optimizes the expansion of the egg whites; I also add a little dried egg white, which guarantees that the egg whites are rich in albumin.

In terms of equipment, I strongly recommend a large, round-bottomed mixing bowl (the bigger, the better) and a flexible bowl scraper to fold in the batter. A candy thermometer is also essential. And of course, if you don't have one already, you'll need to purchase a scale, preferably a digital scale. Because for *macarons*, precision is paramount. Cup measurements are given when possible, but your results will be better if the ingredients are weighed. You'll find all the equipment and the necessary ingredients online or at specialized stores.

On the following pages are the two recipes I use for my cooking classes, published here for the first time. For my *macarons* made using the Italian meringue technique, with different proportions, you won't find the traditional formula of "equal parts confectioners' sugar/almonds," as this is not applicable. The technique that uses French meringue follows immediately afterward.

Keep in mind that each oven has its own quirks. *Macarons* should always be baked using a convection (or fan-assisted) oven, and in fact, this is what I use for all my baking. There are ovens that produce spectacular *macarons* when you use the Italian meringue technique, but produce fragile *macarons* made with the French meringue technique, or vice versa. I've seen every possible permutation when I've given lessons in people's homes. The essential thing is to find the recipe that suits not only you best, but also your oven.

If you are a novice to the world of *macarons*, I recommend that you begin with the Italian meringue method. Although it is longer to prepare, once the batter is all combined, it's perfect, and there is practically no need to do anything further with it. The French meringue method is faster and will have *macarons* in the oven within 10 minutes, but you have to fold the batter in with a scraper, and if you don't know quite when to stop, you may spoil it. I like to use the French meringue method when I make *macarons* using hazelnuts, walnuts, or pistachios. However, I use the Italian meringue method when I use only ground almonds. For details on how to substitute different nuts, see the note on the left.

If you wish, you can color the *macarons* you bake. I use only tiny pinches of powdered food colors. For the praline and pistachio *macarons*, I use no colors at all: the ground nuts take care of that.

A last word of advice: never lose patience and never give up. Without exception, all my students have, in the end, successfully made *macarons*.

Note To make hazelnut *macarons*, you can substitute the entire quantity of ground almonds with ground hazelnuts. For pistachio *macarons*, I use one-third ground pistachios and two-thirds ground almonds, and the same proportions for walnut *macarons*.

Basic *Macarons*
with Italian Meringue

DAIRY FREE
Makes 30 to 40 filled *macarons*
Preparation time: 25 minutes
Cooking time: 13 to 15 minutes per batch
Cooling time: 3 hours
Resting time: 12 to 24 hours

Special equipment: a candy thermometer
and a digital scale

INGREDIENTS
1 ½ cups (4 ¾ oz./135 g) ground almonds
1 ¼ cups (5 ¾ oz./165 g) confectioners' sugar
¼ cup (2 oz./60 g) fresh egg whites

FOR THE MERINGUE
¾ cup (5 ¼ oz./150 g) granulated or caster
  sugar
2 tablespoons plus 1 teaspoon (35 ml) water
¼ cup (2 oz./55 g) fresh egg whites
1 small pinch cream of tartar
½ teaspoon egg white powder
Food coloring, optional

If you have extra-fine ground almonds, there is no need to sift them with the confectioners' sugar. If your ground almonds are somewhat coarse, place them in the mixer with the confectioners' sugar and process for 1 to 2 minutes. If you want *macarons* with a particularly smooth shell, you can then sift the two ingredients together.

Place the ground almonds and confectioners' sugar in a large mixing bowl and add the egg whites. Mix well to make an almond paste and set aside.

Place the sugar in a heavy saucepan over medium heat and carefully pour in the water without splashing. If any grains of sugar happen to settle on the sides of the pan, use a pastry brush dipped in water to brush them down into the syrup. Grains of sugar on the sides might cause the syrup to crystallize—this is what happens during the preparation of a praline paste (see page 18).

Bring the syrup to a boil. As soon as it boils, begin whisking the egg whites with the cream of tartar and the egg white powder in a large bowl. I do not use a stand mixer for this small quantity of whites because, generally speaking, the whisk doesn't reach the bottom of the bowl. I prefer to whip the egg whites with an electric beater. Begin at low speed to eliminate the lumps made by the egg white powder. As soon as they have disappeared, gradually increase the speed and beat until the egg whites form soft peaks.

Check the temperature of the syrup. As soon as it reaches 240°F (116°C), drizzle it into the bowl while the machine continues to beat. When all the syrup has been poured in, continue to beat at medium speed. If you're using food coloring, now's the time to add it.

Continue to beat until the meringue cools to no more than 122°F (50°C). At this stage, you can usually see the patterns left by the beaters in the meringue.

Add 1 or 2 heaping tablespoons of meringue to the almond paste and carefully fold in using a plastic spatula. The bigger the mixing bowl, the easier this will be.

When the mixture is smooth, fold in the remaining meringue in 3 additions, taking care not to deflate the mixture. Scoop up a little of the mixture with the spatula. If it falls back in a ribbon, and is smooth, soft, and shiny, you're ready to go.

To learn how to pipe and bake *macarons*, see pages 41–42.

1 Combine the ground almonds, confectioners' sugar, and egg whites to make an almond paste.

2 Heat the syrup to 240°F (116°C).

3 Drizzle the syrup over the whipped egg whites, keeping the beater running.

4 Fold in, using a bowl scraper.

5 Pipe out with a plain ⅓-inch (8-mm) tip.

6 This is what the baked *macarons* should look like.

Basic *Macarons* with French Meringue

• • • • • • • • • • • • • • •

DAIRY FREE
Makes 30 to 40 filled *macarons*
Preparation time: 15 minutes
Cooking time: 13 to 15 minutes
Cooling time: 3 hours
Resting time: 12 to 24 hours

INGREDIENTS
1 cup plus 1 scant cup (9 oz./250 g)
    confectioners' sugar
1 ½ cups (4 ¾ oz./135 g) ground almonds
    (or ground hazelnuts, or ⅔ ground
    almonds and ⅓ ground pistachios)

FOR THE MERINGUE
¼ cup (2 oz./50 g) sugar
1 teaspoon egg white powder
½ cup (4 oz./115 g) fresh egg whites
1 small pinch cream of tartar
1 small pinch food coloring, optional

• • • • • • • • • • • • • • •

Process the confectioners' sugar and ground almonds for 1 minute, until thoroughly combined. If you like *macarons* with a very smooth shell, sift the dry ingredients together. This is not something I do systematically. For example, if I use 100 percent ground hazelnuts or 50 percent ground pistachios, I don't sift them, because I like the rather rough aspect they give to the *macarons*.

In a small mixing bowl, combine the sugar and egg white powder. If you are using food coloring, add it to the sugar.

In the bowl of a stand mixer fitted with the whisk attachment, or in a large mixing bowl using an electric beater, begin whisking the egg whites. When they increase in volume, add all the contents of the small bowl and whisk until the whites hold firm peaks. To judge the right time to stop, take a little meringue between your thumb and index finger and check that you can no longer feel any sugar crystals. If you can, whisk further. In any case, there is no risk of over-whisking the whites here.

Pour the ground almond-confectioners' sugar mixture into a large mixing bowl and add all the whipped egg whites.

Begin to fold the egg whites in with a scraper. Initially, you'll have to force things a bit and the whites will deflate a little. Once the powdered ingredients and the egg whites are combined, continue to fold in to deflate the batter until it has the right consistency (the verb in French for this process is *macaronner*).

Initially, the mixture will have a pasty texture. To fold in, use a large flexible bowl scraper with the straight edge against your palm. Slice downward through the mixture from the center until you reach the bottom of the bowl. Scoop the mixture upward toward you and fold it toward the center. Give the bowl a quarter-turn and repeat the slicing-scooping movement, rotating the bowl each time, until the mixture is smooth. The action is very similar to the one used to incorporate whisked egg whites into a chocolate mousse with a plastic spatula. As you continue, the mixture will become more fluid. The aim is to obtain a soft, shiny mixture that forms a ribbon as it flows downward when held up with the scraper.

Piping and baking:

When the *macaron* mixture has the required qualities—smooth, soft, shiny, and falls slowly to make a ribbon—it can be spooned into a piping bag. I find it more difficult to pipe *macarons* when the bag is full rather than half-full. More weight in the bag increases pressure, forcing the mixture out faster than one can control easily and making the process awkward.

Preheat the oven to 275°F–285°F (135°C–140°C). Line a baking sheet with a silicone baking mat or draw circles on one side of a sheet of parchment paper and set it, circle-side down, on a baking sheet. Fit a ⅓-inch (8-mm) plain tip on a piping bag.

Block the open end of the tip: either twist the narrow end of the bag and clamp a clothes peg above it, or twist the bag and insert the small knot of the plastic into the tip. This prevents the batter from flowing out while you fill the bag. Fold the top end of the bag outward (you can place it in a suitably sized water pitcher, for example, or hold it in one hand). Spoon in half of the mixture, or the entire quantity if you're comfortable with it.

To close the bag over the *macaron* mixture, twist it round several times, blocking the tightly squeezed twist between the forefinger and thumb of your right hand, if you are right-handed. The other fingers and the palm of the hand will exert the pressure required to pipe out the mixture. When you have done all this, take a deep breath! The calmer you are, the easier the process will be. Remember that it's not a race.

Undo the twist or release the clothes peg to open the nozzle of the tip. Place the piping bag vertically above the first circle on the baking mat, about ¼ inch (6 mm) above it.

Use your left hand to keep the tip in place and begin exerting pressure with your right hand. The mixture will emerge slowly to make a perfect round. When it reaches the perimeter of the mark, stop pressing completely and remove the tip from the shaped *macaron*. Without any further pressure, no more mixture will flow from the tip; simply lift it up. This action forms a little comma shape in the *macaron*. If you start by working slowly, you'll gain confidence as you work and be able to shape the *macarons* with greater ease. I've been teaching people this movement for years now and it gives excellent results. The important thing is to take one's time and pay attention to each stage until you can pipe an attractive *macaron* on automatic pilot.

(continued on page 42)

When the baking sheet is full, tap it lightly on a work surface to deflate the mixture even more. To do this, hold it 4 to 8 inches (10 to 20 cm) above the surface, exactly parallel to it. Repeat several times, until all the small imperfections in the *macarons* are no longer visible. This depends on your mixture and the way you have carried out the folding-in procedure. If the mixture is relatively firm, you will probably need to tap the baking sheet more; if the mixture is relatively soft, you will probably need to do it fewer times.

Bake for 13 to 15 minutes. While the first sheet is in the oven, prepare the next one.

To test for doneness, touch a *macaron* shell. It should offer a little resistance and then return to its original shape. If it separates easily from the little collar that forms around the base, it requires more baking. If the collar is completely set, the *macarons* are already slightly over-baked. You'll have to adapt the baking time to your oven.

When you remove the baking sheet from the oven, leave the *macarons* on it while you place the next sheet in the oven. Leaving them on a hot baking sheet for about 10 minutes extends the baking a little. After this time, slip the parchment paper or mat onto a rack or cool surface and allow to cool completely. Only then can you remove the *macarons* from the parchment paper or mat.

To remove the *macarons*, work carefully and do not pull upward, which might break them. Hold the parchment paper or mat with one hand and with the other, lift up the *macarons* from one side.

You can fill the *macarons* at this stage or the next day and up to 2 to 3 days after baking. The important thing is to store them in an airtight container until you're ready to fill them.

Prepare the filling and sandwich together pairs of *macarons* that are exactly the same size. Place them in an airtight container in the refrigerator to protect them from odors. Allow to rest for 12 hours before serving.

Macarons can be frozen, as long as they are defrosted in their airtight container, which should not be opened at all. They absorb moisture from the air in the same way as moisture condenses on a cold can of soda when it's removed from the refrigerator. They would lose the best of their texture and soften completely.

1 Pour the sugar combined with the egg white powder over the whipped egg whites.

2 Add all the meringue to the dry ingredients (ground almonds and confectioners' sugar).

3 Fold in until the batter is soft, smooth, shiny, and forms a ribbon.

4 Pipe onto a silicone baking mat or parchment paper.

*Macarons hint
at the memories and aftertastes
of vanilla and almonds
the day I fell for you.*

Camila Nicácio

Pistachio and Praline *Macarons*

For 35 filled *macarons*
Preparation time: 20 minutes
Cooking time: 10 minutes
Chilling time: 1 hour
Resting time: 12 to 24 hours

INGREDIENTS

FOR THE ITALIAN MERINGUE
⅓ cup (2 oz./60 g) sugar
1 tablespoon plus 1 teaspoon (20 ml) water
1 ½ tablespoons (⅔ oz./20 g) egg white
½ teaspoon egg white powder
1 small pinch cream of tartar

FOR THE PRALINE FILLING
4 ½ oz. (130 g) praline paste (page 18)
6 tablespoons (3 ¼ oz./95 g) unsalted butter, room temperature

FOR THE PISTACHIO FILLING
4 ½ oz. (130 g) pistachio paste (page 19)
6 tablespoons (3 ¼ oz./95 g) unsalted butter, room temperature
1 teaspoon bitter almond extract

Here are two recipes in one: the recipes for both praline and pistachio fillings made with a butter and Italian meringue base. The two are basically the same, the difference being the use of almond-hazelnut praline paste for one and pistachio paste for the other (see pages 18–19).

To make the *macaron* shells, you can use either the French meringue or Italian meringue method, depending on your oven and the type of *macaron* you are seeking to bake. For praline *macarons*, you may use the French meringue method, replacing all the ground almonds with ground hazelnuts. This will save you from using food coloring and give a lovely natural color.

I have noticed that using ground hazelnuts and pistachios tends to result in *macaron* shells that are a little stronger, which works extremely well with the French meringue method.

Begin with the Italian meringue. Place the sugar in a heavy saucepan over medium heat and carefully pour in the water, without splashing. Grains of sugar on the sides might cause the syrup to crystallize. If any grains of sugar happen to settle on the sides, use a pastry brush dipped in water to brush them down into the syrup. Heat the syrup to 250°F (121°C).

Meanwhile, use an electric beater to begin whipping the egg white with the egg white powder and cream of tartar until the mixture holds firm peaks.

When the syrup reaches 250°F (121°C), drizzle it over the egg whites, whisking continually. Whisk further until the meringue cools to 122°F (50°C). At this stage, the whisks leave clear patterns in the whites.

Cover the bowl of meringue with plastic wrap and chill for at least 1 hour. Clean the whisks of the beater.

For the nut filling, whip the butter in a small mixing bowl for 2 minutes with an electric beater at medium speed. Add the praline or pistachio paste. For the pistachio filling, add the bitter almond extract. Whip until incorporated.

Using a flexible spatula, fold in the cooled Italian meringue, taking care not to deflate the mixture.

Pour the filling into a piping bag fitted with a ½-inch (14-mm) plain tip. Pipe a little filling onto the base of a *macaron* shell and set an equal-sized shell over it to sandwich them together. Press very lightly to spread the filling to the edge.

Immediately transfer the filled *macarons* to an airtight container so that they don't absorb any odors in the refrigerator.

Macarons with Vanilla or Orange Flower Ganache

Makes about 30 filled *macarons*
Preparation time: 15 minutes
Cooking time: 5 minutes
Chilling time: 3 hours
Resting time: 12 to 24 hours

INGREDIENTS
1 batch of plain *macarons* (pages 38–43)

FOR THE VANILLA GANACHE
7 oz. (200 g) white chocolate (sometimes sold as *couverture ivoire*)
7 tablespoons (3 ½ oz./100 g) unsalted butter, diced
Scant ½ cup (100 ml) heavy cream
1 vanilla bean
1 teaspoon concentrated natural vanilla extract

FOR THE ORANGE FLOWER WATER GANACHE
7 oz. (200 g) white chocolate (sometimes sold as *couverture ivoire*)
7 tablespoons (3 ½ oz./100 g) unsalted butter, diced
Scant ½ cup (100 ml) heavy cream
11 drops concentrated orange flower water flavoring
1 drop blue food coloring

Here I divulge to you a recipe I've kept secret for many years. It's not yet published on my blog; only attendees at my *macaron* workshops know about it. Most recipes for ganache with white chocolate use equal parts white chocolate and heavy cream. In my experience, this type of ganache turns runny at room temperature. What I wanted to achieve was a soft, almost translucent ganache. For my first workshop, my goal was to give the participants a recipe with orange flower water. A fine program indeed, but three days before the workshop was supposed to start, I still hadn't figured out the recipe. My many attempts all involved a two-sided problem: the consistency of the ganache on the one hand and the flavor of orange flower water on the other. The flavoring could not be added to the chocolate because it would have ruined the texture of the ganache. Luckily, I finally found a miraculous ingredient: flavoring so concentrated you use no more than a few drops at a time. (If you could have seen my grimace when I added an entire teaspoon!)

Finally, I set off to a famous Parisian pastry shop and analyzed one of their *macarons*. I scraped the ganache off and examined it. I microwaved it to see how it reacted. It occurred to me that if I added butter in addition to cream in the filling, the combination might work. Lo and behold, it did. Just in the nick of time, I finally had a recipe for my ideal ganache. The ganache had the texture I wanted and it stayed set between the *macaron* shells.

When all's said and done, the proportions are simple, but they make a radical difference. The possibilities for variations are endless. Here I give you recipes for vanilla and orange flower water flavors, but you could experiment, for example, with concentrated rose or jasmine water.

I'd like to give you a few details about the ingredients I use. I work on the assumption that no matter where you live, you can buy anything online. You can buy white chocolate at the supermarket, but for a truly luscious ganache, go for a high quality product. I use *couverture ivoire*, a professional product made by several chocolate makers. It's available in small oval shapes or chunks, often in large packages of over 2 pounds. At the end of the day, it's better value than buying bars at the supermarket.

(continued on page 48)

The method is identical for both types of ganache. Place the white chocolate pieces in a large bowl.

Place the heavy cream and diced butter in a small heavy saucepan and add the flavoring. For the vanilla ganache, slit the vanilla bean, scrape the seeds into the saucepan, add the vanilla pod, and the vanilla concentrate. For the orange flower ganache, add the orange flower water flavoring.

Set the saucepan over low heat: the butter needs time to melt before the cream comes to a simmer. If the cream boils while the butter is still in pieces, this is detrimental for the ganache as you will need to increase the temperature in order for the butter to melt. And if you pour cream that is too hot over the chocolate, it may split the ganache, just like a mayonnaise that doesn't emulsify. So take your time! Allow the butter to melt before the cream forms small bubbles.

When the mixture reaches a slow simmer, pour the liquid gradually over the chocolate, scraping the saucepan with a flexible spatula.

Still using the spatula, begin stirring, making a spiral movement in the center of the mixing bowl. When the little whirl in the middle is a uniform color, widen the stirring movements toward the sides of the bowl until the ganache is smooth. For the vanilla ganache, you can leave the vanilla pod in the mixture. For the orange flower water ganache, now is the time to add the drop of food coloring to turn it a lovely pale green that will become even paler as it cools.

Pour the ganache into a small dish and immediately press a sheet of plastic wrap over the surface to prevent a skin from forming. Chill for at least 3 hours, the time required for the ganache to become firm.

After the 3 hours are up, peel off the plastic wrap and have a small taste of the ganache to see just how good it is.

Spoon the ganache into a piping bag fitted with a ½-inch (14-mm) plain tip. The width is necessary to allow the ganache to emerge from the tip without excessive pressure on the bag, which could burst. Pipe a small amount onto the base of a *macaron* shell and set an equal-sized shell over it to sandwich them together. Press very lightly to spread the ganache to the edge.

Immediately place the filled *macarons* in an airtight container so they do not absorb any odors in the refrigerator. Chill for 12 to 24 hours before serving.

You can freeze the *macarons*, but allow them to defrost in their airtight container to prevent them from absorbing humidity from the air. They would lose the best of their texture and soften completely.

Salted Butter Caramel *Macarons*

Makes about 30 filled *macarons*
Preparation time: 10 minutes
Cooking time: 10 minutes, plus cooling time
Resting time: 12 to 24 hours

INGREDIENTS
1 batch of plain *macarons* (pages 38–43),
  plus a small pinch coffee-brown
  food coloring

FOR THE SALTED BUTTER CARAMEL FILLING
¼ cup (60 ml) water
1 ¼ cups (8 ½ oz./240 g) sugar
3 tablespoons (2 oz./60 g) corn syrup
⅔ cup (150 ml) heavy cream, heated
  slightly
1 ¼ sticks. (5 oz./150 g) salted butter,
  room temperature, diced

Its soft caramel center beautifully set off by the hint of salted butter that titillates the taste buds, this is a particularly mouthwatering *macaron*. Probably number one on the *Macaron* Hit Parade! The recipe I give here is not a caramel sauce to which cold butter has been added, but my hitherto unpublished recipe: a caramel that can be prepared in one step, remains soft when cooled, and does not melt at room temperature.

Bake the *macarons*, adding a small pinch of coffee-brown food coloring to the whipped egg whites.

Place the water, sugar, and corn syrup in a heavy saucepan over medium heat and cook until the mixture becomes a dark amber caramel. Be careful not to cook it any further: if it burns, it will be bitter.

Remove from the heat and add the diced butter and warmed cream. (If you add cold cream, the caramel might splutter.) Mix to melt and incorporate the butter.

Return the saucepan to low heat and, stirring constantly, bring the caramel to 237°F (114°C).

Pour into a heat-resistant dish and allow to cool to room temperature, stirring every now and then.

Pour the caramel filling into a piping bag fitted with a ⅓-inch (9-mm) plain tip. Pipe a small amount onto the base of a *macaron* shell and set an equal-sized shell over it to sandwich them together. Press very lightly to spread the filling to the edge.

Place the *macarons* in an airtight container and chill for 12 to 24 hours to enable the flavors of the shells and the filling to meld.

Coconut *Macarons*

Makes about 30 filled *macarons*
Preparation time: 15 minutes
Cooking time: 5 minutes
Chilling time: 3 hours
Resting time: 12 to 24 hours

INGREDIENTS
1 batch of plain *macarons* (pages 38–43)

FOR THE COCONUT FILLING
¾ cup (2 oz./60g) unsweetened shredded
  coconut, plus a little extra to sprinkle
  on half the shells before baking
7 oz. (200 g) white chocolate (sometimes
  sold as *couverture ivoire*)
⅔ cup (150 ml) coconut milk
7 tablespoons (3 ½ oz./100 g) unsalted butter,
  room temperature, finely diced

I'd also like to share with you my luscious coconut ganache in which, instead of cream, I use coconut milk and a little shredded coconut, processed together to make a soft and tasty ganache. It's one of my favorite recipes, one I kept to myself for a long time.

Before baking the *macarons*, sprinkle a little shredded coconut over half of the shells; these will form the tops of the filled *macarons*.

Place ¾ cup shredded coconut in the bowl of a food processor and grind to a finer powder.

Place the white chocolate in a large mixing bowl.

Pour the coconut milk into a small heavy saucepan and add the diced butter. Set the saucepan over low heat; the butter needs time to melt before the milk comes to a simmer. If the milk boils while the butter is still in pieces, this is detrimental for the ganache as you will need to increase the temperature in order for the butter to melt. And if you pour liquid that is too hot over the chocolate, it may split the ganache, just like a mayonnaise that doesn't emulsify. So take your time! Allow the butter to melt before the milk forms small bubbles.

When it reaches a slow simmer, pour the liquid gradually over the chocolate, scraping out the saucepan with a flexible spatula.

Still using the spatula, begin stirring, making a spiral movement in the center of the mixing bowl. When the little whirl in the middle is a uniform color, widen the stirring movements toward the sides of the bowl until the ganache is smooth.

Add the ground coconut and mix in well. (Have a little taste while you're at it.)

Pour the ganache into a small dish and immediately press a sheet of plastic wrap over the surface to prevent a skin from forming. Chill for at least 3 hours, the time required for the ganache to become firm.

Spoon the ganache into a piping bag fitted with a ½-inch (14-mm) plain tip. The tip has to be wide enough for the ganache to come out easily without you having to exert too much pressure on the bag, which could burst.

(continued on page 52)

Salted Butter Caramel Macarons and Coconut Macarons

Pipe a small amount onto the base of a *macaron* shell and set a shell of equal size over it to sandwich them together. Press together very lightly so that the ganache spreads to the edge.

Immediately place the filled *macarons* in an airtight container so they do not absorb any odors in the refrigerator. Chill for 12 to 24 hours before serving.

You can freeze the *macarons*, but allow them to defrost in their airtight container to prevent them from absorbing humidity from the air and softening.

Raspberry *Macarons*

DAIRY FREE
Makes about 30 filled *macarons*
Preparation time: 30 minutes
Cooking time: 15 minutes
Chilling time: 1 hour
Resting time: 12 to 24 hours

INGREDIENTS
1 batch plain *macarons* (pages 38–43),
   plus a small pinch red food coloring

FOR THE RASPBERRY FILLING
1 lb. (450 g) raspberries (fresh or frozen)
2 ¾ cups (1 ¼ lb./550 g) sugar
1 ⅓ oz. (35 g) powdered fruit pectin

Here is the first of two classic, timeless *macaron* fillings featuring fruit. It's worth spending some time studying the method so that you can use it for other types of fruit. The problem with fruit fillings is that they often dampen the shells with the moisture they contain. So everything possible must be done to retain it. We bake the shells for 1 or 2 minutes longer than the usual baking time. If they are drier and firmer, they will withstand the moisture in the filling. For raspberry *macarons*, we make a jam; the difference lies in the percentage of pectin. Since it is relatively high, the jam retains the water contained in the fruit, preventing it from seeping into the baked shells. It is the simplest filling and yet one of the most popular. You can play around with other fruit fillings and use this method to make a firm jam. Store any leftovers in a jar sterilized with boiling water.

Bake the *macarons*, adding a small pinch of red food coloring to the whipped egg whites. Bake for 2 minutes longer than the recommended time to add resistance to the shells.

Place the raspberries in a saucepan over low heat and bring to a simmer. Combine the pectin with some of the sugar. Stir the remaining sugar into the raspberries and cook until completely dissolved. Then stir in the sugar-pectin mixture. Cook for 8 minutes, stirring constantly. The jam must be very firm so that it doesn't moisten the *macarons*.

Remove from the heat, pour into a jar, and allow to cool.

The jam must be at room temperature when you fill the *macarons*. Fill a piping bag fitted with a fairly wide plain tip (about ½ inch or 14–16 mm) so that it flows easily. Pipe jam onto half the shells and sandwich with equal-sized shells. Press together very lightly so that the jam spreads to the edges.

Immediately transfer to an airtight container to prevent them from absorbing odors, and place in the refrigerator for at least 12 hours.

Lemon *Macarons*

Makes about 30 filled *macarons*
Preparation time: 45 minutes
Cooking time: 10 to 15 minutes
Cooling time: 1 hour
Resting time: 12 to 24 hours

INGREDIENTS
1 batch plain *macarons* (pages 38–43),
  plus a small pinch yellow food coloring

FOR THE LEMON FILLING
1 sheet (2 g) gelatin
Zest of an unwaxed or organic lemon
1 egg
2 tablespoons (⅔ oz./20 g) cornstarch
½ cup (4 oz./110 g) sugar
⅔ cup (170 ml) lemon juice
1 ½ sticks (6 ½ oz./190 g) butter, diced
Scant ½ cup (1 ½ oz./40 g) ground almonds

If you use lemon curd to fill your *macarons*, the problem of moisture rears its head. My solution is to add ground almonds and a small amount of cornstarch to the curd to absorb some moisture. The filling nevertheless remains creamy with a pronounced lemony tang. For variations on this theme, use other fruit juices and "set" them with ground almonds and cornstarch.

Bake the *macarons*, adding a small pinch of egg-yellow food coloring to the whipped egg whites. Bake for 2 minutes longer than the recommended time to add resistance to the shells.

Soak the gelatin sheet in a bowl of cold water.

Finely grate the zest of the lemon.

Combine the egg, cornstarch, and sugar until smooth and creamy. Pour in the lemon juice and add the zest.

Pour the mixture into a small, heavy saucepan over low heat and cook, stirring constantly, until the mixture thickens and begins to simmer. Remove from the heat.

Squeeze the water from the gelatin sheet and stir it into the lemon cream mixture until completely dissolved.

Allow the lemon cream to cool to 122°F (50°C) and stir in the diced butter.

When the butter is fully incorporated, stir in the ground almonds.

Pour the lemon cream into a dish and press a sheet of plastic wrap directly on the surface to prevent a skin from forming on the surface. Allow to cool completely to room temperature.

Spoon the cream into a piping bag fitted with a ½-inch (14-mm) plain tip. Pipe a small amount onto the base of a *macaron* shell. Set a shell of equal size over it to sandwich them together, pressing lightly to ensure that the cream spreads to the edge.

Immediately transfer to an airtight container to prevent them from absorbing odors, and place in the refrigerator for at least 12 hours.

My Dad's Walnut Cake

I'm not the only enthusiastic cook in my family. For a start, my mother has always been an excellent cook and it's thanks to her that I enjoy good food and unearthing what makes recipes work. As for my father, he started cooking when he retired, but he prefers to bake cakes. It was sheer serendipity that led to this recipe—and how lucky we all were. The result is just perfect: a moist cake with an unusual texture and a divine flavor from the combination of walnuts and kirsch. It's one of my all-time favorites. Make this cake when it's cold outside and enjoy it as you bask in the warmth of a roaring fire.

Makes one 8-inch (22-cm) cake
Preparation time: 20 minutes
Cooking time: 35 to 40 minutes

INGREDIENTS

1 cup plus scant ½ cup (9 ½ oz./270 g) sugar
6 tablespoons (3 oz./90 g) butter, room temperature, plus more for the pan
4 eggs
½ cup (2 oz./60 g) all-purpose flour
2 ⅓ cups (7 oz./200 g) shelled walnuts
¼ cup (60 ml) kirsch
2 tablespoons water
1 teaspoon almond extract
1 ½ teaspoons (5.5 g) baking powder

Preheat the oven to 320°F (160°C). Line the base of an 8-inch (22-cm) diameter cake pan with parchment paper and generously grease the sides.

Beat the sugar and the butter until combined.

Add the eggs, one by one, beating well after each addition. Pour in all the flour and fold in.

In the bowl of a mixer fitted with the blade attachment, grind the walnuts to a powder. Stir the ground nuts into the batter and then stir in the kirsch, water, and almond extract. The batter will appear surprisingly liquid and you may well think you've added too much kirsch. I was concerned too, the first time, but I assure you that this is crucial to getting the moist texture just right.

At the very last minute, stir in the baking powder until well combined.

Pour the batter into the cake pan and bake for 35 to 40 minutes, keeping a careful eye on it. To test for doneness, insert a cake tester or the tip of a sharp knife into the center: it should come out dry. Another test for doneness I often use is to gently shake the pan to see how the dough reacts. If it doesn't budge, it's done. If you feel that it makes little ripples under the crust, continue baking.

Allow the cake to cool completely in the pan on a rack before unmolding it. You should be able to turn it out without any difficulty, but if it sticks a little round the edges, simply run a knife around the rim.

Caramel and Almond Meringue Cake

Scofa ®

Serves 10
Preparation time: 1 hour
Cooking time: 30 to 40 minutes

Special equipment: a candy thermometer

INGREDIENTS

FOR THE CARAMEL
½ cup (3 ½ oz./100 g) sugar (to make about
    2 ½ oz./70 g ground caramel)

FOR THE ALMOND MERINGUE LAYERS
½ cup plus 1 tablespoon (2 ½ oz./70 g)
    all-purpose flour
1 ⅓ cups (4 oz./115 g) finely ground almonds
Generous ½ cup (2 ⅔ oz./75 g) confectioners'
    sugar
⅓ cup (75 ml) milk
1 scant cup (7 ½ oz./210 g) egg whites
    (about 7 egg whites)
¾ cup (5 ¼ oz./150 g) granulated sugar

FOR THE BUTTERCREAM
3 ½ tablespoons (1 ½ oz./40 g) sugar with a
    little water plus 2 ½ teaspoons (⅓ oz./10 g)
    sugar for the egg yolks
⅓ cup (3 ½ oz./100 g) egg yolks (about
    5 yolks)
1 stick plus 6 tablespoons (7 ¼ oz./210 g)
    butter, softened and diced

Confectioners' sugar for dusting

I regularly contribute to a French culinary magazine called *180°C*, and one of my assignments was to tackle a mysterious cake called the *Scofa*.® The name of the cake is an acronym for its ingredients: S for *sucre* (sugar), C for *caramel* (no explanation needed), O for *oeufs* (eggs), F for *farine* (flour), and A for *amandes* (almonds). And it's as simple as that, but these ingredients together make a delicious almond meringue filled with caramel-flavored buttercream. The cake was originally developed some forty years ago by Carmelite nuns in the town of Niort, France. Later, the recipe was passed on to the Abbey of Ligugé and the Carmelites of Lisieux, where the cake is now produced under license. It's definitely worth the trip to Normandy to taste the authentic cake where it is made.

Of course, I can't help but try to unearth any well-kept secret. So now, you can also make the *Scofa*® at home, because it's not an easy cake to buy—unless you take the train to Lisieux or Niort.

To begin with, prepare a dry caramel. This may sound intimidating, but my method is foolproof. The secret is not to stir. In a small saucepan over medium heat, place 2 tablespoons (1 oz./25 g) sugar. Let the sugar melt, but don't stir it. When it turns a light amber color, swirl the saucepan gently, and add 2 more tablespoons of sugar. Continue, adding 2 tablespoons at a time, gently swirling the saucepan after each addition to distribute the sugar evenly, until all the sugar has a pronounced caramel color. Pour the caramel onto an oiled marble pastry slab or silicone baking mat. Allow to cool completely.

Break into pieces and process in a food processor until reduced to a fairly fine powder. Store in an airtight container until you're ready to incorporate it into your buttercream.

Next, prepare the almond meringue layers. Preheat the oven to 285°F (140°C). Line a 12 x 16 inch (30 x 40 cm) baking sheet with parchment paper.

Place the flour, ground almonds, confectioners' sugar, and milk in a mixing bowl and combine with a wooden spoon.

In another mixing bowl, or in the bowl of a stand mixer, whisk the egg whites until they form soft peaks. Add the sugar and whisk for 1 minute more, until the meringue is firm and glossy.

1 Fold the egg whites into the batter, taking care not to deflate the mixture.

2 Pipe out adjacent bands of batter lengthwise.

3 For the buttercream, add the softened butter to the bowl.

4 Pour the ground caramel into the buttercream.

5 Spread the buttercream evenly over one layer of the almond meringue.

6 Trim the edges of the layered cake neatly.

Spoon some of the whisked egg whites into the almond-milk mixture and fold in carefully. Use a flexible spatula and take care not to deflate the air bubbles that have been incorporated. Fold in the remaining egg whites and stop mixing as soon as the batter is smooth.

Spoon the batter into a piping bag fitted with a plain ⅓-inch (10-mm) tip. Working lengthwise, pipe out bands of batter the length of the baking sheet (making sure they touch one another).

Bake for 40 minutes, until lightly golden and dry on top, but still soft inside. Cool the pan on a rack for 10 minutes, before turning the cake onto the cooling rack and carefully peeling off the parchment paper. Allow to cool completely.

Now make the buttercream. Place the 3 ½ tablespoons (1 ½ oz./40 g) sugar with 1 tablespoon of water in a small saucepan over medium heat and bring to 240°F (116°C).

Meanwhile, whip the egg yolks with the 2 ½ teaspoons (10 g) of sugar for 3 to 4 minutes, until thick and pale. Slowly drizzle the syrup over the yolk mixture, whipping constantly, and whip for 5 minutes at high speed.

(continued on page 60)

Slowly add the diced butter and whip until the mixture is smooth and creamy. Lastly, add 2 ½ oz. (70 g) of the ground caramel and mix to combine.

To assemble the cake, cut the sheet of almond meringue in half crosswise. Spread the buttercream evenly over the less attractive half. Carefully set the other half over the buttercream and trim the sides neatly. Then chill until ready to serve.

Before serving, dust with confectioners' sugar and cut into squares. You can store this cake in an airtight container for 3 to 4 days in the refrigerator.

To vary the recipe, replace the caramel-flavored buttercream with the vanilla cream from the Vanilla Mille-Feuille recipe on page 126 or the praline cream from the Paris-Brest recipe on page 25.

Portuguese Custard Tarts

Pastéis de Nata

These delectable little tarts are found everywhere in Portugal, particularly in Lisbon, where they were created. Legend has it that the monks of the Monastery of the Hieronymites used vast quantities of egg whites to starch their linen, and to use up the yolks (and earn some money), they created these tartlets, which have since become world renowned.

Of all the *pastéis* (*pastel* is the singular) to be found, those made in Belém are the most famous. The Portuguese distinguish between "*pastéis de nata*," found throughout the country, and those made by the *pastelaria de Belém*. In the opinion of many, a *pastel de nata* is no more than an imitation of a *pastel de Belém*. True, they have different textures, but the Belém *pastéis* are all sold while still warm—and that makes them even more appetizing. Each pastry chef has a secret recipe, no doubt better than that of the closest competitor, and we could spend hours speculating on which ingredients and which tricks of the trade make each one so different from the others, and therefore unique.

After systematically tasting the *pastéis* of all of the best pastry shops in Lisbon, I shut myself up in my kitchen to work out a recipe that would combine the best of them all. An all-consuming passion and more than a touch of craziness led me to conduct thirty-five different experiments to make *pastéis* as close as possible to those found in Belém.

Two components are essential for delicious *pastéis*: the puff pastry and the cream filling. There's no getting away from it: the puff pastry must be homemade. One could elect to make it with one "turn" fewer, giving a crunchier texture (like those of Belém), or one extra "turn" for a crispier texture. It was a lengthy process to get to the bottom of the mystery of why the custard filling does not spill over when baked, why it forms a skin on the surface, and still remains creamy without being runny inside. The secret is to prepare the custard cream over a hot water bath. Another important aspect is the temperature of the cream when the tartlets are placed in the oven. If the cream is very cold, the *pastéis* will be creamier. If the cream is at room temperature, the texture will be firmer. To put this recipe together, I tried everything: flour, potato starch, cornstarch, *poudre à crème* (a type of French custard powder), whole milk, low-fat milk, butter, and no butter.

In my wide reading on the subject, I often found information indicating that the baking stage is tricky. But this is because in Lisbon, pastry makers bake their *pastéis* at the astonishingly high temperature of nearly 850°F (450°C)! But their ovens are completely different from those in our kitchens. They diffuse the heat from the bottom. Rest assured, we can make *pastéis de nata* at home. Even with an oven temperature of 465°F (240°C), the result will be perfect.

So here is a recipe that produces a pastry that is as close as possible to the one found in the beautiful town of Belém. But that's no reason not to visit Lisbon and pay tribute to all the pastry makers who are so justifiably proud of their work.

In this recipe, I use vegetable shortening for the puff pastry in preference to butter. I'm not trying to be economical; rather, I find that the crisp texture it gives cannot be equaled. Of course, puff pastry made with butter will be tasty, but too crumbly. With shortening, your puff pastry will be wonderfully crunchy, as you can hear if you do as the locals do: holding the pastry close to their ears and squeezing it lightly between their fingers.

Portuguese Custard Tarts
Pastéis de Nata

· · · · · · · · · · · · · · · ·

Makes 22 tartlets
Preparation time: 30 minutes for the puff
  pastry; 45 minutes for the cream, plus
  cooling time
Chilling time: 1 hour for the cream and 1 hour
  for the pastry
Cooking time: 30 minutes for the stages
  involving the cream, plus 15 to 20 minutes
  for the *pastéis*

Special equipment: fairly deep, flared tartlet
  molds, measuring 1 ¾ inches (4 cm) at the
  base and 2 ¾ inches (7 cm) at the rim

INGREDIENTS
FOR THE CREAM
2 ½ tablespoons (1 oz./25 g) cornstarch
2 tablespoons (½ oz./15 g) whole powdered
  milk
2 cups minus 1 teaspoon (475 ml) whole milk
2 tablespoons (1 oz./25 g) unsalted butter
1 teaspoon vanilla extract
1 generous pinch salt
1 cup (7 oz./200 g) sugar
Scant ½ cup (100 ml) water
1 piece lemon peel from an unwaxed
  or organic lemon, about ½ x 2 inches
  (1 x 5 cm)
1 cinnamon stick
Generous ⅓ cup (3 ½ oz./100 g) egg yolks
3 tablespoons (1 ½ oz./40 g) egg whites

FOR THE PUFF PASTRY
2 ½ cups (10 ½ oz./300 g) all-purpose flour
⅔ cup (140 ml) water with a pinch of salt
6 ¾ oz. (190 g) margarine (choose one
  recommended for baking) or European-style
  butter with at least 84 % butterfat, room
  temperature, plus a little extra to spread over
  the dough and to grease the molds

· · · · · · · · · · · · · · · ·

For the cream:

In a heatproof mixing bowl, dissolve the cornstarch and powdered milk with a little of the whole milk.

Pour the remaining milk into a small saucepan over low heat with the butter, vanilla, and salt. Stir frequently.

In another saucepan over low heat, place the sugar, water, lemon peel, and cinnamon stick, and heat to 234°F (112°C).

When the butter has melted and the milk is simmering gently, gradually pour the liquid over the cornstarch-milk powder mixture, stirring constantly.

Whisk the egg yolks and whites into the cornstarch-milk mixture.

Remove the lemon peel and cinnamon stick from the syrup and pour it gradually over the other mixture.

Set the heatproof mixing bowl over a hot water bath and cook, stirring frequently, until the mixture thickens, about 10 minutes. Pour it into a deep but narrow dish (so that as little as possible will evaporate) and allow to cool to room temperature. Chill for 1 hour.

For the puff pastry:

Combine the flour and water and knead for about 10 minutes. Cover with plastic wrap and chill for 1 hour.

On a lightly floured surface, roll the dough out into a rectangle twice as long as it is wide. The margarine or butter should be malleable enough to shape easily. Spread it over the center of the dough, shaping it into a square with sides the same as the width of the dough. Fold the dough on the left and on the right to meet in the center.

Roll out to a rectangle three times as long as the width. Fold the top third downward and fold the lower third over the other 2 layers. Rotate the dough 90° (keep the fold on the left each time you rotate). This stage is called a "simple turn."

Make another simple turn and once again roll the dough into a rectangle.

With the long side facing you, dip a pastry brush in water and lightly brush the entire surface of the dough. Roll it up to make a long log shape. Using your fingers, spread margarine over the entire surface of the log to prevent it from drying out. Cover in plastic wrap and chill until 1 hour before you assemble the *pastéis*.

(continued on page 66)

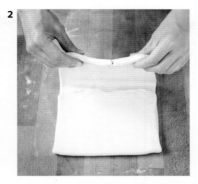

1 Carefully roll the dough into a rectangle 3 times as long as it is wide.

2 Fold the top third downward and fold the lower third over the other 2 layers, to make a simple turn.

3 With the long side facing you, brush the dough lightly with water.

4 Roll the dough tightly to make a long log shape.

5 Set a slice of dough at the base of the mold.

6 Pour the cream into the tart shells.

Preheat the oven to 465°F (240°C), or as hot as possible. Grease the *pastéis* molds.

Gently stretch the log of dough until the diameter is 1 ¼ inches (3 cm) from one end to another.

Cut it into 1-inch (2.5-cm) slices and place them in the prepared molds. Place a piece of dough at the base of each mold and spread it out, using your thumbs as you turn, until it reaches the top.

Pour the cream into the molds, stopping about ¹⁄₁₀ inch (3 mm) short of the top. Place the molds on a baking sheet.

Bake for 15 to 20 minutes, until the surface is caramelized in parts and the cream has risen well.

Remove the sheet from the oven and let cool on a rack for 10 minutes, then carefully turn the *pastéis* out of the molds using a knife. Allow to cool for 30 minutes before serving.

Alicante-Style Nougat
Turrón de Alicante

DAIRY AND GLUTEN FREE
Makes one 6 ½-inch (16-cm) square block
  of nougat
Preparation time: 2 hours
Cooking time: 1 hour

Special equipment: a candy thermometer

INGREDIENTS
2 sheets edible rice paper
3 tablespoons (2 oz./60 g) honey
Scant ½ cup (3 oz./85 g) plus
  2 ½ teaspoons (⅓ oz./10 g) sugar
3 ½ teaspoons (1 oz./25 g) corn syrup
2 ½ tablespoons (40 ml) water
1 tablespoon (½ oz./15 g) egg whites
1 pinch cream of tartar
1 ⅔ cups (9 ¾ oz./275 g) whole blanched
  almonds

Here is my recipe for Alicante *turrón*, a hard nougat-type candy from Spain. I worked for several months to put it together. I hunted for an authentic Alicante *turrón* recipe online, in books on Spanish cuisine, in professional candy-making books—all to no avail. The recipes fell far short of the genuine article. I worked in the dark, modifying my recipes countless times before I finally achieved the result I was hoping for. I had some disastrous experiments, tried several techniques, threw out pounds of honey, sugar, and almonds, and even lost all patience at one stage. But I swore that I would succeed and so I'm proud to share this recipe with you. As you may have gleaned, this recipe is intended mainly for people who enjoy taking up culinary challenges, who are comfortable weighing ingredients with precision, and who are ready to spend the time it takes to succeed.

Using a ruler or cutter, cut the sheets of rice paper to the size of the inside of the confectionery frame or pan. Fit one sheet into the base.

In a small saucepan over low heat, heat the honey, bringing it to 250°F (121°C).

Meanwhile, in another small saucepan over low heat, place ½ cup (3 oz./85 g) sugar, corn syrup, and water. Heat to 300°F (150°C), the hard crack stage.

When the honey is almost at 250°F (121°C), the firm ball stage, use an electric beater to begin whisking the egg whites with 2 ½ teaspoons (⅓ oz./10 g) sugar and the cream of tartar in a large bowl.

When the honey is at 250°F (121°C), drizzle it over the egg whites, whisking continuously.

When the sugar syrup reaches 300°F (150°C), drizzle it over the honey-egg white meringue, continuing to whisk. This makes a type of Italian meringue.

Set the mixture over a hot water bath. And now you're in for a long haul. The meringue has to be stirred continuously over the hot water bath. If you were to stop cooking the candy at this stage, you would have runny nougat that would barely set in the refrigerator. So it's essential to keep cooking it over the hot water bath until all the water contained in the egg whites, honey, and sugar syrup evaporates; the mixture has to dry out. The longer you cook it over the hot water bath, the firmer and more brittle it will be.

(continued on page 70)

To make hard Alicante *turrón*, the paste has to be almost completely dried out. This takes between 45 minutes and 1 hour, but if you double the recipe, it takes longer.

To check the firmness of the meringue as you stir, take a small quantity of the paste and drop it into cold water.

While the nougat paste is drying out, place the almonds in a 350°F (180°C) oven for about 10 minutes, until they are lightly toasted. You may need to ask someone to help you with this, as you'll need to keep stirring the paste.

When the almonds are nicely toasted, reduce the oven temperature to 200°F (100°C) and keep them warm. This means that when you add them to the nougat, the nougat won't harden too quickly because of a drop in temperature.

After about 45 minutes, test the nougat by dropping a small amount into cold water. If it hardens quickly, it is time to add the almonds. In any case, at this stage, you'll be able to tell by the force you have to use to stir—it's a hard job.

Mix the almonds in quickly, because the nougat cools very fast.

Turn the nougat onto the rice paper. Spread it rapidly using your hands. Cover with the second sheet of rice paper, pressing down firmly so that it adheres to the nougat.

Run a knife around the edges so that you can turn the nougat out of the pan. By this time, it should be fairly firm—it's a matter of minutes. Use a rolling pin to roll it to an even thickness. You can turn it over and roll it on the other side too.

Allow to cool completely on a rack.

With a sharp bread knife, cut the nougat into chunks or slices. Alternatively, break it with your hands to give it a rougher look; this method also shows the inside to better advantage.

The nougat must be stored in an airtight container, well protected from all moisture. It will keep for at least a month.

Jijona-Style Nougat
Turrón de Jijona

DAIRY AND GLUTEN FREE
Makes one 4 x 9 inch (11 x 23 cm) block
  of nougat
Preparation time: 1 hour 30 minutes
Cooking time: 1 hour
Resting time: 5 days

Special equipment: a candy thermometer

INGREDIENTS
4 ½ cups (1 ¼ lb./500 g) blanched almonds
½ cup (3 oz./85 g) sugar
⅓ cup (4 ½ oz./130 g) honey
Scant ⅓ cup (2 ⅓ oz./65 g) egg whites
1 pinch cinnamon

After the rather brittle *turrón de Alicante*, I felt I had to explain how to make *turrón de Jijona*, another well-known Spanish nougat traditionally served during the festive season. It has an unusual texture, like powder that's compressed yet somehow melting. If you're not familiar with it, you should certainly taste it. And most people like it after their very first taste. Like the Alicante-style *turrón*, this nougat is also made using a hot water bath. And after that, it must be allowed to rest for at least five days, the time it takes for the sediment to settle. "Sedimentation" is, surprisingly, the appropriate word here. The sedimentation of the Jijona *turrón* is the stage when the paste separates from the oil in the almonds, leaving a nougat that becomes firmer to the touch as it takes on its unique, final consistency. The recipe I give you here is rich in almonds and—you'll find it hard to believe—low in sugar. Serve it in very thin slices.

Preheat the oven to 350°F (180°C). Line a baking sheet with parchment paper. Line a loaf pan with parchment paper for the nougat, with sufficient overhang to fold over and cover the finished product. You may need to use two pieces of parchment.

Spread the almonds evenly on the baking sheet and roast for 12 to 15 minutes, shaking the sheet every 3 minutes so they color all over. Keep a careful eye on them: they should be nicely colored, but certainly not burned. Put the sheet on a rack to cool.

Place the cooled almonds in a sturdy food processer and grind to a fine powder. They should start to form a paste, rendering some of their oil. Process as much as you can. This should take 5 to 8 minutes altogether, but stop running the processor from time to time so that it can cool down. Leave the almond paste in the bowl.

Prepare a hot water bath that is large and stable. You will want to mix without fear of your bowl falling.

Place the sugar and honey in a bowl over the hot water and allow the sugar to dissolve. As soon as the sugar has melted, but before the sugar and honey heat up too much, check the temperature—the syrup should be at about 108°F (42°C). A higher temperature would cook the egg whites.

(continued on page 72)

Stir in the egg whites with a wooden spoon. Continue to stir: the mixture will become pale and gain in volume, like a soft meringue. It becomes more resistant, but keep stirring over the simmering hot water bath for 20 to 25 minutes.

Pour the meringue into the bowl with the ground almonds and allow to cool.

When the mixture reaches room temperature, run the food processor for about 10 minutes, adding a pinch of cinnamon through the funnel after about 5 minutes, until the paste resembles a praline paste. If the motor seems to be overheating, switch it off to allow it to cool. If necessary, process the mixture for longer than 10 minutes; the paste should be soft. The Jijona-style *turrón* goes through several stages: first sandy, it is transformed into a soft paste that breaks into powder when pressed. The stage after that is a paste from which oil seeps out.

Clean the bowl you used over the hot water bath and place the paste in it. Stirring constantly, continue cooking for 15 to 20 minutes to dry it out as much as possible.

Pour the mixture into the loaf pan and tap it gently on a work surface so the bubbles can come to the surface. Fold the parchment paper over the top of the *turrón* and cover the *turrón* with a paper towel.

Allow the nougat to rest for at least 5 days, changing the paper towel every day, or at least every other day. The oil contained in the almonds rises gradually, and the paste becomes increasingly compact as gravity pulls on it.

Changing the paper towel regularly will help wick out the oil and the nougat will take on its unique texture.

When you're ready to serve the nougat, very carefully turn the nougat out of the mold by pulling the strips of parchment paper upward and out of the pan. Slice the *turrón* into very fine slices, pop a piece in your mouth, and savor it.

Sweet Short Pastry Crust

Makes 1 lb. (480 g) pastry
Preparation time: 20 minutes
Chilling time: 1 hour plus 20 minutes

INGREDIENTS
1 ¾ cups (8 oz./220 g) all-purpose flour
1 stick plus 1 tablespoon (4 ¾ oz./135 g)
 unsalted butter, well chilled and diced
Generous ½ cup (1 ½ oz./45 g) finely ground
 almonds
⅓ cup (2 oz./50 g) confectioners' sugar
1 pinch ground vanilla bean, or the seeds of
 1 vanilla bean (slit lengthwise and scrape
 them out)
3 ½ tablespoons (50 g) beaten egg

The secret of a good sweet short pastry is not to overwork the dough as you combine the ingredients. Never mix more than necessary: this results in a crust that is too hard when baked. Of course, you can prepare the dough by hand, but the difficulty is that your hands transmit their natural warmth to the butter, thereby softening it. This causes the dough to clump together even before the egg is added. If you work by hand at any stage, use only your fingertips. However, the simplest, surest technique is to use a stand mixer fitted with the flat beater attachment. If you don't have one, the bowl of a food processor fitted with the blade knife also works well, as does a simple pastry cutter. Combine the dry ingredients with the butter, add the egg last, and incorporate it to make a buttery tart pastry that's crisp and slightly crumbly when baked. Another rule is to respect the chilling time: this gives the gluten time to relax and reduces shrinkage.

Using a stand mixer:
In the bowl of a stand mixer fitted with the flat beater attachment, place the flour, butter, ground almonds, confectioners' sugar, and ground vanilla bean.

Combine at medium speed, stopping the motor as soon as the butter has been completely incorporated into the dry ingredients to make a sandy mixture.

Lightly beat the egg and add it to the bowl. Beat until just combined, and not one moment more! It truly is important not to overwork the dough. Remove the beater and briefly (just for 10 seconds) knead by hand to incorporate any ingredients that may have remained at the bottom of the bowl. Shape into a ball and then flatten to make a disc. Cover in plastic wrap and chill for at least 1 hour.

Making by hand:
Place the flour, diced butter, ground almonds, confectioners' sugar, and ground vanilla bean in a mixing bowl. Working with a pastry cutter, repeatedly cut and mash it into the dry ingredients to form a sandy mixture.

Lightly beat the egg and pour it into the sandy mixture. Continuing to work with the cutter, incorporate the egg. Stop as soon as the dough is smooth.

Shape into a ball and then flatten to make a disc. Cover in plastic wrap and chill for at least 1 hour.

Using a food processor, finishing by hand:
Dice the butter and place it in the freezer for 30 minutes. Place the dry ingredients and butter in the bowl of a food processor fitted with the blade knife, and process until a sandy mixture forms. Transfer the mixture to

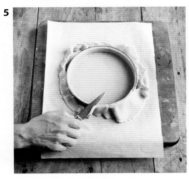

1 Add the beaten egg to the crumbly ingredients.

2 Incorporate until smooth; do not overwork.

3 Roll the dough on a piece of parchment paper.

4 Line the tart ring with the dough, ensuring that it makes a right angle with the rim at the base, or fits snugly into the tart pan.

5 Trim the excess dough, using a sharp knife at a 90° angle to the rim.

6 Baking blind: the flour bag technique.

a mixing bowl. Lightly beat the egg and use your fingertips to work it in to make the dough. Do not overwork: stop as soon as the dough is smooth.

Shape into a ball and then flatten to make a disc. Cover in plastic wrap and chill for at least 1 hour.

Rolling out the dough:
The traditional method of rolling out involves using a floured work surface. This is a method I use less and less, because it tends to add too much flour. I prefer to lightly dust the dough with flour and place it on a sheet of parchment paper. This simplifies the rolling process considerably: you can lift up the paper with the dough, rotate it, and pivot it as you need.

Lightly dust the rolling pin with flour. Work slowly and calmly. I recommend a rolling pin without handles. You should be able to feel the pressure below the palms of your hands as you roll, something that you won't sense if you have handles. Roll from bottom to top, starting and stopping about 1 inch (2 cm) short of the edge. Rotate the paper a few degrees. Roll again, starting and stopping at the same distance from the edge. Keep rotating the dough.

(continued on page 76)

This ensures that the dough is well rolled out and means you won't roll it excessively at the edges. Because you turn the paper each time, the lower and upper edges are rolled out when rotated.

If the dough seems to offer a little resistance to the rolling pin, dust it very lightly with flour both on top and underneath. Continue until it is very thin, under ⅛ inch (2 mm). If this seems dauntingly thin, keep in mind that you may need some practice; it is surprisingly resistant and shouldn't tear.

Grease the tart pan lightly, or the rim of the tart ring. If you're using a tart ring, place it over a baking sheet lined with parchment paper. To line the tart pan or ring, lift the dough off the paper and set it carefully over the pan or ring, ensuring that the dough fits snugly against the rim of the pan, or pressing around the base to make a 90° angle for a ring. If you're using a ring, check that the dough is securely fitted by lifting up the ring slightly to take a peek below.

Trim the excess dough: holding a small, sharp knife at a 90° angle from the rim, run it all the way round. Prick the dough with a fork and place in the refrigerator for 20 minutes or so, while you prepare the filling.

Baking blind (pre-baking):
I suggest using one of two methods to pre-bake a crust.

The first involves the "flour bag," and is widely used by French professionals. It's the method I prefer.

Cut 2 sheets of professional-grade heat-resistant plastic wrap long enough to leave sufficient overhang over the rims. Place one over the unbaked, chilled dough and place the other sheet at right angles to the first.

Pour in enough flour to reach three-quarters way up the rim. Do not press the flour in. Tie the edges of both sheets of plastic together to form a pouch. This ensures that the dough remains close to the rim as it bakes, because the flour swells slightly in the oven.

Bake at 350°F (180°C) for about 15 minutes. Remove the pouch of flour and discard it. Continue to bake until it turns a nice golden color, 10 to 15 minutes more.

The second method is more conventional. Cut a round of parchment paper slightly bigger than the ring or pan you are using. With a pair of scissors, cut a fringe around the rim. Set the parchment paper on the dough and fill with pie weights or dried beans. Bake at 350°F (180°C) for about 15 minutes, discard the parchment paper and weights, and continue to bake until nicely colored.

Yeasted Breton Butter Cake
Kouign Amann

• • • • • • • • • • • • • • •

EGG FREE
Serves 6 to 8
Preparation time: 45 minutes
Resting time: 2 to 3 hours
Cooking time: 30 to 35 minutes

INGREDIENTS

¼ of a 0.6 oz. cake (5 g) of fresh (compressed) yeast

½ cup (125 ml) warm water, divided

1 ⅔ cups (7 ½ oz./210 g) all-purpose flour, plus ½ cup minus 1 tablespoon (2 oz./50 g) to roll out the dough

1 teaspoon salt

1 ¾ sticks (7 oz./200 g) salted butter, room temperature, for the dough (see page 282)

4 tablespoons (2 oz./50 g) salted butter: half for the pan and half for the top of the *kouign amann*

1 cup (7 oz./200 g) sugar plus 2 tablespoons (1 oz./25 g) for sprinkling

• • • • • • • • • • • • • • •

Kouign amann (pronounced "kween-ah-mun"), a classic Breton pastry, comes to us from the small fishing port of Douarnenez in the Finistère department, on the westernmost coast of France. Although it is popularly believed to be a cake going back many, many generations, it was in fact invented in the nineteenth century. *Kouign amann* means "cake" (*kouign*) with "butter" (*amann*). It was the first rather "difficult" recipe I made when I was thirteen or fourteen years old. At the time, it took me over a year (with a few breaks, granted) to get it right. I couldn't find a single cookbook that explained how to make it. For a while, I would carry out experiments after school to get to the bottom of the technique. This required some improvisation, and the result is the recipe below. Since then, I've understood that I did exactly what had to be done, and that I hadn't invented anything new. So here is the recipe that I kept for myself for many years, hoarding it in my blue binder where I kept all the recipes I loved.

Crumble the yeast in a little of the warm water and stir to dissolve. Pour it into a large mixing bowl or the bowl of a stand mixer fitted with a dough hook. Add the flour and salt. Knead in the remaining water.

Knead for at least 10 minutes at medium speed, until the dough becomes smooth and no longer sticks to your hands. If you're working by hand, knead like bread dough until the dough is smooth. Shape into a ball and make a cross-shaped incision on the top.

Lightly press a piece of plastic wrap on top of the dough to prevent it from drying out. Allow to rise for 2 to 3 hours, until at least doubled in volume.

Have all the remaining ingredients, including the flour to roll out the dough (it might be easier to put this in a small bowl), at hand. Be sure to weigh or measure out the flour so that you don't add an unnecessary amount to the dough.

Roll the dough out as much as possible. This stage may take some time, as the dough is very elastic. Keep dusting with flour, using only the flour that you have set aside for this purpose. Roll until you have a rectangle that measures 12 x 20 inches (30 x 50 cm).

(continued on page 78)

Spread the butter as evenly as possible over the surface of the dough, stopping ½ inch (1 cm) short of the edges. Then sprinkle 1 cup (7 oz./200 g) of sugar over it, leaving no sugar-free patches. Press very lightly over the surface to incorporate the sugar into the butter.

Now fold the dough over in thirds lengthwise, and then in thirds crosswise.

Gently roll the dough out, taking care not to crush it: this would make the butter and sugar come oozing out like toothpaste from a tube. If this seems impossible, place the dough in the refrigerator for 20 minutes before trying again. Don't forget to use the measured flour to dust the work surface and the rolling pin.

Once the dough has been rolled out, fold it in thirds lengthwise. Roll out again, turn it 90°, and fold it again in thirds. You'll need to work gently and carefully throughout this process.

Preheat the oven to 350°F (180°C). Butter a 10-inch (26-cm) diameter cake pan with the butter set aside for this purpose. If you wish, you can place a piece of parchment paper cut out to the correct dimensions at the base of the pan and butter that.

Take the dough and using the rolling pin, roll it out to the size of the pan. Dice the remaining butter and scatter it over the top of the dough. Using a knife, make incisions in a criss-cross pattern over the dough.

Bake for 30 to 35 minutes, until nicely golden. Be careful not to over-bake, otherwise you'll have a piece of caramel at the base. Leave in the pan to absorb the butter that will have seeped from the dough. As soon as it has been reabsorbed, place a dish or large plate over the pan, turn it over, and gently shake it until the cake falls onto the dish. Using another dish or large plate, you can then turn the cake over again so that the top is facing upward, with the criss-cross pattern visible. Sprinkle with the remaining sugar.

Tightly wrapped in plastic wrap, *kouign amann* keeps for 4 to 5 days and freezes well. Before serving, reheat it in a hot oven for 5 to 7 minutes.

Breton Flan
Far Breton

Serves 6
Preparation time: 10 minutes
Cooking time: 1 hour

INGREDIENTS
1 scant cup (6 ½ oz./190 g) sugar
4 eggs
2 cups (8 ½ oz./240 g) all-purpose flour
3 cups (750 ml) whole milk
3 tablespoons (2 oz./50 g) salted butter,
    divided
Prunes or raisins, marinated in rum or tea,
    optional
Sliced apples cooked in butter and flambéed
    in Calvados (or other apple brandy),
    optional

Every Breton cook has a secret family recipe for this flan, so there are as many types of *far* as there are Breton cooks. Originally, it was a very simple recipe that contained only baked batter. It was only recently that macerated fruit—prunes, raisins, or apples—began to be added. Of course, you can add whatever pleases you. And you can make it as thick as you like, and even flambé it with Grand Marnier liqueur when you remove it from the oven. Just keep in mind that a traditional *far* is rarely thick, barely 1 inch (1 to 2 cm) high.

Here, I give you a basic recipe that you can vary to your heart's content. With melted salty butter on the top, your *far* will not withstand the onslaught of famished gourmands for long.

If using dried fruit, soak for 1 hour in rum or tea to cover.

Preheat the oven to 320°F (160°C). Using about one-third of the butter, grease the bottom of an 8 x 11 inch (22 x 28 cm) ovenproof dish.

Whisk the sugar and eggs lightly together in a mixing bowl, then whip until foamy. This will create a creamier consistency on the top and a denser texture underneath in the finished flan.

Add half of the flour and whisk briskly, ensuring that no lumps remain.

Pour in one-third of the milk and whisk again. Continue, alternating the flour and milk, until all the ingredients are incorporated and there are no lumps.

Pour the batter into the prepared dish. The baked *far* will not rise any higher than its unbaked height. You'll want a thickness of just under 1 inch (2 cm).

If you're using dried fruit, drain and sprinkle them evenly over the batter. If you're using the apples, no need to drain them first.

Melt the remaining salted butter and pour it carefully over the unbaked *far*. Bake for about 1 hour. Keep a careful eye on it for the last 15 minutes as it may burn.

When you remove it from the oven, the *far* is usually well risen—sometimes quite astonishingly. But as it cools, it deflates and leaves a nice crust on the edges of the dish.

Allow to cool slightly on a rack and serve lukewarm. It's best eaten the day it's made.

Thin Breton Butter Cookies

Galettes Bretonnes

Makes about 50 cookies
Preparation time: 15 minutes
Chilling time: 1 hour
Cooking time: 10 to 12 minutes per batch

INGREDIENTS

1 ⅓ sticks (5 ½ oz./155 g) salted butter,
  room temperature (see page 282)
1 scant cup (6 oz./180 g) sugar
2 tablespoons (1 oz./30 g) beaten egg
2 cups (8 ½ oz./240 g) all-purpose flour
A little low-fat milk to brush the tops

These delicious, delicate cookies, less well known than their thicker cousins (see page 84) originate in the southern area of the Breton department of Finistère on the westernmost coast of France. They are made with so much butter that they taste almost nutty. I'm always surprised to see how many different types of cakes and cookies one can make simply by modifying the proportions of ingredients, and modifying the method and baking time. Since my childhood, these *galettes* have been essential to my afternoon snacks. For a long time, I wondered if I would ever find *the* recipe to make them. As an adult, I visited the factories where they are made and realized that there was no reason not to make them at home. After all, they only contain ingredients that are staples in every kitchen. And so after many attempts to achieve a factory-like product at home, following the listed ingredients to the letter, and without adding or removing anything, I bring you the recipe that recreates the wonderful taste of Breton cookies with salted butter.

Place the butter and sugar in the bowl of a stand mixer fitted with the flat beater attachment or in a mixing bowl. Beat until creamy. Beat in the egg.

Pour in all the flour and continue beating. Stop when all the flour is incorporated. Shape the dough into a ball and then roll it into a log shape just over 2 inches (6 cm) in diameter. Wrap tightly in plastic wrap and chill for 1 hour.

Preheat the oven to 400°F (200°C). Line a baking sheet with parchment paper.

Slice the dough as thinly as possible (paper-thin, about 1 mm thick). Place the rounds on the baking sheet—they won't spread much. If you have a cookie stamp, now is the time to decorate your cookies.

Dip a pastry brush in the milk and brush the tops of the cookies. Lightly press down the edges of the cookies with a finger.

Bake for 10 to 12 minutes, until golden. Transfer the cookies onto a rack to cool completely. Stored in an airtight container they will keep for a week.

Thick Breton Shortbread (left) and
Thin Breton Butter Cookies (right)

Thick Breton Shortbread

Traou mad ®

Makes 20 to 30 cookies
Preparation time: 15 minutes
Chilling time: 30 minutes
Cooking time: 20 minutes

Special equipment: at least 10 small tartlet
rings with 2 ½-inch (6-cm) diameter

INGREDIENTS
1 stick plus 1 tablespoon (4 ½ oz./130 g)
salted butter, room temperature (see
page 282)
½ cup minus 1 tablespoon (3 oz./85 g) sugar
2 tablespoons (⅔ oz./20 g) egg yolk
1 tablespoon (15 ml) whole milk
1 ⅔ cups (7 oz./200 g) all-purpose flour
¼ teaspoon baking powder
Skim milk to brush the tops

Beat the butter and sugar together until soft and creamy.

With a fork, lightly beat the egg yolk and milk in a small bowl. Add the liquid to the butter-sugar mixture and stir in quickly.

In another bowl, combine the flour and baking powder. Pour all the flour into the butter-yolk mixture and stir until smooth. Do not beat or overwork.

Place the dough between 2 sheets of parchment paper and roll out to a ¼-inch (6-mm) thickness.

Chill for 30 minutes or until firm.

Preheat the oven to 400°F (200°C). Line a baking sheet with parchment paper. Lightly grease the tart rings.

Using a tartlet ring, cut out discs of dough and transfer them to the prepared baking sheet. Each shortbread cookie must bake in its own ring. You'll need at least 10 rings per batch.

If you have a cookie stamp, press it down lightly in the dough to create a design. Dip a pastry brush in the milk and brush the surface to make a golden crust.

Bake for 20 minutes, until golden, let cool briefly, then gently push the cookies out of the rings. Allow them to cool completely on a rack and then store in an airtight container for about a week.

Apple Strudel
Apfelstrudel

EGG FREE
Serves 6
Preparation time: 40 minutes
Resting time: 1 hour
Cooking time: 1 hour to 1 hour 15 minutes

INGREDIENTS
FOR THE STRUDEL DOUGH
1 ⅔ cups (7 oz./200 g) all-purpose flour,
   plus a little to dust the dough
Scant ½ cup (110 ml) water
1 tablespoon (½ oz./15 g) butter,
   room temperature
A little oil to brush the dough

FOR THE FILLING
6 apples
Juice of ½ lemon
Generous ⅓ cup (2 oz./60 g) raisins
Scant ½ cup (2 ⅔ oz./75g) walnuts, chopped
½ teaspoon cinnamon
4 tablespoons (1 ¾ oz./50 g) light brown
   sugar

TO FINISH
1 stick (4 oz./125 g) unsalted butter
Confectioners' sugar for dusting

I was intimidated by this recipe for a long time, mainly because it seemed impossible to make at home. I knew the dough was one that had to be pulled until it was paper-thin and that just seemed impossible to me. Curiously, it was when I learned how to make gazelle horns (see page 205) in Casablanca that I realized strudel dough was, in fact, fairly simple. The principle is the same, and so is the dough, the only difference is that the dough for gazelle horns is pulled in oil while strudel dough is pulled on a floured cloth. And so I set to work.

The secret to making a good strudel lies in the dough. It must be very well kneaded so that it is very soft and can be stretched to the utmost. This is the lightest recipe in the book: there is just a little butter to color the top of the dough and the filling contains just a touch of sugar.

For the strudel dough, place all the flour in the bowl of a stand mixer fitted with a dough hook attachment. Set it to low speed and gradually pour in the water.

When the dough forms a ball, add the butter and knead for about 15 minutes, until it is very smooth and soft to the touch. If necessary, add 1 tablespoon water and knead for 5 minutes more, until the dough no longer sticks to the sides of the bowl.

Shape it into a disc, brush the surface with oil, and cover it in plastic wrap. Allow to rest at room temperature for at least 1 hour. During this time, the dough will relax; if you have kneaded it well, it will be very elastic and so you can pull it over an extended surface.

Meanwhile, peel the apples and cut them into bite-sized pieces. Drizzle with lemon juice so that they don't brown. Place them in a mixing bowl and add the raisins, chopped walnuts, cinnamon, and sugar. Mix well. There is no need to plump the raisins in warm water beforehand: they will swell as they bake in the steam from the apples.

Take a clean cloth, preferably ironed smooth, at least 20 x 28 inches (50 x 70 cm) in size.

(continued on page 86)

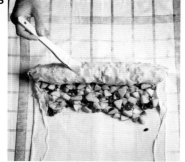

1 Brush the dough with oil, cover it with plastic wrap, and allow it to rest at room temperature.

2 Gently pull the dough with your hands until it is almost transparent.

3 Brush the top part of the dough with melted butter.

4 Use the cloth to help you roll the strudel up.

5 With a soft, dry pastry brush, remove the excess flour as you roll.

6 Generously brush the strudel with melted butter before placing it in the oven.

Remove the plastic wrap from the dough and dust the dough lightly with flour. Spread the cloth flat on a large working surface and sprinkle liberally with flour. If there isn't enough flour, the dough will stick to the cloth.

Set the dough in the center of the cloth and use a rolling pin to roll it toward the edges of the cloth. When you can no long roll with the rolling pin, take the dough with your hands and gently pull it toward the edge of the cloth, taking care not to make any holes. If possible, slip one hand below the dough to help it move toward the edges. You have to spread it over the entire surface of the cloth, and it should be thin enough for you to see any patterns in the fabric. Trim the edges to make a well-defined rectangle.

Preheat the oven to 340°F (170°C). Line a baking sheet with parchment paper.

Spread the apple filling over three-quarters of the surface of the dough leaving a 1-inch (2- to 3- cm) border. Melt the butter and brush the uncovered section of the dough with a little of it.

(continued on page 88)

Pull the border over the apples from both sides and then fold it inward. Using the cloth as a sling, begin rolling up the strudel. As you roll, brush off all excess flour with a soft pastry brush. When you're done, the unbaked strudel will look like a giant sausage. Place the rolled-up strudel on the prepared baking sheet.

Brush the entire surface of the strudel with melted butter. You'll use the remaining butter to brush the strudel while it bakes.

Bake for 1 hour to 1 hour 15 minutes, brushing it with butter every 30 minutes, until nicely golden.

Put the baking sheet on a rack and let the strudel cool slightly, then dust it with confectioners' sugar. Cut generous slices and serve plain or with pouring custard.

Giant Praline Sandwich Cookies

Sablés Géants au Praliné

Makes 12 filled cookies
Preparation time: 20 minutes
Chilling time: 1 hour plus 20 minutes for
   filling to set
Cooking time: 30 minutes per sheet of cookie
   pastry (each sheet is baked in two stages)

INGREDIENTS
FOR THE SWEET PASTRY
1 cup (3 oz./85 g) finely ground almonds
Generous 1 ¾ cups (8 ½ oz./240 g)
   confectioners' sugar
4 ⅔ cups (1 ¼ lb./580 g) all-purpose flour
3 ⅓ sticks (14 oz./400 g) unsalted butter,
   well chilled and diced
Generous ½ cup (4 ¾ oz./135 g) beaten eggs
1 egg, lightly beaten, for the glaze

FOR THE PRALINE FILLING
1 stick (4 oz./120 g) unsalted butter
4 ¼ oz. (120 g) milk chocolate
1 ½ lb. (720 g) praline paste (page 18)

I have always been drawn to good food and the richer it is, the more my brain tries to make me feel guilty, but to no avail. I have to confess: I'm a sucker for delicious things. When I was seventeen, I discovered some giant cookies in a Paris pastry shop. French bakeries often display large butter cookies called *sablés* in their windows. Glued to the window, I marveled at the range of extravagant butter cookies with scrumptious fillings: creamy praline with chocolate, walnuts and caramel, and raspberries. After that, I couldn't get them out of my mind and would bike across the city (burning some calories to ease my conscience) to buy them. The hardest part was choosing which ones to buy. I have never forgotten them, and in fact the pastry shop is still in operation. One day I decided to make them at home so that I could recreate what I like so much.

Of course, if they seem too large to you, you can make half the recipe and cut them into smaller portions. But in my opinion, it's their very extravagance—and their status as guilty pleasures—that make them so special.

Prepare the sweet pastry. Place the ground almonds, confectioners' sugar, flour, and butter in the bowl of a stand mixer fitted with the flat beater attachment. (You can also rub the ingredients together using your fingertips.) Beat until the mixture reaches a sandy texture.

Incorporate the eggs, mixing until just combined. Do not overwork the pastry.

Shape it into a ball, cover with plastic wrap, and chill for 1 hour.

Cut it into 2 equal pieces. On a work surface covered with parchment paper, roll one piece to a thickness of about ⅛ inch (4 mm) to fit onto a 12 x 16 inch (30 x 40 cm) baking sheet. (You'll need a baking sheet with a rim). If necessary, trim off any excess dough. Place the dough on the baking sheet and chill for at least 1 hour.

Repeat with the second piece of dough.

Preheat the oven to 350°F (180°C).

(continued on page 90)

For the first stage of baking, bake the first sheet for 15 minutes. Remove it from the oven and brush the top with the beaten egg. (If you do this before baking, the egg wash will shrink during baking and create unnecessary pressure on the surface.) Using a fork, trace diagonal lines over the surface to make a pattern. Return to the oven and bake for 10 to 15 minutes, until golden all over.

Repeat the procedure for the second sheet of pastry. Allow both sheets to cool on racks.

Meanwhile, make the filling. Melt the butter and milk chocolate together over a hot water bath, or in the microwave oven, working in short bursts.

Add the praline paste and mix until thoroughly combined.

Pour all the chocolate praline mixture over the less attractive sheet of pastry, inverted, spreading it evenly with a spatula.

Carefully set the other sheet of pastry over the filling. Chill for 20 minutes, until the praline filling sets.

Trim the sides and cut the slab into twelve 3 ½-inch (9-cm) squares.

Store in an airtight container.

Giant Praline Sandwich Cookies (top) and
Giant Walnut Sandwich Cookies (bottom)

Giant Walnut
Sandwich Cookies

Makes 12 filled cookies
Preparation time: 20 minutes
Cooking time: 15 minutes
Chilling time: 2 hours

Special equipment: a candy thermometer

INGREDIENTS
1 batch sweet pastry (page 89)

FOR THE WALNUT CARAMEL FILLING
1 ¼ cups (8 ½ oz./240 g) sugar
3 tablespoons (2 oz./60 g) corn syrup
3 tablespoons (50 ml) water
⅔ cup (150 ml) heavy cream, slightly
    warmed
1 ¼ sticks (5 oz./150 g) unsalted butter, diced,
    at room temperature
2 ½ cups (10 ½ oz./300 g) chopped walnuts

Prepare the sweet pastry and bake as for the praline cookies (see page 89).

For the walnut caramel filling, place the sugar, corn syrup, and water in a heavy saucepan over medium heat. Make sure that there are no grains of sugar on the sides of the saucepan. If there are, brush them down with a pastry brush dipped in water.

Cook until the mixture reaches a pronounced caramel color, but don't let it burn.

Remove from the heat and stir in the cream and butter. Return to low heat. The caramel may have hardened and needs to melt again. Heat to 234°F (112°C).

Remove from the heat, stir in the nuts, and transfer the mixture to a bowl to allow it to cool.

Pour all of the walnut-caramel over the less attractive sheet of pastry on the undecorated side, spreading it evenly with a spatula.

Carefully set the other sheet of pastry over the filling. Chill for 2 hours, until the filling sets so that you can cut the cookies easily.

Trim the sides and cut the slab into twelve 3 ½-inch (9-cm) squares.

Store in an airtight container for about a week.

Walnut Caramel Tartlets

Makes 6 tartlets
Preparation time: 20 minutes
Cooking time: 25 to 30 minutes
Chilling time: 1 hour 20 minutes plus 2 hours

Special equipment: a candy thermometer

INGREDIENTS
½ batch sweet short pastry crust (page 74)

FOR THE WALNUT CARAMEL FILLING
1 ¼ cups (8 ½ oz./240 g) sugar
3 tablespoons (2 oz./60 g) corn syrup
3 tablespoons (50 ml) water
⅔ cup (150 ml) heavy cream, slightly warmed
1 ¼ sticks (5 oz./150 g) unsalted butter, diced, at room temperature
2 ½ cups (10 ½ oz./300 g) chopped walnuts

A variation of the recipe for Giant Walnut Sandwich Cookies, these tartlets use the same walnut caramel filling and are equally delicious.

Prepare the sweet short pastry crust, as on page 74.

Line tartlet pans, trim the excess dough, and chill for 20 minutes or so.

In the meantime, prepare the walnut caramel filling. Place the sugar, corn syrup, and water in a heavy saucepan over medium heat. Make sure that there are no grains of sugar on the sides of the saucepan. If there are, brush them down with a pastry brush dipped in water.

Cook until the mixture reaches a pronounced caramel color, but don't let it burn.

Remove from the heat and stir in the cream and butter. Return to low heat. The caramel may have hardened and will need to melt again. Heat to 234°F (112°C).

Remove from the heat, stir in the nuts, and transfer the mixture to a bowl to allow it to cool.

Blind bake the pastry in the tartlet pans, using the flour bag technique (see page 76). As soon as they are golden, fill them with the walnut-caramel mixture.

Chill for 2 hours, until the filling sets.

The tartlets will keep for about a week in an airtight container.

Scandalous Orange Tart

Tarte Scandaleuse à l'Orange

Makes one 8-inch (22-cm) tart
Preparation time: 25 minutes
Cooking time: 45 minutes
Chilling time: 2 hours

INGREDIENTS

½ batch sweet short pastry crust (page 74)

FOR THE ALMOND-ORANGE CREAM

5 tablespoons (2 ½ oz./75 g) butter, room temperature, diced
¾ cup (3 ½ oz./100 g) confectioners' sugar
Finely grated zest of 2 unwaxed or organic oranges
1 cup (3 oz./ 85 g) finely ground almonds
2 eggs
Generous ⅓ cup (90 ml) freshly squeezed orange juice

FOR THE ORANGE CREAM

Scant ½ cup (3 oz./85 g) sugar
1 ½ teaspoons (5 g) cornstarch
1 egg plus 1 egg yolk
Finely grated zest of 1 unwaxed or organic orange
⅓ cup (90 ml) orange juice
6 tablespoons (3 oz./85 g) butter, room temperature, diced

A tart that combines rich, creamy, soft, and crisp textures with the sweet, sophisticated flavors of orange. And butter, butter, and more butter. Yes, it's a scandalously delectable tart. It's scandalously high in calories, even worse, when eaten it doesn't feel as though it should induce any guilt at all. I can't urge you strongly enough to make this scandalous tart: you'll cut it into reasonably sized portions and with its fresh, unusual flavors, no one will suspect what you've used to make it so delectable.

Preheat the oven to 350°F (180°C). Place the rolled sweet short pastry crust in an 8-inch (20-cm) diameter, 1-inch (2.5-cm) deep tart pan with a detachable bottom or tart ring. Fit it in snugly at the base of the rim. If you are using a tart ring, place it on a baking sheet lined with parchment paper. Prick the base of the dough with a fork.

If you have a favorite method for blind baking, proceed as usual. Otherwise, on page 76 you'll find several methods. Bake for 15 minutes. Do not allow the tart to color too much, as it will be baked further with the almond-orange cream. (You'll need to maintain the oven temperature for the next stage.)

Prepare the almond-orange cream. In a mixing bowl, place the butter, confectioners' sugar, orange zest, and ground almonds. Beat with a wooden spoon until creamy.

Beat in the eggs, one by one, and then the orange juice. The cream will appear to curdle—it has lumps at this stage, but this is of no importance, as they disappear during baking. Pour the cream into the tart shell and bake for 30 minutes, until both the crust and the almond-orange cream are a nice golden color.

Carefully remove the tart ring or the rim of the pan and allow the tart to cool completely on a rack.

For the orange cream, combine the sugar, cornstarch, egg, and egg yolk in a saucepan. Add the zest and gradually drizzle in the orange juice. Cook over low heat, stirring constantly. When the cream comes to a boil, remove it from the heat. Allow to cool for 10 minutes.

Whisk in the butter until thoroughly combined. Pour the mixture evenly over the cooled tart and smooth the top.

Chill the tart for at least 2 hours before serving.

Valérie's Chocolate Creams

EGG AND GLUTEN FREE
Makes 5 classic ramekins or a larger number
  of small portions
Preparation time: 5 minutes
Cooking time: 10 minutes
Chilling time: 4 hours

INGREDIENTS
3 cups (750 ml) whipping or heavy cream
  (minimum 30 percent butterfat)
7 oz. (200 g) chopped bittersweet chocolate,
  56 percent cacao
1 ¾ oz. (50 g) chopped bittersweet chocolate,
  70 percent cacao

I was giving a *macaron* lesson at a private home and Valérie, one of the students, kindly invited me to come for lunch before the class began. At the end of the meal, she brought in her chocolate creams. The moment I dipped my spoon into the little dish, I knew I simply had to have the recipe. The cream has just the right degree of firmness, it melts in the mouth, and the taste of cooked chocolate is both rich and reassuring. The recipe is not only extraordinary, it is also very simple, with just a few ingredients. It's a question of proportions.

What's more, it takes only five minutes to make, plus the time it takes to cool. I'd like to once again thank Valérie very warmly for having shared her recipe for this fabulously unctuous chocolate cream dessert.

In a heavy saucepan over low heat, bring the cream to a boil.

Remove from the heat and add the two types of chocolate. Stir with a wooden spoon.

Return to low heat and stir constantly until the chocolate is melted. This should take 1 to 2 minutes. When the cream is perfectly smooth, with no traces of unmelted chocolate, divide it among the ramekins.

Allow to cool completely at room temperature and transfer to the refrigerator for at least 4 hours before serving.

Choose whatever size ramekins you like, but very small ones are a good idea, because these extraordinary cream desserts are quite rich.

Swiss Caramelized
Cream and Sugar Tart
Tarte flambé à la crème et au sucre

EGG FREE
Makes three 8- to 10-inch (20- to 25-cm) tarts
Preparation time: 20 minutes
Chilling time: 1 hour
Cooking time: 8 to 12 minutes

INGREDIENTS
FOR THE PASTRY
1 ⅔ cups (7 oz./200 g) flour
5 tablespoons (3 oz./80 g) unsalted butter,
  well chilled and diced
3–3 ½ tablespoons (40–50 ml) cold water

FOR THE CREAM
¾ cup (6 ½ oz./190 g) heavy cream, double
  cream, or other cream with a high butterfat
  content)
¾ cup (5 oz./140 g) sugar

I first tasted this Swiss specialty in a restaurant in the canton of Vaud. It was mid-winter and we'd just eaten a delicious meal of chicken roasted on an open fire accompanied by *rösti*, grated potato pancakes, sautéed in lard. Then came the long-awaited moment of the flambéed cream tart, thin and crisp. Double Gruyère cream, the local specialty with 50 percent butterfat, is the star ingredient. It is somewhat fluid and is often served with small meringues as a dessert. Since it's not easy to find beyond the borders of Switzerland, you can use a more classic crème fraîche or double cream with a butterfat content that's close to that produced in the Gruyère region. Alternatively, use half mascarpone and half heavy cream. The tart takes little time to prepare and bakes quickly. If you serve it in very small portions, there'll be practically no reason to feel guilty!

For the pastry, place the flour in the bowl of a stand mixer fitted with the flat beater attachment and add the diced butter. (You can also rub the butter in with your fingertips.) Beat at medium speed until the mixture forms fine crumbs.

Gradually pour in the water, beating continuously, until the dough forms a ball. Cover in plastic wrap and chill for 1 hour.

Preheat the oven to 520°F (275°C), or the maximum temperature of your oven.

Divide the dough into 3 equal parts. It's best to roll the dough out on parchment paper. This makes it is easier to manipulate and you'll be able to transfer the dough on the parchment paper directly into the oven.

Dust 1 ball of dough well with flour and roll it as thinly as possible (under ¹⁄₁₀ in. or 1–3 mm, or even thinner if you can). With a single ball of dough, you should be able to shape a 14-inch (35-cm) disc. If it becomes hard to roll, simply place it in the refrigerator for a short time. Flour it again when you recommence rolling. If you're using parchment paper, it's easy to turn the dough over and flour it on the other side.

Cut out an 8- to 10-inch (20- to 25-cm) round and transfer it on the parchment paper to a baking sheet.

(continued on page 100)

In a mixing bowl, combine the cream and sugar. Don't worry if it seems runny: this is because sugar liquefies cream.

Pour one-third of the cream mixture over the round of pastry and spread it almost to the edge (1/10 in. or 3 mm).

Place the tart in the oven for 8 to 10 minutes, keeping a careful eye on it. It bakes very quickly and the top caramelizes.

Prepare the second tart while the first one bakes, and then the third. Make sure you roll the dough out thinly each time.

Serve the tart in thin slices as soon as you remove it from the oven, but take care not to burn your mouth.

Giant Butter Cookies

When I was twelve or thirteen, I used to go to a bakery near where I lived in Paris and drool over the giant butter cookies that stole the limelight in the window. They were so big that they either had to be shared (not my style) or eaten bit by bit (which was just about acceptable). I have never forgotten their taste—they were the ultimate in butter cookies, the benchmark by which I judged all other butter cookies I subsequently ate. For many years, I made recipes that were similar, in the (not-quite secret) quest to recreate the taste I remembered from my teenage years. In the end, I decided to develop my very own recipe, and with each try, I changed the proportions as I fine-tuned my research. Twenty years on, I returned to the very same bakery. It was still there, but sadly it had changed hands and my beloved giant butter cookies weren't sold anymore.

I realized later that there were many similarities between a French regional specialty called the *broyé de Poitou*, an outsized, dense butter cookie, and my ideal butter cookie. That is why I bring you two butter cookie recipes, one for the cookie from the Poitou region, sprinkled with almonds and traditionally broken by hand, and the other that I recreated from memory. For both, I use salted butter, but if you prefer you can use unsalted.

With the two recipes, I explain two different methods for a short butter pastry. I use the creaming method for the *broyé* and the rubbing method for the recipe of my dreams. As always with almond-based doughs, feel free to add a little lemon or orange zest, or 1 ounce (25 to 30 g) of unsweetened cocoa powder for a chocolate variation.

Giant Butter Cookie of Poitou

Broyé du Poitou

Makes one 10-inch (25-cm) butter cookie
Preparation time: 20 minutes
Chilling time: 1 hour 10 minutes
Cooking time: 20 to 25 minutes

INGREDIENTS

1 stick (4 oz./125 g) salted butter, room temperature
⅔ cup (4 ⅓ oz./125 g) sugar
2 ½ tablespoons (1 ⅓ oz./35 g) beaten egg
2 cups (9 oz./250 g) all-purpose flour
1 egg for the glaze
Sliced almonds for sprinkling

In the bowl of a stand mixer fitted with the flat beater attachment, combine the butter and sugar, and mix. When the texture becomes creamy, add the egg and continue to beat. This is known as the creaming method.

Add all the flour and beat just to incorporate. Do not overwork: as soon as the dough is smooth, stop mixing. Over-mixing results in a hard texture, and this is true for any dough that is made without raising agents.

Shape the dough into a ball, flatten it slightly to make a disc, cover with plastic wrap, and chill for 1 hour.

Preheat the oven to 350°F (180°C).

Working on a lightly floured work surface, or even better, on a sheet of parchment paper, roll the dough into a large disc just under ¼ inch (5 mm) thick. If you prefer, you can make this cookie a little thicker, and slightly under-baked in the center.

Using a plate set upside down on the disc, or a tart ring, cut out a 10-inch (25-cm) round. You can make smaller cookies with the extra dough.

Transfer the disc on the parchment paper and chill for 10 minutes.

With your thumb and forefinger, pinch the rim to make an attractive pattern. Brush with the egg glaze and sprinkle with sliced almonds.

Bake for 20 to 25 minutes on the parchment paper set on a baking sheet, keeping a careful eye on it, until it is golden brown all over and firm to the touch. The baking time will depend on the thickness of the dough.

Put the baking sheet on a rack and let cool completely. The traditional method of serving this giant cookie is to place it at the center of the table and give it a blow with your fist—a little violent but a lot of fun for everyone. It breaks into pieces that all the guests can share.

It will keep for 1 week, stored in an airtight container.

Giant Butter Cookie of Poitou (left) and
My Ideal Outsize Butter Cookie (right)

My Ideal Outsize Butter Cookie

Makes two 8- to 10-inch (20- to 24-cm) butter cookies
Preparation time: 20 minutes
Chilling time: 1 hour
Cooking time: 25 minutes

INGREDIENTS
2 cups (9 oz./250 g) all-purpose flour
¾ cup (4 ¾ oz./135 g) sugar
1 stick plus 3 tablespoons (6 oz./170 g) salted butter, well chilled and diced into small cubes
½ teaspoon fleur de sel or other fine flaky sea salt
1 vanilla bean, slit lengthwise and seeds scraped out
¼ cup (⅔ oz./20 g) finely ground almonds
2 tablespoons (1 oz./30 g) beaten egg, plus 1 egg yolk
1 egg, beaten, for the egg glaze

The method I use here involves rubbing the flour into the butter. I add the egg at the end. It's best to work in a cool room because if the butter melts too quickly because it's too warm, or is worked for too long, the dough will begin to clump together before the egg is added. So, ensure that the butter is well chilled. If the weather is too hot, it's best to cream the ingredients, following the method given for the Giant Butter Cookie of Poitou (see page 102), adding the vanilla and ground almonds at the start. The cookie will be less crumbly and crisp, and a little firmer.

Place the flour, sugar, diced butter, fleur de sel, vanilla seeds, and ground almonds in a large bowl and rub in the ingredients with your fingertips until the texture resembles crumbs or sand. As the butter is combined with the flour and sugar, it gradually coats the particles of dry ingredients with fat.

Combine the beaten egg and egg yolk and incorporate them into the sandy mixture. Mix only until combined.

Shape the dough into a ball and flatten to make a disc. Cover in plastic wrap and chill for 1 hour.

Preheat the oven to 350°F (180°C). Line a baking sheet with parchment paper.

Divide the dough in half and roll each half out on a lightly floured work surface or parchment paper to make two 8- to 10-inch (20- to 24-cm) rounds that are less than ⅛ inch (2 to 3 mm) thick.

Using a plate or tart ring, trim the dough to make perfect circles. Use the remaining dough to make small cookies. Chill for 10 minutes.

Brush the surface with a little beaten egg and then bake in batches for 20 to 25 minutes, until a nice golden color all over. Carefully transfer the rounds to a cooling rack and allow to cool completely.

Serve as an accompaniment for ice creams or crème brûlée. Break it up by giving it a good thump with your fist and let guests help themselves to the pieces.

Chocolate Mousse

GLUTEN FREE
Serves 4
Preparation time: 15 minutes
Chilling time: 5 hours

INGREDIENTS
7 oz. (200 g) bittersweet chocolate
1 tablespoon plus 1 teaspoon (¾ oz./20 g)
   salted butter
6 eggs
1 pinch salt

In my opinion, this is the ultimate dessert in terms of simplicity and sheer intensity of its chocolate taste. There's no sugar or cream—just a little butter to facilitate the melting of the chocolate, and so the flavors ring out loud and clear. It's a recipe that takes me back to my childhood.

I advise you to choose a fine quality chocolate with a high percentage of cacao—feel free to select one that contains up to 70 percent. After all, it's the chocolate that should take the limelight here.

Melt the chocolate and salted butter over a hot water bath or in short bursts in the microwave oven. The butter will ensure that the chocolate doesn't firm up as soon as the egg yolks are added.

Separate the eggs. Set the yolks aside and whip the whites firmly with a pinch of salt.

When the melted chocolate is lukewarm, stir in the egg yolks one by one.

Using a flexible spatula, carefully fold in the beaten egg whites, taking care not to deflate the mixture.

Divide the mousse between 4 ramekins, or pour into a serving bowl. Chill for at least 5 hours.

Remove from the refrigerator and serve immediately. When you dip in with your spoon, listen carefully to the tiny noises that the creamy mousse makes—absolutely irresistible!

Almond, Lemon, and Olive Oil Cake
Condat

Makes one 8-inch (22-cm) cake or 8 muffins
Preparation time: 10 minutes
Cooking time: 30 minutes

INGREDIENTS
⅔ cup (4 oz./120 g) sugar
Finely grated zest of 1 lemon, unwaxed
  or organic
3 eggs
3 tablespoons (2 oz./50 g) butter
¼ cup (60 ml) olive oil
Scant ½ cup (2 oz./50 g) all-purpose flour
2 cups (6 oz./170 g) finely ground almonds

This is an extremely tasty almond cake that I made when staying with a dear friend in the small town of Condat in the Limousin region of France. I combined the ingredients a little haphazardly, noting, as always, exactly what I used. This is a recurring practice for me: even if I make something following my instincts, it means I can use the notes if it turns out well. It's also useful if adjustments are necessary. For a moister texture, one needs to add eggs or reduce the flour. For more sweetness, a little extra sugar may be required. In short, everything can be adjusted, and that's how to make a cake that suits your palate.

Serendipitously, this cake turned out well on my first try. I had noted everything on my mobile phone, and as bad luck would have it, it crashed on my return. I lost the notes for all the secret recipes I'd kept on it, a catastrophe for me. Fortunately, I was able to recreate the recipe (it's an easy one), but I've learned my lesson and now write everything down with pen and paper.

You can play around with the flavors, substituting orange zest or vanilla extract for the lemon zest. If you're wary of using olive oil, simply replace it with an equal quantity of melted butter.

Preheat the oven to 350°F (180°C). Grease an 8-inch (22-cm) cake pan or an 8 cup muffin pan.

With your fingers, rub the sugar and lemon zest together. This develops the flavors to the full. Beat in the eggs just enough to dissolve the sugar.

Melt the butter over a hot water bath or in the microwave oven and combine it with the olive oil.

Stir the butter and oil into the batter. Add the flour and ground almonds and stir to combine. There is no risk of lumps forming.

Pour the batter into the prepared pan and bake for 30 minutes, until a cake tester inserted into the center comes out dry. To test for doneness, you can gently shake the pan: it should not wobble at all.

Turn out of the pan and cool on a rack. Dust with confectioners' sugar before serving.

It keeps in an airtight container for a week.

Crunchy Almond Cookies from Cordes-sur-Ciel

Croquants de Cordes-sur-Ciel

DAIRY FREE
Makes about 80 cookies
Preparation time: 25 minutes
Cooking time: 10 minutes per batch

INGREDIENTS
1 ½ cups (9 oz./250 g) whole unpeeled almonds
2 cups (14 oz./400 g) sugar
1 ½ cups (6 ⅓ oz./180 g) all-purpose flour
⅓ cup (2 ⅔ oz./75 g) egg whites

The pastry makers of the picturesque medieval village of Cordes-sur-Ciel near the Pyrenees are justifiably proud of their light, crisp almond cookies. With their domed top and hollow center, they are quite unique. I was lucky enough to see how they are authentically made. Here I follow the baking method to the letter, using only the four ingredients in the original recipe. After several trials at home, I found the proportions that make cookies as similar as possible to those that I enjoyed in the village. The taste is wonderful, they keep for several months when properly stored, and they pair well with ice creams of all flavors.

The surprising thing about this recipe is how a small, seemingly insignificant piece of dough swells up in the oven, practically tripling in size. Each one is uniquely shaped. When they are removed from the oven and cooled, you can hear them crackling and hissing as they reach their final, crisp consistency.

Preheat the oven to 400°F (200°C). Line a baking sheet with parchment paper.

Place the almonds, sugar, and flour in the bowl of a stand mixer fitted with the flat beater attachment, or in a mixing bowl.

Combine the ingredients. Pour in the egg whites and beat in until thoroughly mixed and the dough forms a ball. You don't have to use a stand mixer; using a wooden spoon simply takes longer to incorporate the egg white. But I assure you it works.

Place the dough on a lightly floured surface and cut it in half. Roll the first half into a log with a diameter of just over 1 inch (3 cm), dusting with flour as needed.

Press down lightly on the log of dough with the palm of your hand until it is very thin, about ⅕ inch (5 mm).

Dip a pastry brush in water and brush all the excess flour from the dough. Cut it into slices just under ½ inch (1 cm) thick.

Place the slices on the prepared baking sheet, no more than 8 per 12 x 16 inch (30 x 40 cm) sheet. Bake the first batch for 10 minutes, until puffed up and colored. Immediately slide the parchment paper with the cookies onto a rack. Repeat with the remaining dough.

The cooled cookies will keep in an airtight container for several weeks.

Crunchy Drop Cookies

Craquants

Here are several recipes that are particularly dear to my heart. They are simple and quick to make, and absolutely delicious. I tested them more than ten times to fine-tune them, playing with the proportions and baking times to achieve the type of cookie I had in mind.

In terms of ingredients, these recipes are similar to the specialty made in Cordes-sur-Ciel on page 108, but they also differ in many ways. In my opinion, they are the perfect accompaniment to sorbets and ice creams.

Crunchy Caramel and Hazelnut Drop Cookies;
Crunchy Pine Nut, Orange, and Chocolate Drop Cookies; and
Crunchy Almond and Coffee Drop Cookies

Crunchy Pine Nut, Orange, and Chocolate Drop Cookies

Craquants aux pignons, orange, et chocolat

DAIRY FREE
Makes 25 cookies
Preparation time: 10 minutes
Cooking time: 12 minutes per batch

INGREDIENTS
1 cup plus 1 scant cup (9 oz./250 g)
  confectioners' sugar
¼ cup (1 oz./30 g) unsweetened cocoa
  powder
Scant cup (4 oz./125 g) pine nuts
⅓ cup (2 ⅓ oz./65 g) egg whites
Finely grated zest of 1 orange, unwaxed
  or organic

Preheat the oven to 350°C (180°C). Line a baking sheet with parchment paper.

Sift the confectioners' sugar with the cocoa powder and then combine all the ingredients in a mixing bowl.

Using 2 teaspoons, shape 6 to 8 cookie mounds on the prepared baking sheet.

Bake for 12 minutes, until swelled and nicely colored.

Place the sheets on a rack for 5 minutes before removing the cookies from the paper. Repeat the baking process with the remaining dough.

Allow the cookies to cool completely before storing them in an airtight container. They will keep for 2 weeks.

Crunchy Caramel and Hazelnut Drop Cookies

Craquants au caramel et noisettes

DAIRY FREE
Makes 30 to 36 cookies
Preparation time: 10 minutes
Cooking time: 13 to 15 minutes per batch

INGREDIENTS

2 cups (7 oz./200 g) sugar
2 ½ cups (10 ½ oz./300 g) chopped hazelnuts
½ cup (2 oz./60 g) all-purpose flour
1 generous pinch ground vanilla
½ teaspoon salt
⅓ cup (3 oz./85 g) egg whites

Preheat the oven to 350°F (180°C). Line a baking sheet with parchment paper.

Combine the sugar, hazelnuts, flour, ground vanilla, and salt in a mixing bowl.

Add the egg whites and stir in with a wooden spoon, or use your hands, until the mixture is smooth.

Drop tablespoons of the batter onto the prepared baking sheet, no more than 6 per sheet, as they spread a lot. Flatten them with the back of a spoon.

Bake for 13 to 15 minutes, preferably in the top third of the oven, until nicely colored and puffed up.

Place the sheets on a rack for 5 minutes before removing the cookies from the paper. Repeat the baking process with the remaining dough.

Allow the cookies to cool completely before storing them in an airtight container. They will keep for 2 weeks.

Crunchy Almond and Coffee Drop Cookies

Craquants aux amandes et café

DAIRY FREE
Makes 25 cookies
Preparation time: 10 minutes
Cooking time: 12 to 15 minutes per batch

INGREDIENTS
Generous ¾ cup (5 ¼ oz./150 g) whole
  almonds, unpeeled
1 cup plus 1 scant cup (9 oz./250 g)
  confectioners' sugar
2 ½ tablespoons (1 ¼ oz./35 g) egg whites
1 teaspoon coffee extract

Preheat the oven to 350°F (180°C). Line a baking sheet with parchment paper.

Place the almonds in a food processor and process until roughly chopped. Transfer them to a mixing bowl and add the confectioners' sugar, egg whites, and coffee extract. Mix well.

Using a teaspoon, drop 6 small mounds on each prepared baking sheet.

Bake for 12 to 15 minutes. They swell and crack, and are done when they no longer expand.

Place the sheets on a rack for 5 minutes before removing the cookies from the paper. Repeat the baking process with the remaining dough.

Allow the cookies to cool completely before storing them in an airtight container. They will keep for 2 weeks.

Flemish Vanilla Waffles
Stroopwafels

Makes about 30 filled cookies
Preparation time: 20 minutes
Rising time: 2 hour 30 minutes minimum
Cooking time: 1 to 2 minutes

Special equipment: a waffle maker

INGREDIENTS
FOR THE WAFFLE WAFER DOUGH
2 ¼ cups (9 ½ oz./270 g) all-purpose flour
2 ¾ tablespoons (⅔ oz./20 g) powdered milk
5 tablespoons (2 ½ oz./75 g) butter, room
    temperature
1 egg
½ teaspoon dry active yeast
3 tablespoons (40 ml) warm milk
¼ cup (3 oz./80 g) corn syrup

FOR THE VANILLA FILLING
1 ½ cups (7 oz./200 g) confectioners' sugar
1 stick (4 oz./120 g) butter
1 tablespoon (⅔ oz./20 g) corn syrup
1 vanilla bean, seeds scraped
½ teaspoon vanilla extract
½ teaspoon ground vanilla

These delicious little waffle wafer cookies come to us from the Low Countries of northern Europe. Thin, soft, and generously filled with vanilla-scented syrup, they are open to adaptation. You might want to try filling them with rum and brown sugar.

Before I begin, I must tell you that I tried out a large number of recipes. The one here includes corn syrup, which retains the moisture in the vanilla filling—it has a tendency to dry out, otherwise—and in the wafers. If you prefer not to use it, replace the syrup in the batter with ¼ cup (2 oz./50 g) of granulated sugar. If you omit it from the filling, keep in mind that the consistency will be even softer.

For the waffle wafer dough, place all the ingredients in the bowl of a stand mixer fitted with the dough hook attachment, or in a mixing bowl if you are kneading by hand.

Knead for 10 minutes at medium speed, until the dough pulls away from the side of the bowl and you can shape it into a ball.

Cover with plastic wrap and leave to rise in a warm place for at least 2 hours 30 minutes; it may not double in volume but it swells.

Weigh out small balls of dough, ½ oz. (16 g) each. It's important to weigh so that you can make even, nicely shaped wafers.

Switch on the waffle maker (not a Belgian waffle maker, as the grid will be too large for the cookies). The best way to cook them would be with an old-fashioned waffle iron, but you'd need a gas burner or an open stove.

Place a ball of dough on each small grid and press the sides down as hard as you can while the waffles cook. This ensures that they are flat. Cook for about 1 minute and remove as soon as they are golden, no darker, so that they remain as soft as possible.

Immediately slice each waffle horizontally, leaving one side hinged, and place in a plastic bag to cool. Seal the bag to retain the steam. If you were to let them dry on a rack, they would be crisp.

For the filling, combine all the ingredients in a mixing bowl. Stir with a spoon until the mixture is smooth and creamy.

(continued on page 116)

When the waffles have cooled, open the bag and place a spoonful of filling inside each one. Be generous with the filling. Spread it evenly with a knife and then close the waffle like a sandwich.

If you wish, you can trim the waffles with a round cookie cutter after they are filled. This is purely to improve the aesthetics of your waffles and not essential.

Store the waffles in a plastic bag; this is the best way to keep them soft. They keep very well for about 5 days if properly wrapped.

Spice Cookies
Speculoos

EGG FREE
Makes about 40 thin cookies
Preparation time: 20 minutes
Chilling time: 2 to 12 hours
Cooking time: 13 to 15 minutes per batch

INGREDIENTS
FOR THE SPICE MIX
2 ⅛ teaspoons cinnamon
¼ teaspoon ground ginger
¼ teaspoon gingerbread spice mix
⅛ teaspoon ground cardamom
⅛ teaspoon ground aniseed

FOR THE DOUGH
2 teaspoons spice mix
Scant cup (6 oz./170 g) dark brown sugar
1 ¼ sticks. (5 oz./150 g) butter, room temperature
2 tablespoons milk
2 cups (9 oz./260 g) all-purpose flour

Thin *speculoos* are northern European cookies whose unique flavor comes, in part, from the spices they contain, but perhaps more importantly from the type of sugar used: brown *vergeoise*, a beet sugar from northern France. As a substitute, many people believe raw sugar will do, but I disagree. The readily available, moist brown sugar found in the US and UK is a perfect substitute for the original dark *vergeoise* of this recipe and reproduces the authentic flavor. I'm revealing to you my spice mix, a secret I'd kept to myself until now. Do keep to my measurements, right down to the perfectly level one-eighth of a teaspoon! I tested the recipe several times before I was sure of the result. I don't use any raising agents, neither baking soda nor baking powder. It's the butter that aerates the dough. If you want to make attractive molded *speculoos*, a raising agent would mean that the pattern will be lost. But there are no strict laws regarding *speculoos* forms and you can shape them however you like. Having experimented with several methods, I can assure you that this recipe never fails to recreate the taste of the delightful cookies.

Begin with the spice mix. It's a good idea to double the quantities and store half for future use. All you need to do is combine them well in a small bowl.

Place the sugar in a large mixing bowl. Add the spices, stir well, and enjoy the fragrance that wafts up.

Ensure that the butter is very soft. Add it to the sugar with the milk and mix until creamy.

Add all the flour and stir quickly until just combined; do not overwork if you want to achieve the best texture. Shape the dough into a ball and place it on a sheet of plastic wrap. Shape it into an elongated brick by beating it on the work surface. Wrap tightly in plastic wrap and chill for a minimum of 2 hours and up to 12 hours.

Preheat the oven to 375°F (190°C). Line a baking sheet with parchment paper.

Cut the dough block into very fine slices, ⅕ inch (5 mm) thick. Place on the prepared sheet, spaced 1 inch (2.5 cm) apart, and bake for 13 to 15 minutes, until lightly browned. Cool on a rack and store in an airtight container.

Spice Cookies (left) and
Oatmeal, Walnut, and Chocolate Cookies (right)

Oatmeal, Walnut, and Chocolate Cookies

• • • • • • • • • • • • •

EGG FREE
Makes 4 dozen cookies
Preparation time: 20 minutes
Chilling time: 2 hours
Cooking time: 15 to 20 minutes

INGREDIENTS
Scant ½ cup (1 ¾ oz./50 g) walnuts
1 ¾ cups (5 ¼ oz./150 g) oatmeal, regular or
   quick-cooking
2 sticks (8 ½ oz./240 g) salted butter, room
   temperature
⅔ cup (4 oz./125 g) sugar
1 ½ cups (6 ½ oz./185 g) all-purpose flour
Generous ½ cup (3 ½ oz./100 g) chocolate
   chips

• • • • • • • • • • • • •

It was rather hard to know what to call these. They're not quite *sablés*, the French version of shortbread, nor are they really American drop cookies. I never tire of testing new ways of making crisp cookies, and I like nothing better than being in my kitchen, randomly adding ingredients to a mixing bowl to see what the outcome is. Sometimes, the result is not a success. For this recipe, I played the mad professor. I extracted the dominant elements of a classic American oatmeal cookie and injected them into a well-known small French cookie, the *sablé diamant*, a butter cookie coated in sugar that makes it sparkle like a diamond. I anxiously waited to see what would come out of the oven, but the baked result was reassuring, and it held well as it cooled. For this recipe, I processed the oats with walnuts to make a very tasty powdery mixture. After adding flour and butter, the result was beyond my expectations. Chocolate chips added the final touch.

Place the walnuts and oatmeal in the bowl of a food processor and process for 1 minute, until a fine powder forms.

Place the butter and sugar in a mixing bowl and beat until creamy. Stir in the ground walnut-oatmeal mixture and flour, and stir until just combined.

Stir in the chocolate chips; do not overwork. Divide the dough in half. Roll each half into a 1 ½-inch (4-cm) diameter log and wrap tightly in plastic wrap. Chill for at least 2 hours to firm up the dough.

Preheat the oven to 350°F (180°C). Line a baking sheet with parchment paper.

Cut the logs of dough into slices just under ½ inch (1 cm) thick, keeping in mind that they will not spread too much. Place on the prepared sheet, spaced 1 inch (2.5 cm) apart, and bake for 15 to 20 minutes, until nicely golden. Keep a careful eye on them as they bake—and remember, no one knows your oven and its quirks better than you do.

Allow to cool completely on a rack (repeat baking process with the remaining dough), and store in an airtight container for up to a week.

Traditional Parisian Custard Tart

Flan Parisien

Makes one high-sided 9-inch (24-cm) tart
Preparation time: 1 hour
Chilling time: 30 minutes for the crust,
  3 hours for the flan
Cooking time: 40 to 50 minutes

INGREDIENTS

FOR THE STARCH PASTRY CRUST
2 sticks (8 oz./225 g) butter, well chilled
  and diced
2 cups (9 oz./250 g) all-purpose flour
⅓ cup (1 ¾ oz./50 g) potato starch
Heaping ½ teaspoon (3 g) salt
2 ½ tablespoons (1 oz./30 g) sugar
2 ¾ teaspoons (½ oz./15 g) egg yolk
4 tablespoons (55 ml) milk

FOR THE FLAN FILLING
1 ⅔ cups (11 oz./315 g) sugar, divided
1 small pinch ground vanilla bean
1 cup minus 2 ½ tablespoons (4 ½ oz./130 g)
  cornstarch (or *poudre à crème*, in which
  case there's no need for vanilla extract)
1 teaspoon vanilla extract
⅔ cup (5 ⅔ oz./160 g) beaten eggs
3 ½ tablespoons (2 oz./60 g) egg yolks
5 ¼ cups (1.3 liters) low-fat milk
2 tablespoons (1 oz./30 g) unsalted butter

What do I expect when I bite into a Parisian custard tart? A freshly made, crisp crust and a smooth, dense filling. I tried several recipes but didn't manage to achieve exactly what I wanted—namely, the kind of flan those of us who grew up in Paris ate after school. All my attempts lacked that little *je ne sais quoi*, until the pastry chef of Le Valentin in Paris agreed to take me on a four-day course to teach me all he could. That was when I discovered the explanation for my previous failures, a missing ingredient called *poudre à crème*. Rest assured, although the name literally means "powder for cream," it's not a powder that makes a cream when mixed with water. It's a substitute, and a better one at that, for flour or cornstarch. This ingredient, familiar to all French professionals, makes all the difference. You can find it online or at specialized baking stores. Surprisingly enough, it is just flavored cornstarch, but the texture, flavor, and fragrance of the flan is always much better when it's included. Initially, I was rather skeptical about this powder, but it truly does help the flan retain moisture and gives it a special consistency. So now you have the secret. I've been using it for all my pastry creams since I discovered it, and I'm always satisfied with the results. If you can't get hold of *poudre à crème*, simply substitute an equal amount of cornstarch and add a bit of vanilla extract.

The recipe here also includes a "starch pastry crust," which is made with potato starch instead of flour. When it's baked, it's surprisingly good—so flaky and buttery it could be mistaken for puff pastry.

For the pastry crust:
Place the diced butter, flour, potato starch, salt, and sugar in the bowl of a stand mixer fitted with the flat beater attachment. Mix until the mixture reaches a fine, sandy texture. Of course, you can also prepare it by hand, rubbing the ingredients with your fingertips.

In a small bowl, mix together the egg yolk and milk. Pour it into the flour-butter mixture and mix until the dough is smooth. It will probably seem quite soft, particularly if you're making it on a hot day. Cover it with plastic wrap and chill for 30 minutes.

(continued on page 122)

Lightly dust a pastry board with flour, or cover it with parchment paper. Roll the dough out very thinly, to under ⅛ inch (2 mm). If the weather is warm, work in stages. If the dough is difficult to roll out when you begin, return it to the refrigerator for a few minutes to firm it up. I've made this flan in all kinds of weather and have concluded that it's more difficult when the temperatures are high. But I assure you, it's still feasible.

If you are using a dessert ring, set it on a baking sheet lined with parchment paper. A springform pan is also perfect; line the base with parchment paper and grease the rim. Transfer the dough to the ring or pan and set it firmly in. Run a knife around the top of the rim to remove all excess dough. Prick the base with a fork and return to the refrigerator until you are ready to use it.

For the flan filling:
Preheat the oven to 350°F (180°C). Place 1 scant cup (6 ½ oz./180 g) sugar, the ground vanilla bean, and cornstarch in a mixing bowl. Stir in the whole eggs and egg yolks, and vanilla extract if using.

In a large saucepan over low heat, bring the milk, butter, and remaining sugar to a boil.

As soon as it comes to a boil, drizzle it over the custard powder–egg mixture, whisking constantly. Combine well and return the liquid to the saucepan.

Bring to a simmer over low heat, and simmer for 3 to 4 minutes, whisking constantly.

Pour the flan filling into the tart shell and smooth the top. Bake for 40 to 50 minutes, keeping a careful eye on it, until it is well risen and nicely colored. Allow to cool on a rack completely. It will deflate.

Once cooled, remove the tart ring and chill for at least 3 hours before serving.

A last word of advice: if you prefer the top of your flan to be nicely browned, bake it as soon as you pour the filling into the crust. If you prefer a marbled top, place the unbaked, filled tart, with plastic wrap pressed directly onto the flan filling, in the refrigerator overnight. The next day, remove the plastic wrap and increase the baking time slightly. The surface will be lighter than shown in the photo, and slightly marbled.

Tiramisù

Tiramisù literally means "pick me up" in Italian and it really does keep to its word. A single spoonful of this creamy dessert is an instant pick-me-up. With this recipe, you'll be able to make a light, airy, deliciously soft and creamy tiramisù, and what's more, it won't be runny at all. This is just how I like my tiramisù to be. Feel free to adapt the recipe and make it with fruit: instead of soaking the ladyfingers in coffee, use a little kirsch or eau-de-vie, and insert a layer of fresh raspberries between the layers of mascarpone cream. Fresh pears or peaches with a few crumbled shortbread cookies will add an original, tasty touch to your dessert. For a tiramisù without any alcohol, soak the ladyfingers with coffee and finely grate a little orange zest over them before smothering them with cream.

I often double the quantities to make a second layer of both ladyfingers and mascarpone cream, and you may want to do so too.

Serves 4 to 6
Preparation time: 25 minutes
Chilling time: 3 hours

INGREDIENTS
1 cup (250 ml) strong coffee
2 extra large (US) or large (UK) eggs
Scant ½ cup (3 oz./80 g) sugar
2 ½ cups (1 ¼ lb./500 g) mascarpone
Scant ¼ cup (1 oz./30 g) confectioners' sugar
2–3 tablespoons Amaretto liqueur
8 oz. (250 g) ladyfingers
Unsweetened cocoa powder for dusting

Prepare the coffee and set aside.

Separate the eggs. Place the yolks in a mixing bowl with the sugar and with an electric beater, whisk until the mixture is as pale and thick as possible, about 3 minutes.

Add the mascarpone and whip until the texture is light and airy. Beating the mascarpone until it resembles whipped cream gives the tiramisù its lovely texture and ensures that it holds its shape.

Make sure your beaters are perfectly clean, grease-free, and dry. In another mixing bowl, whip the egg whites. When they begin to hold soft peaks, add the confectioners' sugar. Continue whipping until the meringue mixture holds firm peaks.

Using a flexible spatula, fold the egg whites into the whipped mascarpone, taking care not to deflate the mixture.

Stir the liqueur into the coffee.

Dip the ladyfingers into the coffee mixture just to moisten them. Be careful not to soak them.

Pack the ladyfingers tightly in a 7 x 10 inch (18 x 24 cm) dish. Pour the mascarpone cream over the ladyfingers, spreading it evenly. If you're making a second layer, repeat the process. Chill for at least 3 hours.

Just before serving, sprinkle the entire dessert with cocoa powder that you've pushed through a small sieve. A dusting of cocoa powder around individual portions is very attractive, so you may want to plate the tiramisù before serving.

Vanilla Mille-Feuille

A few years ago, I participated in a tasting session of vanilla mille-feuilles—or napoleons, as this dessert is called in many countries—that was organized by a friend. Paris's best pastry chefs were represented and some of the chefs even came to assemble the mille-feuilles themselves at the last minute. We weren't there to grade the masterpieces (that wasn't the point), all made of the finest quality. Instead I was able to savor them and understand what I truly love about this dessert.

For this mille-feuille, it is clear that it's best to make one's own puff pastry. This is not as difficult as it might seem, and with a little effort, you'll soon acquire the knack. A key ingredient is butter. Professional bakers and pastry chefs in France use a butter with a butterfat content of 84 percent. This means that the butter doesn't soften easily, but has a malleable texture which allows it to be rolled with the dough. This recipe also works well with regular-quality butter. Just check that it contains at least 82 percent butterfat.

To make the vanilla cream, I suggest combining a denser-than-usual pastry cream with whipped cream that includes mascarpone. I also highly recommend using a whipping cream stabilizer to ensure that the luscious filling retains its texture.

Serves 6 to 8
Preparation time: 2 hours
Chilling time: 2 to 3 hours
Cooking time: 25 to 30 minutes for the puff
 pastry and 10 minutes for the vanilla cream

INGREDIENTS
FOR THE PASTRY CREAM
3 tablespoons (2 oz./50 g) unsalted butter
1 cup (250 ml) low-fat milk
1 teaspoon vanilla extract
⅓ cup (2 ½ oz./70 g) sugar, divided
3 tablespoons (1 ¾ oz./50 g) egg yolks
3 tablespoons (1 oz./30 g) cornstarch

FOR THE PUFF PASTRY
2 cups (9 oz./250 g) all-purpose flour
1 teaspoon (5 g) salt
5 tablespoons (2 ½ oz./70 g) butter,
 well chilled and diced
½ cup (125 ml) cold water
2 sticks (9 oz./250 g) butter, room
 temperature
Confectioners' sugar

FOR THE WHIPPED CREAM
 WITH MASCARPONE
¾ cup (6 ½ oz./190 g) whipping or
 heavy cream, well chilled
⅔ cup (5 oz./150 g) mascarpone, well chilled
1 teaspoon vanilla extract
Seeds of 2 Madagascar vanilla beans
¼ cup (1 ¾ oz./50 g) sugar
⅓ oz. (10 g) whipping cream stabilizer
 (see page 280)

First prepare the pastry cream. Place the butter, milk, vanilla extract, and half the sugar in a heavy saucepan over low heat and bring to a boil.

In a mixing bowl, place the remaining sugar, egg yolks, and cornstarch. Whisk for about 3 minutes until the yolks become pale and thick. When the milk boils, pour it gradually over the egg yolk mixture, whisking constantly. Return the liquid to the saucepan over low heat and bring to a simmer, stirring constantly.

Allow to simmer for 1 minute and then pour into a heatproof bowl. Immediately press a piece of plastic wrap onto the surface to prevent a skin from forming. Allow to cool then place in the refrigerator for up to a day.

For the puff pastry, combine the flour, salt, and chilled diced butter in the bowl of a stand mixer fitted with the flat beater attachment. Beat until crumbly. Add the water and mix until the dough holds together. Do not overwork. It may not look very attractive, but it will improve later. Shape the dough into a rectangle just under 1 inch (2 cm) thick. Cover with plastic wrap and chill for at least 2 to 3 hours.

An hour before you make the puff pastry, bring the remaining butter to room temperature. Set the chilled dough on a lightly floured surface. Roll into a rectangle twice as long as the width, ¼ inch (6 mm) thick.

It's important for the butter and dough to be the same consistency for best incorporation. If necessary, roll the butter between 2 sheets of plastic wrap to soften and shape it into a square equal to the width of the dough. Set it in the center of the dough.

Fold the dough at each side over the butter, ensuring that the edges meet to make a line down the middle. Rotate the dough 90° and roll out evenly with a rolling pin, making sure that the edges are parallel and straight. Shape it into a rectangle three times as long as the width.

Fold the upper part downward and fold the lower part upward to meet it. Rotate the dough 90° and roll out again to the same dimensions. Fold the upper part downward and fold the lower part upward to meet it. Fold in half to make a double turn. Rotate the dough 90° again, keeping the fold on the left. Fold in thirds, as above, and then fold in half to make another double turn.

Cover tightly in plastic wrap and chill for 30 minutes.

Repeat the procedure to make 2 more double turns. Chill for 30 minutes.

Preheat the oven to 400°F (200°C). Roll the dough into a rectangle about ½ inch (1 ½ cm) thick and cut it into 3 equal parts.

Working on a piece of parchment paper, roll each part into a very thin rectangle, under ⅛ inch (3 mm). Don't worry if the edges aren't perfectly straight: you'll be trimming them later.

Transfer the sheet of dough on the parchment paper to a baking sheet. Set a perforated baking sheet over it. If you don't have one, protect the dough with a sheet of parchment paper and set an oven-proof rack over it. This step is not essential but prevents the pastry from rising too much.

Bake for 25 to 30 minutes. If the upper baking sheet rises, set a weight over it. When the puff pastry has stopped rising (about halfway through the baking process), remove the upper sheet to color the surface of the pastry evenly until it reaches a lovely golden brown. Let the pastry cool on a rack. Repeat with the remaining pieces of pastry.

When they are cool enough to touch, use a serrated knife to cut the pastry pieces to size. Sift confectioners' sugar over the surface.

Turn on the broiler in your oven and return the pastry to the oven for just 1 minute to caramelize the surface.

For the whipped cream with mascarpone, place a mixing bowl in the refrigerator to chill it well. This helps the cream whip up.

Just before serving, prepare the vanilla cream. Place the whipping cream, mascarpone, vanilla extract, and vanilla seeds in the chilled bowl. In a separate bowl, combine the sugar and whipping cream stabilizer.

Begin whisking the cream mixture. When it holds soft peaks, add the sugar. Whisk until the cream holds firm peaks. With the stabilizer, there is little danger of over-whisking.

(continued on page 128)

1 Fold the upper and lower ends toward the center and fold in half.

2 Carefully roll out the pastry.

3 Set a rack or perforated baking sheet upside down over the dough to be baked.

4 Trim the edges of the baked puff pastry.

5 Sift confectioners' sugar over the surface.

6 Using a piping bag, cover the puff pastry with vanilla cream, either in long strips or small dollops.

Take the pastry cream from the refrigerator and whisk until very smooth. Weigh about 8 oz. (200 to 250 g) of the pastry cream. With a flexible spatula, fold a little of the whipped cream into it, working carefully so as not to deflate the mixture.

Gradually add the remaining whipped cream, folding in carefully just until completely incorporated.

Spoon the mixture into a piping bag fitted with a ½-inch (14-mm) plain tip. Pipe a layer of cream on the first sheet of puff pastry. You can pipe out long strips, as shown in the step-by-step photo, or small dollops, as shown on the facing page.

Set a second sheet of puff pastry over it, pipe a layer of cream over the surface, and top with the last sheet of puff pastry. Dust with confectioners' sugar sifted through a small sieve. If you wish, you can use a stencil or make strips.

The mille-feuille is best served as soon as possible. It is at its very best within 2 hours of assembly: the pastry remains crumbly until the cream begins to moisten it. My advice is to prepare the cream ahead of time and store it, in the piping bag, in the refrigerator. When it's time for dessert, all you'll have to do is the last step.

Almond Tuiles

Tuiles aux amandes

Makes 24 tuiles
Preparation time: 10 minutes
Chilling time: 1 hour
Cooking time: 10 to 12 minutes per batch

INGREDIENTS

⅔ cup (5 oz./140 g) beaten egg whites (about 5 egg whites)
2 ⅔ cups (9 oz./250 g) sliced (flaked) almonds
1 cup minus 3 tablespoons (5 ½ oz./160 g) sugar
3 tablespoons (1 oz./30 g) all-purpose flour
3 tablespoons (2 oz./50 g) unsalted butter, melted

Since I was a child, I've always loved almond tuiles, the cookies that take their name from the roof tiles whose shape they resemble. But not just any tuiles: they have to be large-sized, smothered with almonds, and, most importantly, nicely browned. I've treasured the recipe I give you here for many years, because it has all the elements I'm so fond of. It reminds me of the many times I would go out with my parents to enjoy an ice cream at a famous Parisian ice cream parlor. The bowls always came garnished with a large tuile. Since then, I've been making almond tuiles to serve with my ice creams and sorbets.

In a large mixing bowl, place the sliced almonds, sugar, and flour and stir to combine.

Stir in the egg whites.

Pour the butter into the mixture. Stir until the mixture is smooth and the almonds are evenly distributed.

Place the bowl in the refrigerator for 1 hour.

Preheat the oven to 340°F (170°C). Line a large baking sheet with parchment paper.

Drop the mixture by tablespoons on the prepared sheet, no more than 6 per sheet. Flatten each small heap of dough with the back of a fork or spoon to make it as thin as possible, shaping them into ovals. The finer and smoother the tuiles are, the more regularly they will bake and the more evenly they will color.

Bake the tuiles for 10 to 12 minutes, keeping a careful eye on them. When finished, the tuiles should be nicely golden both in the center and around the edges.

Remove the sheet from the oven and use a spatula to remove each tuile. Immediately drape them over a rolling pin to give them their final curved shape. Repeat with the remaining dough.

The trick is to remove the tuiles as quickly as possible from the sheet because they cool and firm up very fast. The tuiles are best eaten the day they are made, but if you must keep them for a day or two, place them in an airtight container once fully cooled, since they don't react at all well to moisture.

(continued on page 132)

If your tuiles do soften a little, just pop them into a 340°F (170°C) oven for 3 to 4 minutes. They will soften and become malleable again, and you'll be able to return them to their proper shape.

Other ideas for giving the cookies an attractive shape: roll parchment paper around a broomstick, ensuring there are no folds in it, and place it between the seats of two chairs; wrap around bottles on their side; or use baguette baking pans turned upside down.

Shortbread

Just count to 3—yes, it's as simple as that to bake shortbread. Once again, it's all a question of proportions: 1 part of sugar for 2 parts of butter and 3 parts of flour. It's a foolproof formula for shortbread baked in pans.

Making plain shortbreads shaped in rectangles or other shapes is a little more complicated because the dough softens somewhat and they don't retain their shape. I've changed the proportions for my Plain Shortbread so that the cookies retain not only their pleasing forms but also their rich, delicious buttery taste. I've kept the 1–2–3 proportions for my Millionaire's Shortbread and Pecan Caramel Shortbread—in both cases, the dough bakes in a square pan and is then topped with a decadent layer of caramel made with light or dark brown sugar.

As a teenager, I loved shortbread so much that I would cross Paris to buy it at an English store. With the three recipes given here, I've recreated the exact taste of butter, caramel—and indulgence. A diabolical combination!

Plain Shortbread

Place the butter and sugar in a bowl and cream together.

Add all the flour and beat in just until the dough is smooth.

Roll the dough out on a sheet of parchment paper to a thickness of just under ½ inch (1 cm) and then chill for 30 minutes, until it is firm to the touch.

Preheat the oven to 300°F (150°C).

Using a knife, cut the dough into rectangles.

To score the typical shortbread indentations, I use the end of a small wooden paintbrush, but you can use any slightly pointed small object, like a toothpick.

Bake for about 20 minutes, keeping a careful eye on them, until the shortbread is barely colored. It's fine if they are a very light biscuit color, but they should be no darker.

This dough spreads much less than the version using the 1–2–3 proportions, and can be made in special shortbread molds. These are often round or eight-sided with floral patterns. Just put the raw dough into them, remove any excess, turn the mold over, and tap them to get the shaped dough out.

• • • • • • • • • • • • • • •

EGG FREE
Makes 1 ⅓ lb. (600 g) cookies
Preparation time: 15 minutes
Chilling time: 30 minutes
Cooking time: 20 minutes

INGREDIENTS
1 ½ sticks (6 ⅓ oz./180 g) salted butter, room temperature
½ cup (3 ½ oz./100 g) sugar
2 ⅔ cups (11 ½ oz./325 g) all-purpose flour

• • • • • • • • • • • • • • •

Plain Shortbread (top),
Pecan Caramel Shortbread (center), and
Millionaire's Shortbread (bottom)

Millionaire's Shortbread

EGG FREE
For an 8-inch (21-cm) square pan
Preparation time: 40 minutes
Cooking time: 25 minutes baking,
   plus 15 minutes for the caramel
Chilling time: 2 hours

INGREDIENTS
FOR THE 1–2–3 SHORTBREAD DOUGH
1 stick (4 ¼ oz./120 g) salted butter,
   room temperature
⅓ cup (2 oz./60 g) sugar
1 ½ cups (6 ⅓ oz./180 g) all-purpose flour

FOR THE CARAMEL TOPPING
¾ cup (5 oz./150 g) light brown sugar
¼ teaspoon salt
1 heaping tablespoon (1 oz./25 g) honey
1 ½ sticks (6 oz./175 g) butter
1 14-oz. (397-g) can sweetened condensed
   milk
7 oz. (200 g) milk chocolate

Preheat the oven to 350°F (180°C). Line the cake pan with parchment paper.

Place the butter and sugar in a mixing bowl. If you have a stand mixer, use the flat beater attachment to mix until the texture is creamy.

Stir or beat in the flour just until it is incorporated.

Scrape the dough into the prepared pan and spread it out with your hands. Use the back of a large spoon to even the top.

Bake for 25 minutes, until golden on the top. Unlike my method for plain shortbread, where I bake until the dough is only pale, here I prefer it to color a little. Set aside to cool slightly in the pan.

For the caramel, place the brown sugar, salt, honey, and butter in a heavy saucepan over low heat. Bring to a boil and simmer for 3 to 4 minutes.

Stir in the condensed milk, mixing well. Bring back to a simmer over low heat. Continue to simmer, stirring constantly, for 8 to 10 minutes, until thickened.

Pour the caramel over the baked shortbread and allow to cool completely. Chill for 2 hours.

Melt the chocolate over a hot water bath or in short bursts in the microwave oven. Pour it over the set caramel, spreading it evenly. You can use a spatula and draw wavy patterns, or tilt the pan to make a smooth surface (as I did for the photo on page 135).

After about 10 minutes, when the chocolate begins to set but is not yet firm, cut into 16 portions using a sharp knife dipped into hot water after each cut.

Store the shortbread in an airtight container.

The 1–2–3 formula can be applied using ounce measurements as follows: 3 oz. sugar; 6 oz. butter; and 9 oz. flour. This will make a slightly larger quantity. You won't need to change the quantities for the caramel topping, however.

Pecan Caramel Shortbread

EGG FREE
For an 8-inch (21-cm) square pan
Preparation time: 30 minutes
Cooking time: 25 minutes baking,
  plus 15 minutes for the caramel
Chilling time: 1 hour

INGREDIENTS
FOR THE 1–2–3 SHORTBREAD DOUGH
1 stick (4 ¼ oz./120 g) salted butter,
  room temperature
⅓ cup (2 oz./60 g) sugar
1 ½ cups (6 ⅓ oz./180 g) all-purpose flour
(Or use the quantities given in ounces
  in the previous recipe)

FOR THE CARAMEL TOPPING
¾ cup (8 oz./150 g) dark brown sugar
¼ teaspoon salt
1 heaping tablespoon (1 oz./25 g) honey
1 ½ sticks (175 g) butter
1 14-oz. (397-g) can sweetened condensed
  milk
9 oz. (250 g) pecans

To make the dough, follow the recipe for millionaire's shortbread on the facing page.

Bake until golden.

While the shortbread is baking, prepare the caramel following the recipe for millionaire's shortbread, substituting dark brown sugar for light brown sugar. Pour the caramel, still hot, over the baked shortbread.

Immediately scatter the pecans over the caramel and press them in lightly.

Allow to cool completely. As the caramel will be rather soft, chill for 1 hour before cutting it into 16 portions.

Upside-Down Apple Tart
Tarte Tatin

EGG FREE
Makes one 8-inch (21-cm) diameter tart
Preparation time: 2 hours
Cooking time: 20 minutes for the apples
    plus 25 to 40 minutes baking

INGREDIENTS
About 12 apples, such as Golden Delicious
1 stick (4 oz./120 g) salted butter, divided,
    plus extra to grease the pan generously
Scant ⅔ cup (4 ½ oz./120 g) sugar, divided
1 batch puff pastry (page 126)

With caramelized apples, softened in butter, nestled in a wonderfully crisp crust moistened with caramel, who can resist a *tarte tatin*? This tart (that legend has it was made by mistake by the two Tatin sisters, whose customers liked it so much they kept it on their menu) is, however, a hard one to get just right. And I know what I'm talking about. All the experiments I conducted gave results that were satisfactory in terms of taste, but they didn't look good. What I was after was something that was aesthetically as near to perfection as possible. I tested almost ten versions before I made this one. One version rendered too much juice after baking; yet another was too sweet; sometimes the apples were over-baked underneath and underdone on top; for another, the caramel was too light. And very often, turning out the tart from the pan proved disastrous.

I've found a solution to all these problems. With this tart, you can make several tartlets or one large tart. Here, I give you my recipe using puff pastry, but you can also use short pastry. To make the task easier, I advise cooking the apples separately in a pan rather than directly in the pan in the oven. This allows you to get them golden all over and to achieve the right degree of doneness and color.

What's more, any surplus juices stay in the pan. As the apple quarters soften, they are easier to handle, which means you can pack them in tightly to add an evermore generous dimension. To achieve the lovely caramel color, I prepare a caramel with butter that I pour directly into the pan before arranging the apples tightly in it.

Prepare the apples: peel, core, and quarter them.

Place 3 tablespoons (1 ½ oz./40 g) of the butter and ¼ cup (2 oz./50 g) of the sugar in a large, high-rimmed saucepan over high heat.

Add the apple quarters and stir well with a wooden spoon, or even better, shake the pan to flip the apples. Since the heat is high, you'll need to keep a careful eye on them, but there's little danger of them burning. The water that the apples render prevents the caramel from burning. But stay close by, shaking the pan and turning the apples over from time to time so that they are nice and golden all over. When they are tender and lightly coated in a pale caramel, they are ready. This should take 10 to 15 minutes.

(continued on page 140)

Remove from the heat and allow to cool in the pan. This will soften them even further, and enable you to pack them more tightly in the cake pan.

Preheat the oven to 375°F (190°C). Butter an 8-inch (21-cm) diameter cake pan, making sure the sides are particularly well buttered. If you have a pan with a slightly sloping rim, that's even better.

I prefer to prepare the final caramel first in a saucepan, but it's quite possible to make it directly in the cake pan. So why add this extra step? If you do happen to overcook the caramel, you can start again without having to butter the pan again. All you need to do is to pour it as soon as you consider that the color is right.

Place 3 tablespoons (1 ½ oz./40 g) of the butter and ⅓ cup (2 oz./60 g) sugar in a saucepan over medium heat and add a splash of water. Bring to a boil and continue to cook until it is a nice amber color. If the sugar crystallizes, it's not too serious because it will melt again beneath the apples during baking.

When the caramel reaches a golden amber color, pour it into the buttered pan and allow to cool. Sprinkle the remaining sugar on the rim, turning and shaking it to distribute it evenly.

When the apples are cool enough to handle, arrange them attractively in the pan. Since they're already cooked, you'll be able to pack them in tightly. Dice the remaining butter and scatter over the apples.

Bake for 10 to 15 minutes. The apples swell as they heat and the caramel below them melts.

Meanwhile, roll the puff pastry out thinly on a sheet of parchment paper. Using a plate larger than the cake pan, cut out a circle. Freeze the surplus pastry for another use.

Remove the pan from the oven and set the disc of pastry over the apples. Use a spatula to fold the extra pastry inward.

Return the pan to the oven and bake for 20 to 30 minutes, until the puff pastry is golden and thoroughly baked.

Allow to cool completely in the pan. Don't think of turning it out when you remove it from the oven, or you'll have a disaster on your hands. When it has cooled, pass the base of the pan over a burner or electric plate, just enough to warm it up slightly. Place a serving dish over the pan and turn it all over. Carefully remove the pan, in case a few obstinate apples are stuck to it, unbeknownst to you. If they are, you can pack them back in their place.

Serve accompanied by a dollop of heavy cream, crème fraîche, or a scoop of vanilla ice cream.

Strawberry Tart
Tarte aux fraises

Serves 6
Preparation time: 1 hour
Chilling time: 3 to 12 hours
Cooking time: 30 minutes
Cooling time: about 1 hour

INGREDIENTS
½ batch sweet short pastry crust (page 74)

FOR THE PASTRY CREAM
3 tablespoons (2 oz./50 g) egg yolks
1 pinch ground vanilla bean
1 teaspoon vanilla extract
⅓ cup (2 oz./60 g) sugar, divided
2 ½ tablespoons (1 oz./25 g) cornstarch
1 cup (250 ml) low-fat milk
2 tablespoons (1 oz./25 g) unsalted butter

FOR THE PISTACHIO CREAM
2 oz. (50 g) ground pistachios
⅓ cup (2 oz./50 g) confectioners' sugar
1 ½ teaspoons (5 g) cornstarch or custard
    powder
3 tablespoons (2 oz./50 g) unsalted butter,
    melted and cooled
1 teaspoon bitter almond extract
2 tablespoons (1 oz./30 g) beaten egg

TO FINISH
8 oz. (250 g) strawberries, washed
    and carefully dried
A little pistachio paste (page 19),
    for decoration

When it's strawberry season, it's time to make strawberry tarts. Usher in the sunny days of summer with this tart—the ground almonds and fresh butter in the sweet crust underscore the fragrantly flavored strawberries nestled in a pistachio cream.

I'd advise preparing the pastry cream a day ahead. This will ensure that it's sufficiently chilled when you need to use it.

For the pastry cream, combine the egg yolks with the ground vanilla bean, vanilla extract, half the sugar, and cornstarch in a mixing bowl. Whisk to combine.

In a heavy saucepan over medium heat, bring the milk to a boil with the remaining sugar and the butter. As soon as the milk comes to a boil, pour it gradually over the yolk–cornstarch mixture, whisking constantly. When it is thoroughly combined, return the liquid to the saucepan over low heat.

Bring to a simmer, stirring constantly, and simmer for 3 to 4 minutes.

Pour the pastry cream into a dish and press a piece of plastic wrap directly on the surface. Allow to cool completely and then place in the refrigerator for between 3 and 12 hours.

When you're ready to bake, roll the pastry dough out very thinly, to a thickness of under ⅛ inch (2 to 3 mm). Line a 7-inch (18-cm) tart ring, 1 inch (2.5 cm) deep, with the dough, as explained in the sweet pastry recipe on page 75. (You can also use a tart pan.) Place the lined tart ring in the refrigerator.

Preheat the oven to 350°F (180°C).

In a mixing bowl, place the ground pistachios, confectioners' sugar, cornstarch, and butter and mix. Whisk in the bitter almond extract and egg until smooth. Spread the pistachio cream over the unbaked crust.

Bake for about 30 minutes. The baking time will depend on what you see, so keep an eye on the tart. It should be a lovely golden color both on top and underneath. Allow to cool completely on a rack.

Now it's time to take the pastry cream from the refrigerator. Transfer it to a large mixing bowl and whisk for 1 or 2 minutes, until very smooth, creamy, and glossy. Spread it over the pistachio cream.

(continued on page 142)

Cut the strawberries into halves, carefully removing the stem. Arrange them attractively on the tart.

To decorate, crumble a little homemade pistachio paste between your fingers and sprinkle it over the tart.

Chill the tart until you wish to serve it—as soon as possible for the finest taste and texture.

Strawberry-Pistachio Layer Cake

Fraisier Pistache

Makes one 8- inch (20-cm) cake, to serve 8 to 10
Preparation time: 2 hours
Chilling time: 2 hours
Cooking time: 13 to 15 minutes for the
  Genovese sponge
Make a day ahead: Genovese sponge,
  pastry cream, and pistachio paste

Special equipment: an 8-inch (20-cm) dessert
  ring or springform pan, or individual dessert
  rings of the same height, and a strip of
  food-safe acetate

INGREDIENTS

FOR THE GENOVESE SPONGE
3 eggs, room temperature
½ cup (3 ½ oz./100 g) sugar
¾ cup plus 2 tablespoons (3 ½ oz./100 g)
  cake flour
2 tablespoons (1 oz./30 g) unsalted butter,
  melted and cooled

FOR THE PASTRY CREAM
1 ½ tablespoons (1 oz./25 g) egg yolks
1 small pinch ground vanilla bean
1 teaspoon vanilla extract
2 tablespoons (1 oz./25 g) sugar, divided
½ cup minus 1 tablespoon (110 ml) milk
1 ½ teaspoons (5 g) cornstarch
1 tablespoon (½ oz./15 g) unsalted butter

FOR THE CUSTARD CREAM
1 ¾ tablespoons (1 oz./30 g) egg yolks
⅓ cup (2 ½ oz./70 g) sugar, divided
Scant ⅓ cup (70 ml) milk

(continued on page 147)

This is my version of the classic *fraisier*, which is a layered cake of Genovese sponge, mousseline cream, and fresh strawberries. I use a pistachio-scented buttercream, one that, despite its ingredients, is very light and airy thanks to intensive beating. It's so airy that one might wonder what happened to the butter! Homemade pistachio paste gives it a remarkable texture and a pronounced taste. The cream is deliberately not very sweet, as I don't want to overshadow the delicate freshness of the strawberries, and the Genovese sponge is moistened with kirsch. In my opinion, this is the ultimate cake to spoil your friends and family with in summer. I prefer to keep the decoration simple, but you can certainly dot the top with whipped cream, sliced strawberries, or peeled green pistachios. The strawberries I use are fragrant French Gariguette strawberries: you should use the tastiest, freshest strawberries you can find—in season, of course.

For the Genovese sponge:
Preheat the oven to 350°F (180°C). Line a rimmed 12 x 16 inch (30 x 40 cm) baking pan with parchment paper.

Place the eggs and sugar in the bowl of a stand mixer fitted with the whisk attachment, or use an electric hand beater with a large mixing bowl.
Whip at high speed for 10 minutes, until the mixture is light and foamy.

Carefully stir in the flour, folding it in as if you were making a chocolate mousse.

Pour half of the batter over the prepared baking pan and spread as evenly as possible. You don't need to spread it all over, as you'll be using a cake ring to cut the sponge into a disc. Transfer the pan of batter to a rimmed baking sheet.

Bake for 13 to 15 minutes, keeping a careful eye on the sponge, which should be just lightly golden and spring back when touched. Be careful not to overbake.

As soon as you remove the sponge from the oven, turn it over and carefully peel off the parchment paper. Use the dessert ring (or springform pan) to cut out a disc (or smaller discs) and allow it to cool on a rack.

Repeat the procedure with the remaining batter. The cakes can be made up to a day ahead.

(continued on page 146)

1 Fold the flour carefully into the batter with a flexible spatula.

2 Spread half the batter over a prepared baking sheet and smooth it over.

3 Place the halved strawberries around the rim of the cake, against the food-safe acetate.

4 When the butter is whipped with the custard cream and the pistachio paste has been incorporated, add the chilled pastry cream.

5 Pipe the mousseline cream between all the strawberries.

6 Carefully top the cake with the disc of almond paste.

For the pastry cream:

Place the egg yolks in a mixing bowl with the ground vanilla bean, vanilla extract, half the sugar, and the cornstarch. Whisk for about 3 minutes, until the mixture begins to turn pale.

Bring the milk to a boil with the other half of the sugar and the butter. When it comes to a boil, pour a little over the egg yolk–cornstarch mixture, whisking constantly. Continue to whisk and then return the mixture to the saucepan of milk, whisking steadily. Over low heat, bring to a simmer, whisking continuously, and allow to simmer for 3 to 4 minutes.

Pour the pastry cream into a dish or bowl and press a piece of plastic wrap directly onto the surface. This prevents a skin from forming. Allow to cool completely and then chill. The pastry cream can be made up to a day ahead.

For the custard cream:

Whisk the egg yolks with one-third of the sugar until thick and pale.

Over low heat, bring the milk to a boil with the remaining sugar. When it boils, pour it slowly over the yolk-sugar mixture, stirring constantly.

Return the mixture to the saucepan over low heat and continue to cook, whisking continuously to incorporate as much air as possible and give the custard a very creamy texture. Do not allow it to come to a simmer.

2 sticks (9 oz./250 g) unsalted butter, room
  temperature
3 oz. (85 g) pistachio paste (page 19)

FOR THE SYRUP
Scant ¼ cup (2 oz./50 g) sugar
Scant ¼ cup (50 ml) kirsch
1 ¼ lb. (600 g) strawberries, washed and
  carefully patted dry

Confectioners' sugar to dust the pastry board
5 oz. (150 g) green almond paste

. . . .

If you have a candy thermometer, remove the custard from the heat when it reaches 187°F–189°F (86°C–87°C), when it is cooked. If you don't have a thermometer, you can tell that it is ready when it thickens and coats the back of a spoon.

Pour it into the bowl of a stand mixer fitted with the whisk attachment (or use an electric beater). Whisk at medium speed until the custard cream cools to room temperature; it will have a wonderful light, airy texture.

Pour into a bowl, cover with plastic wrap, and chill for at least 1 hour.

To assemble the cake:
Begin by assembling the components of the mousseline cream. Place the butter in the bowl of a stand mixer fitted with the whisk attachment (or use an electric beater) and whisk at high speed for 5 minutes. Pour in the chilled custard cream and whisk at high speed for a further 2 minutes. Initially, the mixture may not look like a cream, but don't be discouraged. Just continue whisking and it will become perfectly smooth.

Add the pistachio paste and whisk for 3 minutes. Lastly, add the chilled pastry cream and whisk for 2 to 3 minutes. The mousseline cream is ready.

Cut a piece of food-safe acetate to fit around the inside rim of the dessert ring and fit it in. Place the dessert ring on a baking sheet lined with parchment paper and carefully transfer a layer of Genovese sponge to the base.

For the syrup:
Combine the sugar with ¼ cup (50 ml) of water and bring to a boil to dissolve the sugar. Measure out ¼ cup (50 ml) of syrup, mix with the kirsch, and use this to moisten the sponge generously using a pastry brush. Store any leftover syrup in the refrigerator.

Choose several strawberries of the same size and cut them in half lengthwise. Arrange them on the outside of the circle, with the cut side against the food-safe acetate. Arrange the other strawberries on the sponge, ensuring that they are no higher than the top of the dessert ring.

Transfer the mousseline cream to a piping bag fitted with a plain wide tip. Pipe out cream between each strawberry on the outside edge of the cake, and then fill the other gaps. Smooth over with an offset spatula.

Set the second sponge layer over the mousseline cream and moisten it with the kirsch syrup.

On a work surface dusted with confectioners' sugar, roll out the green almond paste very thinly, under ⅛ inch (2 mm) thick. Cut it into a circle of the same dimensions as the dessert ring and place it carefully over the top of the cake.

Chill the cake for at least 2 hours. Just before serving, remove the dessert ring and carefully remove the food-safe acetate. Decorate the cake as you wish.

Cherry Clafoutis
Clafoutis aux cerises

• • • • • • • • • • • • •

Serves 6
Preparation time: 25 minutes
Cooking time: 35 minutes

INGREDIENTS
1 ¼–1 ½ lb. (600–700 g) sweet cherries
(lower weight if pitted, higher weight
if unpitted)
1 scant cup (4 ½ oz./125 g) confectioners'
sugar
½ cup plus 1 teaspoon (2 ¾ oz./80 g)
cornstarch
¾ cup plus 1 tablespoon (2 ½ oz./70 g)
finely ground almonds
1 small pinch ground vanilla bean
2 extra large (US) or large (UK) eggs
1 cup plus scant ½ cup (350 ml) heavy
or whipping cream
2 tablespoons (1 oz./25 g) melted butter,
plus 2 tablespoons (1 oz./25 g) to grease
the dish

• • • • • • • • • • • • •

To pit or not to pit, that's the eternal dilemma when it comes to making a cherry clafoutis. If you go to the Limousin region of France, the home of this summer dessert, and make a clafoutis with pitted cherries, you may be given short shrift. Tradition has it that the pits exude flavor as the clafoutis bakes. However, I've experimented making clafoutis both with and without pits, and in my opinion and those of my testers, there is no difference in the taste.

And yes, I'll make my confession: I far prefer a clafoutis with pitted cherries, as it's simpler to enjoy. Here is my version, a richer one than the traditional recipe, with ground almonds and cream.

Preheat the oven to 400°F (200°C).

Butter a dish approximately 6 x 8 inches (15 x 20 cm) in size.

Wash the cherries well and pat them dry. If you've opted to pit them, now's the time to do so.

Prepare the batter: combine the confectioners' sugar, cornstarch, ground almonds, and ground vanilla bean in a mixing bowl.

Add the eggs and mix well. Stir in the cream and melted butter.

Dot the cherries around the dish, pour in the batter, and bake for 35 minutes, until the top is golden.

Serve warm or cold—both are equally delicious.

Italian Hazelnut Sandwich Cookies
Baci di Dama

EGG FREE
Makes about 20 cookies
Preparation time: 40 minutes
Chilling time: 20 minutes
Cooking time: 20 minutes per batch

INGREDIENTS

1 ¼ sticks (5 oz./150 g) butter, room
 temperature
1 cup minus 2 tablespoons (2 ⅔ oz./75 g)
 finely ground almonds
1 cup minus 2 tablespoons (2 ⅔ oz./75 g)
 ground hazelnuts
¾ cup (5 oz./150 g) sugar
1 cup plus 2 tablespoons (5 ¼ oz./150 g)
 flour
3 ½ oz. (100 g) bittersweet chocolate
7 oz. (200 g) hazelnut paste (page 20)

This recipe comes to us from Piedmont in northern Italy, a major hazelnut-producing region. The name means "kisses of the lady." But I actually discovered it not in Turin, but in Venice, at a local café that had a large selection of cakes on offer. I loved that café and would go back every morning during my stay for my morning ritual: an espresso and two *baci di dama*. These little kisses are irresistible: two crisp hazelnut and almond cookies sandwiched together with chocolate *gianduja*, a hazelnut paste that melts in the mouth. Using a scale will help you make identically sized cookies that are easy to sandwich.

Preheat the oven to 285°F (140°C) using fan heat, if possible. Line a baking sheet with parchment paper.

Place the butter, ground nuts, and sugar in a bowl and beat until creamy.

Add all the flour and mix in, just until incorporated. Don't overwork the dough.

For this recipe, I'd advise you to weigh each of the balls you make: this will enable you to make *baci di dama* that are all identical. I make balls that weigh ½ oz. (14 g), but if you like, you can make them even smaller. Just make sure to roll them so that they are perfectly spherical.

Arrange the cookie balls on the prepared baking sheet, about 20 at a time.

Bake for about 20 minutes, depending on how your oven behaves. The *baci di dama* must rise to a rounded shape, their surface ever so slightly cracked, and most importantly, they shouldn't be too colored. Let them cool on a cooling rack and repeat with the remaining dough.

Prepare the filling. Melt the chocolate in the microwave oven in short bursts, stirring each time, or over a hot water bath, and then mix well with the hazelnut paste until fully combined.

Spoon the chocolate-hazelnut paste—*gianduja*—into a piping bag fitted with a ½-inch (14-mm) plain tip. Freshly made *gianduja* solidifies very quickly, so don't dawdle. Pipe a small amount of *gianduja* onto the bottom of one cookie, then sandwich a second cookie on top. Repeat with the remaining cookies. As soon as you have finished filling them all, place them in the refrigerator for about 20 minutes to set the *gianduja* once and for all. Once it has set, you can remove the cookies from the refrigerator and store them in an airtight container for a few days.

Black Forest Cake
Forêt noire

This is my version of the Black Forest cake, a classic German layer cake made with whipped cream, chocolate, and preserved cherries. I knew exactly what combination of tastes and textures I wanted to achieve: a crisp chocolate casing, smooth whipped cream, a chocolate Genovese sponge generously moistened with kirsch, Italian preserved cherries, and chocolate-flavored whipped cream. In combination, these elements make for an extraordinary dessert, light despite its rich components. I'll explain in detail what you need to do to make this cake. But in fact, it's very simple to put together. Read through the key stages once or twice rather than rushing headlong into the recipe. But even making the chocolate band around the cake is child's play. And if you find it too daunting after all, you can always just use classic chocolate shavings for the decoration.

You can bake the Genovese sponge as a single cake and cut it into three layers, or bake it in thin layers and make smaller two-layer cakes.

For the chocolate Genovese sponge, preheat the oven to 350°F (180°C). Line the base of an 8-inch (20-cm) cake pan with parchment paper and grease the rim. If you're making small cakes, line a large baking sheet with parchment paper (see step-by-step instructions on page 154).

Place the eggs and sugar in the bowl of a mixer fitted with a whisk (or use an electric beater) and whisk at maximum speed for 5 minutes. Reduce the speed to medium and whisk for an additional 10 minutes. The mixture should have increased considerably in volume and be light and airy.

Sift the flour and cocoa powder together and use a flexible spatula to fold the mixture gradually into the egg-sugar mixture, taking care not to deflate the batter. Continue until the mixture is smooth. Then carefully stir in the melted butter until well combined.

Pour the batter into the cake pan or over the prepared baking sheet. For the cake pan, bake for 25 to 30 minutes, until a cake tester inserted into the center comes out dry; it must be springy to the touch. For the baking sheet, spread the batter evenly to a thickness of ⅕ inch (5 mm). Bake for 15 minutes. Do not allow it to dry out; it should be springy to the touch.

Turn out of the pan or take the sponge off the baking sheet and carefully peel off the parchment paper. Allow to cool on a rack.

(continued on page 154)

Makes one 8-inch (20-cm) cake or several
   individual 1 ¾-inch (4.5-cm) high cakes,
   depending on your dessert rings
Preparation time: 2 hours
Cooking time: 15 minutes, or 25 to 30
   for a single cake
Freezing time: 30 minutes plus 3 hours
Chilling time: 5 hours

Special equipment: the rim of an 8 ½-inch
   (22-cm) springform pan to assemble the
   large cake, or dessert rings ½ inch (1 cm)
   larger than the size of the individual cakes,
   and an acetate cake collar to fit into the rim
   or pastry rings for the chocolate band

INGREDIENTS
FOR THE CHOCOLATE GENOVESE SPONGE
3 eggs
½ cup (3 ⅓ oz./95 g) sugar
⅔ cup plus 1 tablespoon (3 ¼ oz./90 g)
   cake flour
3 tablespoons (⅔ oz./20 g) unsweetened
   cocoa powder
2 tablespoons (1 oz./30 g) butter, melted
   and cooled

FOR THE SYRUP
1 18-oz. (510-g) jar Amarena cherries in syrup,
   drained (reserve the syrup)
Scant ½ cup (100 ml) kirsch
A little water

FOR THE WHIPPED CREAM WITH
   MASCARPONE
1 scant cup (7 oz./200 g) mascarpone
¾ cup (200 ml) whipping cream or heavy
   cream (30 to 35 percent butterfat)
⅓ cup (2 oz./50 g) confectioners' sugar

(continued on page 155)

1 Cut discs in the layer of baked Genovese sponge.

2 Spread a layer of cream around the inside rims of the pastry rings.

3 Place a disc of sponge at the base of the rings, use a pastry brush to moisten with syrup, and dot with cherries.

4 Pipe out the chocolate whipped cream.

5 Using a spatula, spread the chocolate over the acetate strip.

6 Surround the frozen cake with the strip of chocolate.

For the 3-layer version, cut the cake horizontally into equal thirds. For the 2-layer cakes, cut discs of sponge with a diameter ½ inch (1 cm) smaller than the dessert rings you'll be using to assemble the Black Forest cake. If you have 5-inch (12.5-cm) rings, cut 4 ½-inch (11 cm) discs. If you only have one ring, simply trim the sponge to the right size.

To moisten the sponge, combine some of the syrup from the cherries with the kirsch and a little water. Taste and adjust accordingly.

Place the mascarpone, whipping cream, and confectioners' sugar in a bowl and place the bowl, with the beaters, in the refrigerator for 30 minutes. When the ingredients and equipment are well chilled, the cream will whip quickly and easily. Whip until the mixture holds firm peaks.

Place a disc of sponge on a baking sheet or other base lined with parchment paper.

Spread a generous layer of the mascarpone cream around the inside rim of the springform pan (or rings). Set the ring over the layer of sponge. Moisten the sponge generously with the syrup and dot with a few cherries.

FOR THE CHOCOLATE WHIPPED CREAM

1 ¼ cups (300 ml) whipping cream or heavy
  cream (30 to 35 percent butterfat)
5 oz. (150 g) bittersweet chocolate
1 heaping tablespoon (⅓ oz./10 g)
  confectioners' sugar

FOR THE CHOCOLATE COLLAR

3 ½ oz. (100 g) bittersweet chocolate

• • • • • • • • • • • • • •

Place the springform rim (or rings) in the freezer so that the cream can firm up. This should take about 30 minutes. This will prevent it from spilling out against the rim of the ring when you add the next layers.

When the mascarpone cream is firm, place the whipping cream in a clean bowl, with the beaters, in the refrigerator.

Melt the chocolate in the microwave oven in short bursts, stirring each time, or over a hot water bath. Allow to cool to lukewarm.

Whip the cream with the confectioners' sugar until it holds firm peaks. Add the melted chocolate and whip until smooth.

Spoon into a piping bag and pipe the cream between the cherries, adding some of it over them.

Set a second layer of sponge over the chocolate whipped cream. Moisten well with the syrup-kirsch mixture and dot with a few cherries. If making the 3-layer version, repeat the layer of chocolate whipped cream, sponge, and cherries.

Pipe a layer of chocolate whipped cream on top and smooth with a knife or offset spatula. If there seems to be too much, smooth it into a slightly rounded dome.

Place in the freezer for about 3 hours, or until firm.

To remove the pastry rings, briefly blow a hairdryer around the sides. Carefully ease the rings off and return the cake to the freezer while you make the chocolate collar.

Cut a strip of food-safe acetate a little bigger than the perimeter of the pastry ring or springform pan, and the same width as the height of the rim (1 ¾ in./4.5 cm), and place it on a flat surface.

Melt the chocolate in the microwave oven in short bursts, or over a hot water bath. Using a spatula, spread the melted chocolate over the acetate strip. Carefully pick it up and place it around the frozen whipped cream. In just 1 minute, the chocolate will cool completely and you can remove the acetate strip. Pull it off gently but smoothly and you'll have a perfectly smooth chocolate collar for the cake.

To finish, pipe out small dollops of mascarpone cream on top of the cake. Set a cherry on the top and chill for 5 hours before serving. The wait will be agony!

The Americas

Pecan Pie

Makes one 8-inch (20-cm) pie, to serve 6
Preparation time: 35 minutes
Cooking time: 35 to 40 minutes

INGREDIENTS
FOR THE SWEET PASTRY CRUST
½ batch sweet pastry (page 74)

FOR THE PECAN-MAPLE SYRUP FILLING
3 eggs
3 tablespoons (1 ½ oz./40 g) melted
  unsalted butter
1 cup minus 2 ½ tablespoons (6 oz./170 g)
  brown sugar
1 ½ tablespoons (½ oz./15 g) all-purpose
  flour
1 teaspoon maple extract, optional
⅔ cup (8 ½ oz./240 g) corn syrup
¼ cup (3 ½ oz./100 g) maple syrup
1 ½ cups (6 ¾ oz./190 g) shelled pecans

This pecan pie is so good, it's practically sinful. It's also the ultimate in contrasting textures: a crisp pastry crust paired with a rich, dense filling stuffed with crunchy pecans. My version includes maple syrup. The secret to achieving the special melting texture of the filling is using corn syrup.

The method I give here uses a tart ring with no base, something used by French professionals and many amateurs. Using a pastry ring gives excellent results for the crust and makes it easier to test for doneness on the bottom of the tart dough, but of course you can use a pie plate or a tart pan with a detachable base.

Roll the sweet pastry dough out very thinly to less than ⅛ inch (2 to 3 mm). Line an 8-inch (20-cm), 1 ¾-inch (4-cm)high tart ring with the dough and set on a baking sheet lined with parchment paper. Alternatively, use a tart pan or pie plate lined with parchment paper. When you transfer the dough to the ring, make sure to press the tart around the rim so that it makes a right angle with the base. With a sharp knife, trim the surplus dough in brief, sure movements from the inside of the ring to the outside (see photo 5 on page 75).

Preheat the oven to 350°F (180°C).

Prepare the pecan-maple syrup filling. In a mixing bowl, place all the ingredients except the pecans. Combine well with a whisk and then stir in the pecans.

Prick the tart shell with a fork and pour in the pecan mixture.

Bake for 35 to 40 minutes. The filling rises to surprising heights! When the pie is done, the crust should be golden and the filling should be risen and starting to crack. Remove from the oven. If you're using a tart ring, remove it carefully, and transfer the pie to a rack to cool. If you're using a tart pan, remove carefully with the paper, and slide the pie onto a rack to cool. The filling will settle as it cools.

Serve the pie warm with a scoop of vanilla ice cream and whipped cream, or chilled, straight from the refrigerator. It will remain crisp for at least 2 days.

Cocoa Brownies

Makes 16 brownies
Preparation time: 25 minutes
Cooking time: 20 minutes

INGREDIENTS

6 tablespoons (3 oz./90 g) unsalted butter
4 tablespoons plus 2 teaspoons (2 ½ oz./
   70 g) salted butter
⅔ cup (2 ¾ oz./80 g) unsweetened cocoa
   powder
1 cup plus scant ½ cup (9 ½ oz./270 g) sugar
1 teaspoon vanilla extract
1 teaspoon water
2 extra large (US) or large (UK) eggs
½ cup (2 oz./60 g) all-purpose flour
1 cup (4 oz./120 g) walnuts

This classic American bar cookie can be dated back to the late nineteenth century and most likely originated in Chicago. These melt-in-the mouth chocolate treats are traditionally made without raising agents and are best when slightly under-baked. I brought back this recipe from the US many years ago, after a stay with a family in Maine to improve my language skills. It uses unsweetened cocoa powder instead of chocolate and browned butter instead of regular butter. In France, browned butter is known as *beurre noisette*—hazelnut butter—and these soft-textured brownies do indeed exude notes of hazelnut.

Preheat the oven to 300°F (150°C). Line an 8-inch (20-cm) square pan with parchment paper.

Place both butters in a heavy saucepan over medium heat and bring to a boil. When the melted butter begins to foam and darken, immediately remove from the heat. It becomes a hazelnut color, and if the bottom of the saucepan is just a little darker—but not burnt—it will be even better. So now you've made brown butter!

Sift the cocoa powder into the sugar and combine. Stir the mixture into the brown butter and whisk briskly.

Whisk in the water and vanilla extract until smooth.

Allow to cool for 5 minutes.

Beat in the eggs one by one, combining well each time.

When the batter is smooth, pour in all the flour. Whisk just until smooth and stir in the walnuts.

Pour the batter into the prepared baking pan and smooth over with an offset spatula. Bake for 18 to 20 minutes, no longer! If you prolong the baking time, the brownies will lose their luscious texture. A thin crust should form on the top, and if you gently shake the pan, the batter should not move at all.

Allow to cool in the pan and cut into 16 portions. Stored in an airtight container, the brownies will keep for 5 to 7 days.

Utterly Decadent Brownies

My dear friend Sébastien contributed this recipe for utterly decadent iced chocolate brownies. The brownies themselves are just as we like them: soft, rich, and sticky. The quantity of sugar in the recipe may seem surprisingly high, but, combined with the eggs, it's how the brownies achieve a truly remarkable consistency. A bonus: this is a one-bowl recipe and a surefire solution to those sudden and uncontrollable cravings for something chocolaty and sweet.

Makes 16 brownies
Preparation time: 30 minutes
Cooking time: 25 to 30 minutes

INGREDIENTS
FOR THE BROWNIES
7 oz. (200 g) bittersweet chocolate
1 ¼ sticks (5 oz./150 g) unsalted butter
1 cup plus 1 scant cup (13 ¾ oz./390 g) sugar
2 extra large (US) or large (UK) eggs
1 teaspoon vanilla extract
¾ cup plus 2 tablespoons (100 g) all-purpose flour
7 oz. (200 g) walnuts, or other nuts of your choice

FOR THE ICING
2 oz. (60 g) bittersweet chocolate
2 tablespoons (1 oz./30 g) unsalted butter
Scant ¼ cup (50 ml) milk
1 generous cup (5 oz./150 g) confectioners' sugar

Preheat the oven to 310°F (155°C). Line an 8-inch (20-cm) square pan with parchment paper, leaving the paper to extend beyond the sides of the pan.

To make the brownies, place the chocolate and butter in a bowl set over a hot water bath and melt. You can also melt the ingredients in the microwave oven, working in short bursts at the highest level, and stirring after each burst. When combined, pour in all the sugar and mix in well.

Beat in the eggs, one by one, and stir in the vanilla.

Fold in the flour, stirring until just combined and there are no lumps left.

Stir in the nuts. Pour the batter into the prepared pan and bake for 25 to 30 minutes, depending on how soft you like your brownies. I'd advise you to under-bake them slightly for the best texture. A fine crust should form on the top, the sides should rise up a little, and if you gently move the mold, the batter should not move at all. Those are the best indications of doneness.

Allow to cool completely in the pan.

To make the icing, melt the chocolate with the milk and butter in a bowl over a hot water bath or in the microwave oven.

Stir together well and mix in the confectioners' sugar.

Pour it over the top of the brownie pan and allow to cool.

Using the parchment paper as a sling, lift the slab of brownies out of the pan and cut it into 16 squares. And then, test your willpower.

Photo page 167

Cheesecake

Makes one 9-inch (22-cm) cake
Preparation time: 45 minutes
Cooking time: 40 minutes
Cooling time: 2 hours
Chilling time: 24 hours

INGREDIENTS

FOR THE CRUST

7 ½ oz. (210 g) digestive biscuits or other dry,
  crumbly cookies
7 tablespoons (3 ½ oz./100 g) butter, melted
1 tablespoon plus 2 teaspoons (⅔ oz./20 g)
  sugar

FOR THE FILLING

2 lb. (900 g) cream cheese, room temperature
¼ cup (1 ¼ oz./35 g) all-purpose flour
1 ½ teaspoons vanilla extract
1 ¼ cups (9 oz./250 g) sugar
Juice of 1 lemon, divided
Zest of ½ lemon
1 cup (8 ½ oz./235 g) sour cream or
  crème frâiche
2 eggs plus 1 egg yolk

FOR THE LEMON TOPPING

⅔ cup (5 ¼ oz./150 g) sour cream or
  crème fraîche
1 tablespoon plus 2 teaspoons (⅔ oz./20 g)
  sugar
2 teaspoons lemon juice (from the lemon
  used for the filling)

The French have their own variety of cheesecake; much lighter and airier than a classic American cheesecake. But I happen to love the dense and decadent American version. This is the genuine New York cheesecake in all its glory. If you like, you can serve it with a berry sauce or lemon topping. For the crust, you can use your favorite dry cookies. I like to use English digestive biscuits for their flavor, but in place of the classic graham-cracker crust, you can also use *speculoos* (see page 118), Breton shortbread (see page 84), or a combination of several of your favorite cookies.

Preheat the oven to 350°F (180°C) and line the base of a 9-inch (22-cm) springform pan with parchment paper. Open the pan, place the paper inside and shut the pan to hold it in. Butter the sides of the pan.

Grind the cookies to a fine powder. In a bowl, combine thoroughly with the sugar and melted butter.

Put the mixture into the pan and press it down with the back of a spoon to make an even crust. Bake for 10 to 15 minutes, until nicely colored.

Meanwhile, prepare the filling. Place the cream cheese, flour, vanilla extract, and sugar in the bowl of a mixer fitted with the flat beater attachment and beat at minimum speed for 2 minutes. This creates the creamy texture you're aiming for. You can also use a hand whisk; the important thing is not to over-beat.

Add 2 teaspoons of lemon juice to the cheese mixture. Add the lemon zest, sour cream, eggs, and egg yolk. Run the beater just enough to incorporate the ingredients.

Increase the oven temperature to 400°F (200°C).

Pour the filling in the crust and bake for 10 minutes, then lower the temperature to 195°F (90°C) and cook for an additional 30 minutes. The cheesecake will be set on the edges and slightly wobbly in the center.

Turn off the oven and allow the cake to cool in the oven until it reaches room temperature. This takes about 2 hours.

Place the cheesecake, still in the springform pan, in the refrigerator for no less than 24 hours! That's the time required to get the texture perfectly creamy.

(continued on page 164)

To serve, you can either drizzle the cake with a berry coulis (as I did for the photo) or make a lemon topping. For the topping, combine the cream, sugar, and lemon juice. When thoroughly mixed, pour over the cheesecake and spread with an offset spatula. Return to the refrigerator for at least 1 hour and serve well chilled.

Choc Chip Bars

These choc chip bars are very similar to blondies. The dough is baked in a pan and then cut into bars, instead of being dropped in spoonfuls for round cookies. The results are chewy and delicious, especially for fans of the flavor and texture of uncooked cookie dough. I've held on to this recipe for twenty years. It was given to me by my American host family. And you should keep it handy too, for whenever you need a quick treat.

Preheat the oven to 310°F (155°C). Line a 9-inch (23-cm) square pan with parchment paper, placing one piece in one direction and another piece in the other direction.

In a mixing bowl, combine the eggs, salt, sugar, brown sugar, and vanilla extract. Add the melted butter and mix well.

In another mixing bowl, combine the baking soda with the flour.

Pour all the flour into the batter and mix until smooth. Stir in the chocolate chips. And your dough is ready!

Pour the dough into the pan and smooth it with the back of a spoon.

Bake for 30 minutes, until a fine crust has formed on the top. Allow to cool completely before turning carefully out of the pan.

Cut into 16 pieces and shoo away all the eager kids who'll be clamoring loudly around you.

· · · · · · · · · · · · · ·

Makes 16 bars
Preparation time: 15 minutes
Cooking time: 30 minutes

INGREDIENTS
2 extra large (US) or large (UK) eggs
½ teaspoon salt
1 cup minus 3 tablespoons (5 ½ oz./160 g)
    granulated sugar
1 scant cup (7 oz./200 g) brown sugar
1 teaspoon vanilla extract
1 ⅔ sticks (6 ¾ oz./190 g) butter, melted and
    cooled to lukewarm
1 teaspoon baking soda
3 cups (13 ½ oz./380 g) all-purpose flour
1 ⅔ cups (10 oz./300 g) chocolate chips (milk
    or bittersweet, or a combination)

· · · · · · · · · · · · · ·

Choc Chip Bars (left) and
Utterly Decadent Brownies (right)

Giant New York Walnut and Chocolate Cookies

Makes 5 giant cookies
Preparation time: 15 minutes
Freezing time: at least 4 hours
Cooking time: 15 to 20 minutes

INGREDIENTS

1 scant cup (4 oz./120 g) walnuts
1 medium (US) or small (UK) egg
½ cup (3 ½ oz./100 g) granulated sugar
⅔ cup (4 oz./125 g) light brown sugar
1 stick (4 oz./125 g) unsalted butter, melted
   and cooled to lukewarm
1 generous pinch salt
½ teaspoon vanilla extract
1 ¾ cups (8 oz./225 g) all-purpose flour
1 heaping cup (7 oz./200 g) bittersweet
   chocolate chips

In New York City, not far from Central Park, there's a bakery called Levain that sells enormous and decadent cookies. On a visit to New York, I had to try them. I loved them so much, I brought some back home to France, where I set to work to reproduce the recipe. After many attempts, I think I managed to get as close to the original as possible. What's special about these cookies is that they are very crisp on the outside and very soft and chewy on the inside. If you think I've made a mistake by omitting baking powder and baking soda, I assure you that it's by design! This way the cookies hold the shape you give them—as much as possible—when you pop them into the oven.

Roughly chop the walnuts. Lightly beat the egg.

In a large mixing bowl or the bowl of a stand mixer, combine the granulated and brown sugar. Pour in the melted butter, salt, and vanilla extract and combine until creamy.

Pour in the beaten egg, stirring or beating constantly, until fully incorporated.

Pour in all the flour and stir to combine.

Stir in the chopped walnuts and chocolate chips.

Finish kneading the dough by hand to distribute the walnuts and chocolate chips evenly.

To make these utterly decadent cookies, divide the dough into 5 balls of equal weight, 6 ½ oz. (185 g). Of course you can make them smaller, but it's their exceptional size that ensures that the cookies remain soft inside and have a crisp crust.

Take a ball and pull at it with your hands to give it a rough look. This method increases the surface of the crust. Repeat for the other balls. Place the cookies on a baking sheet and freeze for at least 4 hours, or up to 12 hours.

Preheat the oven to 425°F (220°C). It's the high temperature that will quickly bake the crust before the inside gets baked.

Place the frozen cookies in the oven for 15 to 20 minutes, keeping a careful eye on them so that they don't burn, but turn a lovely golden color.

(continued on page 170)

1 Prepare all the ingredients.

2 Work in the walnuts and chocolate chips.

3 The dough is now ready.

4 Pull at the ball of dough to increase the surface that will be crisp.

5 Place the cookies in the freezer for at least 4 hours before baking them.

Because all ovens have their quirks, I strongly advise you to stay close to yours while the cookies bake, especially if you've opted to make a smaller size.

Allow them to cool for about 10 minutes on the baking sheet and transfer carefully to a cooling rack.

The giant cookies will be at their most scrumptious 30 minutes after coming out of the oven: the inside will have firmed up just slightly, the chocolate will still be half-melted, and the crust will bear its name proudly.

Giant Oatmeal-Cranberry Cookies

Giant Oatmeal-Cranberry Cookies

Makes 5 giant cookies
Preparation time: 15 minutes
Cooking time: 15 to 20 minutes

INGREDIENTS
½ cup (3 ½ oz./100 g) granulated sugar
⅔ cup (4 oz./125 g) light brown sugar
1 stick (4 oz./125 g) unsalted butter,
   room temperature
1 medium (US) or small (UK) egg
½ teaspoon vanilla extract
1 cup plus scant ½ cup (6 oz./175 g)
   all-purpose flour
1 pinch salt
2 cups (6 oz./175 g) oatmeal, regular
   or quick-cooking
⅔ cup (3 ½ oz./100 g) dried cranberries
   or raisins (or a combination of the two)

Here's another recipe inspired by the bakery Levain in New York City. These cookies are so big that two or three people could probably share one! After I'd finished testing the walnut and chocolate cookies (see page 168), I tried my hand at this oatmeal recipe. The important thing was fine-tuning the quantity of oatmeal to use. I had to increase it several times over the course of my trials. I wanted to make the same type of cookie that was crisp on the outside and soft inside. Even more, I wanted them to taste just as good two days after baking. Like their giant chocolate cousins, these oatmeal-cranberry cookies don't call for baking powder or baking soda.

Preheat the oven to 375°F (190°C).

Combine the granulated sugar, brown sugar, and butter in the bowl of a mixer fitted with a flat beater attachment. If you don't have a stand mixer, no need to worry; you can work with a wooden spoon.

Beat until the mixture is creamy. Add the egg and vanilla extract. Beat for 1 minute, until the mixture is smooth.

Stir in the flour, salt, and oatmeal until the mixture reaches the consistency of a dough. Lastly, add the cranberries. Use your hands to work them in so that they are evenly distributed.

Divide the dough into 5 balls of equal weight, around 6 oz. (170 g) each. With your hands, pull at the dough to give them a very rough look.

What's different from the previous recipe is that you don't need to freeze the dough. You can bake them directly for 15 to 20 minutes, keeping a careful eye on them. A lovely golden crust must form on the top. And don't worry if they don't look all that well baked in the center—they'll be even better for it.

Allow to cool for 10 minutes on the baking sheet and transfer to a rack to cool completely.

Photo page 171

Three Classic Cookies

In addition to the spectacularly textured giant cookies on the previous pages, I'd like to share three other cookie recipes: classic chocolate-chip cookies made with oat flour, double chocolate-chip cookies, and peanut butter chip cookies. The method for making the cookies is the same; all that changes are the ingredients.

The recipe for classic chocolate-chip cookies is the one I make most often at home. I first discovered it on an exchange trip with a family in Florida when I was thirteen years old. The cookies had everything I loved: chocolate (bittersweet and milk), walnuts, and ground oats. Each time I make them, they disappear in the blink of an eye.

The double chocolate-chip cookies have a soft and tender inside and a crumbly shortbread texture on the edges.

In the peanut butter chip cookies, the soft texture of the chips offsets the chewy interior perfectly. Note that these cookies are flatter than the other ones.

In all three recipes, you may vary the cookies with nuts of your choice. And instead of using chocolate chips, you can consider chopping up big chunks of your favorite chocolate bar.

For all three recipes, preheat the oven to 350°F (180°C). Line a cookie sheet with parchment paper.

For the first stage, use the bowl of a stand mixer fitted with the flat beater attachment. But don't worry if you don't have a stand mixer: a wooden spoon, your arm muscles, and a little extra time will achieve the same result. Combine the two types of sugar and the butter, beating for 2 minutes until creamy.

Beat in the egg (or eggs), vanilla, and the melted chocolate if you're making the double chocolate cookies. Don't worry if the mixture seems to curdle a little. This is not serious—it may be due to hot weather; when you add the following ingredients, it will all come right.

In another mixing bowl, combine all the ingredients listed in Stage 2. Pour them into the mixture in the stand mixer and beat in for about 1 minute, until thoroughly combined.

Add the ingredients in Stage 3 and work in rapidly. Switch off the mixer and work in the chips and other optional ingredients with your hands, just until evenly distributed.

(continued on page 174)

Makes about 50 classic chocolate-chip cookies
Preparation time: 20 minutes
Cooking time: 8 to 10 minutes per batch

INGREDIENTS
STAGE 1
1 cup plus 3 tablespoons (8 oz./225 g)
   granulated sugar
1 cup minus 1 tablespoon (6 ¾ oz./190 g)
   light brown sugar
2 sticks (8 oz./225 g) butter, room temperature
2 eggs
1 teaspoon vanilla extract

STAGE 2
2 ½ cups (10 ½ oz./300 g) all-purpose flour
2 ½ cups (7 oz./200 g) rolled oats, finely
   ground in a food processor
½ teaspoon salt
½ teaspoon baking powder
½ teaspoon baking soda

STAGE 3
1 heaping cup (7 oz./200 g) bittersweet
   chocolate chips
Heaping ½ cup (3 ½ oz./100 g) milk
   chocolate chips
½ cup (2 ½ oz./65 g) chopped walnuts

Makes about 50 double chocolate-chip cookies
Preparation time: 20 minutes
Cooking time: 8 to 10 minutes per batch

INGREDIENTS
STAGE 1
1 cup plus scant ¼ cup (8 oz./230 g)
   granulated sugar
1 scant cup (7 oz./200 g) light brown sugar
2 sticks plus 3 tablespoons (9 ½ oz./270 g)
   butter, room temperature
2 eggs

(continued on page 174)

1 teaspoon vanilla extract
4 oz. (120 g) bittersweet chocolate, melted
   and cooled to lukewarm

STAGE 2
3 cups plus 1 scant cup (1 lb./480 g)
   all-purpose flour
Scant ½ cup (2 oz./60 g) unsweetened cocoa
   powder
1 teaspoon salt
½ teaspoon baking powder
1 teaspoon baking soda

STAGE 3
7 oz. (200 g) bittersweet chocolate, in chunks
6 oz. (170 g) milk chocolate, in chunks

Makes about 30 peanut butter chip cookies
Preparation time: 20 minutes
Cooking time: 8 to 10 minutes per batch

INGREDIENTS
STAGE 1
⅓ cup (2 ½ oz./70 g) granulated sugar
1 scant cup (7 oz./200 g) light brown sugar
1 ½ sticks (6 oz./170 g) butter, room
   temperature
1 egg
1 teaspoon vanilla extract

STAGE 2
1 ¾ cups (8 oz./230 g) all-purpose flour
3 tablespoons (1 oz./30 g) cornstarch
½ teaspoon baking powder
1 teaspoon baking soda

STAGE 3
6 oz. (180 g) peanut butter chips

• • • • • • • • • • • • • • •

Using either your hands or an ice cream scoop, shape balls of dough. If you want them all to be identical, you can weigh them. I think a good weight is 1 ¼ oz. (35 g) per ball.

Place the balls on the cookie sheet, no more than 6 to 8 per sheet. Of course, you'll need to bake several batches to use up all the dough. Bake for 8 to 9 minutes, until golden around the edges but barely baked in the center. As they cool down, the dough will become firmer, and it's when they're slightly under-baked that they're the most delicious.

Transfer to a rack and let cool. They are best eaten still slightly warm.

Keep in mind that the soft peanut butter cookies spread a lot when baked; they are also very thin (though their texture is deliciously soft). The double chocolate cookies will be almost the same shape when baked as when raw, and the classic cookies are somewhere in between.

Should you want to freeze your cookies, you can either freeze the raw dough or prepare the balls of dough and place them on a baking sheet. Freeze the baking sheet, well covered in plastic wrap. You can also freeze the balls of dough in plastic bags, but only once they're very firm. This way, they are ready to be baked. If you bake frozen cookies straight from the freezer, the center will be even less baked than otherwise, so it's a good idea to defrost them partially before baking.

Chocolate-Chip Scones

EGG FREE
Makes 6 large scones
Preparation time: 10 minutes
Chilling time: 1 hour
Cooking time: 25 to 30 minutes

INGREDIENTS
1 ¾ cups (8 oz./225 g) all-purpose flour
7 tablespoons (3 ¾ oz./110 g) butter,
   well chilled and diced
2 pinches salt
⅓ cup (3 oz./75 g) sugar, plus a little extra
   for sprinkling
1 teaspoon baking powder
Scant ½ cup (110 ml) orange juice
⅔ cup (4 oz./125 g) chocolate chips

I really love the enormous scones I find in the US, very distant cousins of the more restrained British scones. The dough can be prepared in just a few minutes, with perfect results. What's special about this recipe is the fact that it uses orange juice instead of cream or buttermilk to moisten the dough. The juice imparts a lovely color to the scones and the flavor pairs well with the chocolate chips.

Place the flour, butter, salt, sugar, and baking powder in the bowl of a stand mixer fitted with the flat beater attachment, or in a mixing bowl.

Beat or rub in with your fingertips until the mixture forms crumbs.

Pour in the orange juice and mix just until combined.

Incorporate the chocolate chips and *voilà*, the dough is ready!

Shape it into a ball and flatten it into a thick 7- to 8-inch (18- to 20-cm) diameter disc.

Cover it in plastic wrap and chill for 1 hour. This will firm it up and enable you to cut it into triangles.

Preheat the oven to 350°F (180°C). Line a baking sheet with parchment paper. Cut the disc into 6 slices and bake for 25 to 30 minutes, keeping a close eye on them. They should be nicely golden.

Eat the scones warm. They are best eaten the day they are made.

Granola Bars

DAIRY AND EGG FREE
Makes 9 large bars
Preparation time: 25 minutes
Cooking time: 45 to 50 minutes

INGREDIENTS
DRY INGREDIENTS
2 ¼ cups (6 oz./180 g) oats, regular or
  quick-cooking
⅔ cup (2 oz./55 g) unsweetened dried
  shredded coconut
Scant ½ cup (3 oz./90 g) dark brown sugar
6 tablespoons (1 ½ oz./45 g) wheat germ
Heaping ⅓ cup (2 oz./60 g) dried cherries,
  sliced in half
¾ cup (2 ½ oz./70 g) dried cranberries
½ cup (2 ½ oz./70 g) pumpkin seeds
⅔ cup (2 ¾ oz./80 g) sunflower seeds
½ cup (2 ¾ oz./80 g) untoasted sesame seeds
½ cup (2 oz./60 g) raw cashews, roughly
  chopped
⅔ cup (2 oz./50g) sliced (flaked) almonds
¼ cup (1 ½ oz./40 g) raisins
¼ teaspoon salt

LIQUID INGREDIENTS
6 oz. (180 g) brown rice syrup
¼ cup (3 oz./80 g) honey
Generous ⅓ cup (3 oz./90 g) canola oil
1 tablespoon vanilla extract
1 tablespoon (15 ml) water

I discovered granola bars, relatively unknown in France, for the first time at an organic grocery store in New York City and fell in love immediately. For several months, I wondered obsessively how granola bars were made. Every time I went to New York, I would rush to buy a supply. One day, I decided to try and use my instincts to make them myself. In my first attempts, when I would bake the granola bars, all the ingredients separated as if they had oil running between them. Luckily, I thought to try cooking the granola in a saucepan, and the problem was solved. To recreate exactly what I liked so much about the store-bought granola bars, I followed the list of ingredients on the label to a T, and took inspiration from what the bars looked like. Feel free to adapt and change the nuts, seeds, and dried fruit as you wish.

Preheat the oven to 320°F (160°C). Line an 8-inch (21-cm) square pan with parchment paper.

Combine all the dry ingredients in a large mixing bowl.

In a large pot over low heat, combine all the liquid ingredients and bring to a simmer.

Add the dry ingredients and stir thoroughly with a wooden spoon. Continue cooking over low heat, stirring constantly and checking that the bottom of the pot does not burn.

The ingredients first absorb all the liquid and then begin to form a sticky mass. This takes 7 to 8 minutes.

Pour the mixture into the prepared pan, packing it compactly, and smooth it with the back of a spoon or offset spatula.

Bake for 35 to 45 minutes, until lightly golden on top. The sides should be just a little darker. Allow to cool to room temperature in the pan and then turn out of the pan. This will be very easy with the parchment paper.

Cut into 9 bars, cover them tightly in plastic wrap, and store in an airtight container for several weeks.

Caramelita Bars

EGG FREE
Makes 9 large bars
Preparation time: 20 minutes
Cooking time: 35 to 40 minutes

INGREDIENTS

FOR THE BASE

1 stick plus 3 tablespoons (5 ¾ oz./160 g)
  butter, very soft or just melted
Generous ¾ cup (6 oz./170 g) brown sugar
  (or light brown sugar)
1 cup plus scant ½ cup (6 ¼ oz./175 g) flour
¼ teaspoon baking soda
1 ¼ cups (3 ½ oz./100 g) oats

FOR THE FILLING

¾ cup (8 ¾ oz./250 g) caramel sauce
  (homemade or store-bought)
1 scant cup (3 ½ oz./100 g) whole pecans
5 oz. (150 g) chocolate, roughly chopped

FOR THE CRUNCHY TOPPING

5 tablespoons (2 ½ oz./70 g) butter, very soft
  or just melted
2 ½ tablespoons (1 ¼ oz./35 g) brown sugar
3 tablespoons (1 ¼ oz./35 g) granulated
  white sugar
½ cup plus 1 tablespoon (2 ½ oz./70 g) flour
Scant ½ cup (1 ¼ oz./35 g) oats

I have just unwittingly pressed the button on a huge calorie bomb. It's about to explode, so turn the page quickly before you yield to the temptation of all this butter. I ate these Caramelita Bars for the first time in San Francisco and have always remembered them fondly. So now I bring you my version: a moist, soft dough made with oats, a layer of caramel, pecans, and chocolate, covered with a crispy oat topping. I did say a bomb. You've been warned!

Preheat the oven to 350°F (180°C). Line an 8-inch (21-cm) square pan with parchment paper.

For the base, begin by combining the butter and brown sugar. Add the flour, baking soda, and oats.

Mix with a flexible spatula until just smooth. Spread out evenly on the base of the prepared pan. Flatten gently, but don't crush it.

Bake for 15 minutes.

Remove from the oven and pour the caramel sauce over the base. It'll melt immediately. Add the pecans and chopped chocolate, spreading them evenly over the caramel.

For the crunchy topping, combine all the ingredients as for the base; it should have a crumbly texture. Scatter evenly over the filling, in large clumps.

Bake for 20 to 25 minutes, until the topping obtains a light golden color.

Cut into 9 generous portions—or a larger number of small ones, if you want to ease your conscience.

Caramel-Pecan
Sticky Buns

Makes about 12 buns
Preparation time: 40 minutes
Rising time: 3 to 4 hours
Cooking time: 25 to 30 minutes

INGREDIENTS

FOR THE DOUGH

⅓ oz. (10 g) fresh (compressed) yeast
Scant ⅔ cup (140 ml) low-fat milk, warmed
2 ⅔ cups (11 ½ oz./330 g) all-purpose flour
⅓ cup (2 ½ oz./70 g) sugar
2 pinches salt
1 large (US) or medium (UK) egg
1 stick plus 1 tablespoon (4 ½ oz./130 g)
   butter, room temperature, diced

FOR THE CARAMEL TOPPING

Scant ½ cup (3 ½ oz./100 g) brown sugar
7 tablespoons (3 ½ oz./100 g) salted butter
1 tablespoon (20 g) honey
1 teaspoon vanilla extract
Generous ½ cup (2 ½ oz./65 g) whole pecans,
   roughly chopped

FOR THE CINNAMON-SUGAR AND
PECAN FILLING

¼ cup (2 oz./50 g) brown sugar
1 ½ teaspoons cinnamon
3 tablespoons (1 ½ oz./40 g) butter, melted
   and cooled
½ cup (2 ½ oz./65 g) chopped pecans

FOR THE STICKY GLAZE

Generous ⅓ cup (3 oz./70 g) brown sugar
5 tablespoons (3 oz./70 g) butter
3 ½ tablespoons (55 g) sweetened
   condensed milk
1 teaspoon vanilla extract
½ teaspoon cinnamon
A few chopped pecans for sprinkling

These sticky buns are stuffed with cinnamon, brown sugar, and crunchy pecans—a classic trio of American ingredients. Totally regressive and high-calorie, the buns are so appetizing and fragrant that we can forgive them all their sins. Waiting for them while they bake, filling the kitchen with a wonderful scent, is nothing short of torture.

Prepare the dough. Dissolve the yeast in the warm milk. Place the flour, sugar, and salt in a mixing bowl. It's easier to knead the dough using a stand mixer fitted with a dough hook. If you don't have one, simply knead by hand.

Pour the yeast-milk mixture into the bowl, add the egg, and knead at medium speed for about 10 minutes, until the dough is soft, sticky, and elastic. Add the butter and continue for another 10 minutes or so, until the dough pulls away from the sides of the bowl. If some of it remains stuck, scrape it off and incorporate it into the rest.

Cover with a cloth and allow to rise at room temperature for 1 hour 30 minutes, until doubled in volume.

Meanwhile, make the caramel topping. Place the brown sugar, butter, honey, and vanilla in a heavy saucepan over medium heat and bring to a boil. Mix well: there should be no lumps.

When all the sugar has dissolved, pour the caramel into a 10-inch (24-cm) diameter, 2-inch (5-cm) deep cake pan. Sprinkle with the chopped pecans and set aside.

For the filling, combine the brown sugar and cinnamon.

Place a large sheet of parchment paper on your work surface. This will keep it clean and save you from adding unnecessary flour to your sticky buns.

Roll the dough out to a 12 x 16 inch (30 x 40 cm) rectangle. If necessary, use your hands to shape it, particularly at the corners, if it doesn't roll out into the rectangle you want.

To fill the buns, brush the melted butter over the entire surface of the dough. Sprinkle with all the cinnamon and brown sugar mixture and then with the chopped pecans.

Using the parchment paper to help you, roll the dough into a log lengthwise. The final diameter should be 2 ½ to 3 inches (6 to 8 cm).

(continued on page 182)

Cut into slices 1 ¾ to 2 inches (4 to 5 cm) thick. Transfer them carefully to the pan and place them over the caramel and pecans at the bottom. You may need to reshape them slightly to give them a nice, round shape.

Allow the sticky buns to rise for 1 hour 30 minutes to 2 hours, until they fill the pan.

Preheat the oven to 350°F (180°C). Bake the buns for 25 to 30 minutes, until nicely golden.

Immediately turn the buns onto a cooling rack, taking care not to burn yourself. Place the rack of buns over a large baking sheet or tray for the final stage of the recipe.

Prepare the sticky glaze. In a small, heavy saucepan over medium heat, combine all the ingredients and bring to a boil. Boil for 2 minutes and pour over the top of the cake. Sprinkle with a few chopped pecans and serve warm or cool.

Canadian Sugar Tart

Makes one 7-inch (18-cm) tart
Preparation time: 30 minutes
Cooking time: 30 minutes

INGREDIENTS
½ batch sweet pastry (page 74)
½ cup (2 oz./60 g) all-purpose flour
1 cup plus scant ½ cup (10 ½ oz./300 g)
   brown sugar
¼ cup (60 ml) milk
1 cup (250 ml) heavy cream

The sugar tart is a specialty of Quebec. In northern France and Belgium, other versions of sugar tarts are familiar. Here, the crust is crisp and the filling is rich and sweet. Cream, brown sugar—and that's practically it! It's delectable, especially when temperatures drop outside.

Prepare the sweet pastry and fit it into a 7-inch (18-cm) tart ring or pan with a 1-inch (2.5-cm) rim lined with parchment paper.

Preheat the oven to 350°F (180°C).

In a heavy saucepan, combine the flour and brown sugar. Stir in the milk and cream.

Set the saucepan over low heat and bring to a boil, stirring or whisking constantly so that the bottom of the saucepan doesn't burn.

When the creamy mixture comes to a boil, simmer a little until it thickens slightly. Pour it into the raw crust.

Bake for about 30 minutes, until the crust is golden and the filling has risen.

As it cools, the filling will return to its pre-baking depth. Allow to cool on a rack, but don't put it in the refrigerator. The tart is best served warm, or at least at room temperature, but definitely not chilled.

Brazilian Tapioca Crêpes

EGG AND GLUTEN FREE
Makes 10 to 12 crêpes
Preparation time: 15 minutes
Sedimentation time: 12 hours or overnight
Resting time: 1 hour 20 minutes
Cooking time: 35 minutes

INGREDIENTS
3 ¼ cups (14 oz./400 g) tapioca flour
1 ⅔ cups (400 ml) water
Sliced bananas, sweetened condensed milk,
  freshly grated coconut, dulche de leche,
  goiabada (page 192), or yogurt, for filling

I first tasted this unusual and delicious dessert in Rio de Janeiro, but at first I couldn't quite figure it out. It was called tapioca, but didn't look anything like the tapioca pearls I knew from home. In fact, this crêpe is made with tapioca flour. Tapioca flour comes from the manioc root, also known as cassava, and has a high degree of moisture. This means that tapioca flour can be used to make a crêpe that cooks in a pan all on its own without any added ingredients. It's quite magical. Since it only cooks on one side, the crêpe has an ever-so-lightly grilled taste—utterly delicious! The crêpe can be filled with whatever you please. And contrary to what you might think, tapioca flour is not that hard to find. You can buy it in Asian supermarkets and online.

Place the tapioca flour in a large mixing bowl and pour in the water. Mix well. The mixture should look like milk. Allow the sediment to sink for 12 hours; do not touch it at all during this period!

After 12 hours, you'll see that the water has risen to the top and the starch has gathered at the bottom. To empty the bowl of the water, simply pour it into the sink: the starch will not pour out with the water. At this stage the surface of the flour will be very shiny and you'll be able to gently press your finger into it. But if you push too hard, the paste will offer some resistance.

Allow it to rest for an additional hour. More water will rise to the surface. Pour it off and mop up any excess by placing several sheets of paper towel on top of the flour for 20 minutes. The process is done when the surface of the flour is quite dull, with no more shine. If there is still some water remaining, simply mop it up with more paper towels.

Break up the paste using a fork. Place the pieces in a fine-mesh sieve and push through to make a fine powder.

To prepare the tapioca crêpes, heat a non-stick pan over medium heat. Using a spoon, evenly spread a layer of powder about ⅕ inch (5 mm) thick over the pan. Do not press it down.

Cover with the lid and cook for 2 to 3 minutes. Remove from the pan and add the filling of your choice.

Fold the tapioca crêpe in two and serve.

Brazilian Cornmeal-Parmesan Cake
Bolo de Fubá

Makes one 9-inch (23-cm) bundt cake
Preparation time: 30 minutes
Cooking time: 45 minutes

Special equipment: 9 ½-inch (24-cm) bundt
cake pan

INGREDIENTS
1 ½ cups (9 oz./250 g) yellow cornmeal
1 cup plus scant ½ cup (360 ml) low-fat milk
1 ¾ cups (12 ½ oz./350 g) sugar
¾ cup (185 ml) neutral-flavored vegetable oil
½ cup (3 oz./90 g) grated Parmesan
⅔ cup (3 oz./75 g) all-purpose flour
3 eggs
2 teaspoons ground aniseed
1 tablespoon baking powder

Brazilian cuisine joyfully combines elements of cultures as diverse as Amerindian, Portuguese, and African. *Fubá* exemplifies this synthesis. Corn was cultivated by the Indian peoples in Brazil before the arrival of the Portuguese, but the word used for corn flour, *fubá*, comes from Kimbundu, the language spoken by slaves from Angola. In Portuguese, *bolo* means cake. To make this *fubá* cake, you'll need cornmeal. And even though it contains Parmesan cheese, it is indeed a cake, and a delicious one at that. The taste of cheese disappears during baking, leaving a uniquely moist texture. I find this sort of culinary paradox fascinating and that's why I've included *bolo de fubá* in this book.

If you can't find cornmeal, grind polenta in the food processor until it is finely processed.

Place the cornmeal, milk, sugar, and oil in a large pot and mix well. Set over low heat and bring to a boil, whisking constantly so that no lumps form as it cooks. When it reaches a soft polenta texture, allow to simmer for 2 minutes. Remove from the heat and allow to cool for 20 minutes, until it reaches a lukewarm temperature.

Preheat the oven to 375°F (190°C). Butter a 9 ½-inch (24-cm) bundt cake pan and dust with flour (or spray with non-stick spray).

Whisk in the grated Parmesan, flour, eggs, aniseed, and baking powder until thoroughly combined. Pour the batter into the pan and bake for 45 minutes, until a cake tester comes out dry.

Turn the cake out of the pan and allow to cool on a rack.

The *bolo de fubá* keeps for 3 to 4 days.

Bolo de fubá/
a recipe from afar/that you may never know/
until the moment/when pulled from the oven,/
its fragrance smells/like home.

Camila Nicácio

Brazilian Guava Jelly Roll
Rocambole

Serves 6 to 8
Preparation time: 50 minutes
Cooking time: 3 to 4 minutes
Chilling time: 2 hours

INGREDIENTS
3 jumbo (US) or extra large (UK) eggs,
   total weight 7 oz. (200 g)
1 cup (7 oz./200 g) sugar
1 ¾ sticks (7 oz./200 g) unsalted butter,
   melted and cooled
1 ⅔ cups (7 oz./200 g) all-purpose flour

FOR THE FILLING
1 ½ lb. (750 g) *goiabada* (page 192)

Even though jelly rolls and rolled cakes of one sort or another can be found in many parts of the world, this version is typically Brazilian. It comes from the north-east of the country, and it is filled with *goiabada*, a popular guava paste (a recipe for it is on the next page). The paste is highly addictive and is an essential part of what makes this cake so good. You can also make *rocambole* with dulce de leche from Argentina.

In Brazil, the cake is made in varying thicknesses. In Recife, the dough is very thin and the diameter of the cake is relatively wide. You can also make several batches of cake and roll them up together. The version I give here is the simplest, but also, in my opinion, the best. What's important is that you combine the ingredients without beating the egg whites too stiffly. This makes for a batter that barely rises and bakes very quickly. Surprisingly, the proportions are those of pound cake, one quarter eggs, one quarter sugar, one quarter flour, and one quarter butter.

Preheat the oven to 350°F (180°C). Cut out two 12 x 16 inch (30 x 40 cm) sheets of parchment paper and set one on a pastry board. Have a baking sheet large enough to hold the paper close at hand. Whip the eggs and sugar together until pale and thick. Whisk in the melted butter.

Fold in the flour with a flexible spatula. Pour half the batter onto 1 sheet of the parchment paper. Using a spatula, spread it out thinly and evenly to cover the paper entirely. Now you have the exact shape needed, and any excess can be easily cleaned from the board or baking sheet. Carefully, transfer the batter on the paper to the baking sheet.

You'll see that the batter will take no longer than 3 to 4 minutes to bake. It must not color. It sets like pancake batter and that's quite enough. If you bake it for too long, it'll become breakable and it will be very hard to roll it all up. The cake is more like a barely cooked pancake than a sponge base.

Remove from the oven, turn over onto a clean baking sheet and carefully peel off the parchment paper. Repeat the procedure with the remaining batter to make a second rectangle. If necessary, trim the edges of the cake so that they are perfectly straight. Place the *goiabada* in the microwave oven or in a saucepan with 2 to 3 tablespoons of water to melt it, if necessary. This is much easier with homemade guava paste.

Spread the *goiabada* thinly over each of the cake layers. Roll the first cake up evenly, making sure to roll tightly when you start. Place this roll on the second layer and roll up again to make a snail shape. Cover in plastic wrap and chill for at least 2 hours to allow the *goiabada* to firm up again before serving.

Guava Paste
Goiabada

DAIRY, EGG, AND GLUTEN FREE
Makes three to four 1-lb. (450-g) jars of paste
Preparation time: 25 minutes
Cooking time: 2 hours

INGREDIENTS
2 ¼ lb. (1 kg) red guavas
½ cup (120 ml) water
3 cups (1 lb. 5 oz./600 g) sugar

Carefully wash the guavas; you're going to be using the peel. Cut them in half and scoop out the seeds in the center with a spoon. Set aside the guava halves.

Strain the flesh around the seeds, adding a little water to dilute it and make it easier for the flesh between the seeds (which contains pectin) to get through the sieve.

Cut the remaining flesh with the skin into cubes and place it in a large pot with the water, sugar, and strained guava flesh. Over low heat, slowly bring to a boil. Allow to boil for 2 hours, taking care to avoid any *goiabada* splatters (they're hot!). Stir regularly to ensure that the bottom of the pot doesn't burn.

When the *goiabada* is done, it has the texture of a fruit jelly, and should come away easily from the bottom of the pot. It's important to check the consistency of your *goiabada* regularly. To do so, drop a small quantity in a bowl and place it in the refrigerator, just as you would do for jam, to see whether it gels.

Goiabada can be stored for several months in sterilized jars.

Carrot Cake

Carrot cake has only been around since the 1960s, but it's an established classic of American cuisine. With its thick cap of cream cheese frosting, it is absolutely divine. After many attempts at getting the recipe right, the one I give you here has all the important ingredients: raisins, pecans, spices, and, of course, carrots! It's the grated carrots that give the cake its wonderfully tender texture. I like to bake carrot cake in a loaf pan instead of a traditional round cake pan.

For my recipe, I use an amazingly large amount of frosting by French standards. But of course it's just the right quantity for this cake. The frosting is utterly delicious. I guess what I love most about this recipe is the combination of all those different elements in one delicious cake.

• • • • • • • • • • • • • • • • •

Makes one 9 x 5 inch (23 x 12 cm) loaf cake
Preparation time: 30 minutes
Cooking time: 40 to 50 minutes
Chilling time: 5 hours total

INGREDIENTS
FOR THE CARROT CAKE
⅛ teaspoon nutmeg
⅛ teaspoon cloves
¼ teaspoon ginger
2 teaspoons cinnamon
½ teaspoon baking soda
1 teaspoon baking powder
½ teaspoon salt
1 ¾ cups (7 ¾ oz./220 g) all-purpose flour
¾ cup (5 ¼ oz./150 g) granulated sugar
¾ cup (5 ¼ oz./150 g) light brown sugar
3 eggs
¼ teaspoon vanilla extract
1 cup minus 2 tablespoons (220 ml) oil
1 cup (4 ½ oz./120 g) chopped pecans
3 oz. (80 g) raisins
7 oz. (210 g) grated carrots (about 2 well-
 packed cups)

FOR THE CREAM CHEESE FROSTING
1 ¾ sticks (7 oz./200 g) unsalted butter,
 room temperature
1 lb. 1 oz. (480 g) cream cheese
1 cup plus 1 heaping cup (9 ½ oz./270 g)
 confectioners' sugar
½ teaspoon vanilla extract
1 pinch vanilla powder
A few whole pecans for decoration, optional

• • • • • • • • • • • • • • • • •

Preheat the oven to 340°F (170°C). Line a large loaf pan with parchment paper.

In a mixing bowl, combine the spices, baking soda, baking powder, salt, flour, granulated sugar, and brown sugar.

In another mixing bowl, place the eggs, vanilla extract, and oil. Mix until well combined. Pour the liquid mixture over the dry ingredients and whisk carefully until the mixture is smooth. Stir in the pecans and raisins.

Stir the grated carrots into the batter.

Pour the batter into the prepared loaf pan and bake for 40 to 50 minutes, until a cake tester inserted into the middle of the cake comes out dry.

Turn out of the pan; the parchment paper should make this very easy. Immediately cover the cake in heat-resistant plastic wrap so that all the steam it contains is retained inside to give it a lovely moist texture. Allow to cool completely.

When the cake has come to room temperature, prepare the frosting. With an electric beater, combine the butter, cream cheese, and confectioners' sugar. Add the vanilla extract and vanilla powder and whip.

Cut the cake horizontally into 3 equal parts. Keep in mind that you'll be using about half of the frosting for the layers and the other half for the top and sides of the cake. Carefully place the base of the cake in the loaf pan and spread a layer of frosting just under ½ inch (1 cm) thick over it.

Place the second layer of the cake over the frosting and spread another layer of frosting over it. Set the third layer of the cake over the frosting.

(continued on page 194)

Place the loaf pan in the refrigerator for at least 2 hours to set the frosting. Dip the base of the pan in hot water so that you can unmold the cake easily.

To finish, generously cover the outside of the cake with the remaining frosting. If you wish, you can use a small spatula to draw little waves over the top, and decorate the carrot cake with whole pecans.

Chill for at least 3 hours before serving.

Brazilian Coconut Pudding Cakes
Quindins

GLUTEN FREE
Makes 24 *quindins*
Preparation time: 20 minutes
Cooking time: 45 minutes
Cooling time: 4 hours
Chilling time: 2 hours

Special equipment: a 24 cup mini-muffin pan

INGREDIENTS
1 ⅓ cups (3 ½ oz./100 g) unsweetened dried shredded coconut
¾ cup (200 ml) lukewarm water
2 cups (14 oz./400 g) sugar, plus a little extra for the pan
3 tablespoons (2 oz./50 g) butter, plus a little extra for the molds
12 egg yolks, total weight 7 ¾–8 ½ oz. (220–240 g)

I first ate a *quindim* (in the singular) at the Confeitario Colombo café in Rio de Janeiro. And to tell you the truth, I didn't like it. Why not? I had no idea what was inside. Then I had another, and another, and soon I was hooked. When I found out how *quindins* are made, I was bewitched. Just think: you mix all the ingredients in a blender, pour the batter into aluminum molds, and then, as the *quindins* bake, the batter separates into a flan on the bottom and a coconut sponge on top!

Quindins are a real pleasure to eat and what's more, a good way of using up extra egg yolks.

The molds traditionally used are small (1 ½ inches or 4 cm) and made of rigid aluminum. But because they are hard to find, you can use other shapes and sizes, like a standard mini-muffin pan, the only constraint being the rigid aluminum (don't use disposable pans). Even in Brazil, shapes and sizes vary.

Preheat the oven to 330°F (165°C).

Butter the muffin cups. When the butter has set, dust them lightly with sugar, tapping out any excess. This will ensure you'll be able to unmold the *quindins* easily.

Soak the shredded coconut in the water for 5 minutes.

Place the sugar and butter in a blender. Add the coconut and water (if it hasn't all been absorbed by the coconut!). Pour in the egg yolks.

Blend for 2 minutes, until the mixture is smooth. Fill each muffin cup to the top with the mixture—it won't rise or swell.

Place the pan in an ovenproof dish and pour in boiling water to two-thirds of the height of the molds.

Bake for 45 minutes, until the surface of the *quindins* becomes a lovely golden color. The coconut floats during baking, which creates the sponge layer.

Leave the *quindins* in the pan and allow to cool for at least 4 hours.

Carefully run a knife between the crusts and the cups, then gently take the *quindins* out of the pan. Chill for 2 hours before serving. They'll be deliciously refreshing with an attractive sheen.

Brazilian Flan
Pudim de Leite

• • • • • • • • • • • • • •

GLUTEN FREE
Serves 6 to 8
Preparation time: 15 minutes
Cooking time: 1 hour 15 minutes to
    1 hour 30 minutes, or more
Chilling time: 3 hours

Special equipment: an 11-inch (28-cm)
    savarin pan

INGREDIENTS
FOR THE CARAMEL
¾ cup (5 ¼ oz./150 g) sugar, divided

FOR THE CREAM
2 14-oz. (397-g) cans sweetened condensed
    milk
Enough low-fat milk to fill the 2 cans of
    condensed milk (3 ¼ cups/800 ml)
5 eggs

• • • • • • • • • • • • • •

Pudim de leite is a Brazilian dessert served throughout the country. It's not much different from a French *crème caramel*, but it's easier to make and the texture is quite firm, yet still creamy. Like many Brazilian desserts, the custard is prepared in the blender. This recipe uses condensed milk, which plays an important role in the final taste and texture. Its caramelization in the cooking process gives *pudim de leite* a slight caramel flavor. Just one spoon of this dessert and I guarantee that you'll be won over.

In Buenos Aires, Argentina, I once discovered a fantastic dessert that I later realized was a close relative of *pudim de leite*. I'd enjoyed an extraordinary meal of grilled meat, fried potatoes, and creamed spinach, accompanied with an excellent red wine, and then I had a dessert I have never forgotten: a small flan, like the *pudim de leite*, served in a bowl with a scoop of vanilla ice cream, some walnuts, freshly whipped cream, and dulce de leche. A decadent combination, but it was out of this world. I'd go so far as to say it was perfect. The serving style is an idea you can try at home now that you have the recipe for the *pudim de leite*. One more thing: *pudim de leite* is pronounced "poodeem dee lay-chay."

Preheat the oven to 350°F (180°C).

Place one-third of the sugar in a heavy saucepan over medium heat. Allow it to melt without stirring. Add the next third and allow to melt, and then add the last third. You should have a lovely amber-colored caramel.

Pour it into the savarin pan, tilting the pan so that the caramel coats the base evenly.

Prepare the cream. Pour the sweetened condensed milk into a blender. Then fill the empty cans of condensed milk with low-fat milk and pour them into the blender.

Add the eggs. Blend for 1 minute, until perfectly smooth.

Pour the mixture into the pan over the caramel. Place the pan in an ovenproof dish and pour in enough boiling water to reach halfway up the pan. Cover with a sheet of foil and bake for 75 to 90 minutes, until the cream has set, but still wobbles a little in the center like a set jelly. You can also test with the tip of a knife or cake tester, which should come out dry.

If the *pudim* is still not done, extend the cooking time until it sets.

Allow to cool completely and then chill for 3 hours. Just before serving, fill your kitchen sink with very hot water and dip the lower part of the pan into it. Turn the *pudim de leite* onto a serving dish and serve in slices.

North Africa and
the Middle East

Moroccan Biscotti
Fekkas

Makes 3 lb. (1.5 kg) cookies
Preparation time: 20 minutes
Cooling time: 4 hours (minimum) to 12 hours
Cooking time: 20 minutes plus 20 minutes

INGREDIENTS

½ cup (3 ½ oz./100 g) whole almonds, unpeeled or peeled
⅔ cup (3 ½ oz./100 g) raisins
1 cup plus 1 scant cup (9 oz./250 g) confectioners' sugar
3 eggs
Scant ½ cup (100 ml) oil
7 tablespoons (3 ½ oz./100 g) melted butter, cooled
1 teaspoon vanilla extract
1 tablespoon (11 g) baking powder
6 cups (1 ¾ lb./770 g) all-purpose flour
1 generous pinch salt

Morocco is known for its pastries, the most famous being gazelle horns (see page 205). But *fekkas*, though less well known, are just as delicious. They are *bis-cuits* in the true sense of the word: twice (*bis*) cooked (*cuits*), just like Italian biscotti. After the dough is first baked in long loaf shapes, *fekkas* are sliced and returned to the oven. My dear friend Touria was happy to share the recipe she's been fine-tuning over the years, becoming so renowned that her friends and family sometimes call on her for large orders, several pounds at a time. *Fekkas* are absolutely addictive. They take effect immediately; soon your own friends and family may well start ordering large quantities from you, too.

First prepare the almonds and raisins. Using a sharp knife, cut each almond into 6 or 7 slices. Then put the raisins into a large mug or bowl and, with a pair of scissors, snip them as you would cut fresh herbs. The pieces should be small, so that the almonds and raisins can be evenly distributed in the dough.

Preheat the oven to 350°F (180°C). Line a baking sheet with parchment paper.

Mix the confectioners' sugar into the eggs until just combined; no need to mix until pale and thick. Pour the oil, melted butter, and vanilla extract into the mixture, stirring with a wooden spoon or working the ingredients in with your hands. Then stir in the baking powder, almonds, and raisins until just combined.

Gradually add the flour and salt to the mixture. When all the flour has been incorporated, you should be able to shape the dough easily.

Divide it into 5 equal balls. Roll each ball into a 1 ½-inch (4-cm) diameter log. Place the logs on the prepared baking sheet. You can bake all the loaves at once as long as they don't touch.

Bake for 20 minutes, or until the loaves are lightly golden.

As soon as you remove the loaves from the oven, cover them with a clean cloth. Then wrap everything in heat-resistant plastic wrap: the baking sheet, the loaves, and the cloth. This retains the moisture in the *fekkas*. Allow to cool completely, for at least 4 hours. At this stage, if you are making a smaller batch, you can freeze some of the loaves and then finish baking them another time.

(continued on page 204)

Line another baking sheet with parchment paper.

With a sharp knife, one that can cut cleanly without breaking the *fekkas*, especially around the almonds, slice the loaves thinly and at an angle. Place the slices on the baking sheet and bake for 20 minutes, rotating the sheet halfway through to ensure that they are all evenly colored. As you know, ovens have the annoying habit of browning the cookies more in front than in the back, or the other way round.

Allow the *fekkas* to cool completely before storing them in an airtight container. They keep for up to a month. You can also freeze them at this stage and defrost them to serve another time.

Moroccan Gazelle Horns
Kaab el ghzal

INGREDIENTS
FOR THE DOUGH
2 ½ cups (10 oz./300 g) all-purpose flour
2 teaspoons orange flower water
1 pinch salt
⅔ cup (150 ml) water (you may need a little
    more or less)
1 tablespoon (½ oz./15 g) butter
A little oil for brushing

FOR THE FILLING
3 cups (1 lb./500 g) almonds, preferably
    unpeeled
2 cups (13 oz./375 g) sugar
½ teaspoon cinnamon
2 tablespoons melted butter
1–2 tablespoons orange flower water
6–7 crystals gum arabic, optional
A small bowl of oil

· · · · · · · · · · · · ·

I'd always wanted to learn how to make Moroccan gazelle horns, with their paper-thin pastry encasing an almond filling delicately flavored with cinnamon and orange flower water. On a visit to Morocco, I met Touria, Lalla Myriam, and her mother, Lalla Fatima, a lovable grandmother straight out of a storybook. The three women know all the secrets of their country's cuisine. My patience was rewarded, because what I learned far exceeded my expectations.

For gazelle horns, they told me that it was important to peel the almonds myself. Immersing almonds in boiling water to be able to easily peel them gives the nuts a tender texture that you can't achieve otherwise. Though if you want to make things easier for yourself, you can use ground almonds (almond flour). One ingredient traditionally incorporated in the pastries is gum arabic, which improves the consistency of the filling. But if you can't find any, it's not essential.

Place the flour in a large mixing bowl with the orange flower water and salt. Add water little by little, mixing it in with your hands, just until the flour has absorbed the water. Now you can put the dough in the bowl of a stand mixer fitted with a dough hook (or continue by hand). If you add the water without doing the kneading by hand, there's a risk of adding too much water. Add the butter and knead for 10 to 15 minutes. The dough should be very soft and silky to the touch.

Brush a large dish with oil. Divide the dough into balls each weighing about 3 ½ oz. (90 to 100 g). Brush them with oil so that they don't dry out and place them in the dish. Cover with plastic wrap and chill for at least 1 hour.

Meanwhile, prepare the filling. Immerse the almonds in boiling water for 5 minutes. Rinse them under running water and remove the skins. If you only have blanched almonds, of course this will speed up the task. However, the almonds will be less tender. To remedy this, add an extra tablespoon of orange flower water to the filling. Do the same if you're using ground almonds.

Process the peeled almonds with the sugar to form a fine powder that sticks lightly to the fingers. If necessary, add a little water to achieve this consistency.

Mix in the cinnamon and melted butter using your hands. Then add the orange flower water. If you are using gum arabic, crush it with a mortar and pestle and incorporate it into the filling.

(continued on page 206)

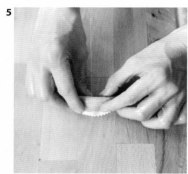

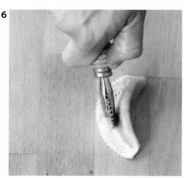

1 Roll the balls of filling into log shapes.

2 Divide the dough into balls and brush with oil.

3 Fold the dough over the log-shaped almond filling.

4 Use a pastry wheel to cut out half-moons.

5 With both hands, shape the gazelle horns.

6 Trim the excess pastry.

It's best to weigh the portions of almond filling to ensure that your gazelle horns are identical. Prepare balls of filling weighing ½ to ⅔ oz. (15 to 20 g).

Roll each ball of filling into a small oblong log.

Keep a small bowl of oil at hand.

Oil the work surface (a marble pastry slab if possible, or even better, cedar wood). Lightly oil the chilled dough again. With a rolling pin, thinly roll one ball of dough into a rectangle. You'll need to finish shaping it by hand as follows: take the edges and pull the dough lightly, lifting it up a little outward to make it even thinner. The dough becomes very thin. If it's been well kneaded, it should be very malleable and easily stretched, but do be careful not to tear it.

Place 2 or 3 logs of filling on the length of the rectangle of dough. Fold the dough over the logs of filling and press down at the join, to seal the dough.

Using a pastry wheel, separate the gazelle horns, following the shape of the filling. You don't need to cut them with great precision because you'll be cutting them a second time, closer to the filling.

(continued on page 208)

Take a gazelle horn, pulling sharply upward to separate it from the rest of the dough. Flatten it between your fingers to give it its final shape.

Using the pastry wheel, trim the excess dough to give the gazelle horn its finished shape.

Use the remaining rolled-out dough. Trim the edge, place 3 logs of filling on it, and repeat the procedure. Continue until all the dough and balls of filling have been used up.

Oil a baking sheet or line it with parchment paper. Place the gazelle horns on the sheet to allow them to form a crust and dry out. This takes no less than 24 hours and is a very important stage for ensuring the crispness of the dough.

Preheat the oven to 320°F (160°C). With a thin needle or toothpick, pierce 3 small holes at the top of each gazelle horn to enable air bubbles to escape during baking. Bake for 15 to 20 minutes, depending on your oven. The gazelle horns should be only very lightly colored.

Serve warm, accompanied by hot mint tea.

*From generation to generation
the recipe is passed on effortlessly;
who will whisper the memories
of Moroccan gazelle horns?*

Camila Nicácio

Date and Walnut Pastries

Ma'amoul

EGG FREE
Makes about 40 pastries
Preparation time: 45 minutes
Chilling time: 20 minutes
Cooking time: 20 minutes

INGREDIENTS
FOR THE DOUGH
1 cup plus 3 tablespoons (7 oz./200 g)
    fine semolina
½ cup (2 ½ oz./70 g) confectioners' sugar
1 ⅓ cups (6 oz./165 g) all-purpose flour
7 tablespoons (3 ½ oz./100 g) butter,
    well chilled and diced
4 tablespoons (60 ml) orange flower water

FOR THE FILLING
8 oz. (230 g) moist dates
1 cup (3 ½ oz./100 g) walnuts

These small, elegant pastries have a delicate, haunting flavor. The recipe I give here has very little added sugar: the filling is made only of dates and walnuts. Using sculpted wooden molds gives the pastries pretty motifs which remain visible after baking because the dough contains no eggs or raising agents. You can, however, make *ma'amoul* without using the sculpted wooden molds: they will be less of a feast for the eyes, but the taste will be just as good.

To make the dough, place all the ingredients except the orange flower water in a bowl and beat until they form a fine, sand-like powder. You can do this in the bowl of a stand mixer fitted with a flat beater attachment. Stir in the orange flower water and knead or mix until the dough forms a ball.

Cover the dough in plastic wrap and chill for 20 minutes while you prepare the filling.

Pit the dates and process them in the bowl of a food processor until they form a paste.

Add the walnuts and process again, just enough for small pieces of nuts to remain.

If you don't have a special *ma'amoul* mold (see photo overleaf), simply roll and fill small balls that you can bake directly. You'll need to weigh balls of dough of ½ oz. (14 g) and balls of filling of just under ⅓ oz. (8 g).

Using your thumb, make a cavity in the ball of dough large enough to hold the filling. Carefully close the dough over the filling and roll it between your hands to make a nice spherical shape.

If you have a *ma'amoul* mold, the procedure is the same, but you'll need to adapt the size of your balls and filling to fit the mold. This is very easy. Before you start forming the pastries, place a ball of dough without any filling in the mold and remove the excess. I have developed this recipe using proportions of 64 percent of dough for 36 percent of filling (yes, you've read that correctly). But it's simpler to use the following proportions: two-thirds dough to one-third filling.

Press the sphere into the mold to imprint the motif on it. Then turn the mold over and tap the handle against the edge of the work surface to make an attractively sculpted pastry.

(continued on page 210)

209

The first time you do this, it's likely that the *ma'amoul* pastries won't come out easily. You'll certainly have to rap hard for the first 10 cakes. But the butter in the dough eventually greases the mold lightly, and after that, the cakes come out far more easily.

Preheat the oven to 295°F (140°C) while you shape the *ma'amoul* pastries. Line a baking sheet with parchment paper. Carefully transfer the *ma'amoul* pastries on the blade of a wide knife to the parchment paper.

Bake for 20 minutes. They should remain a very light biscuit color. When cool, store in an airtight container for up to a few weeks.

Moroccan Coconut Balls

Makes about 50 cookies
Preparation time: 40 minutes
Cooking time: 10 to 12 minutes

INGREDIENTS
FOR THE DOUGH
3 large egg yolks
⅔ cup (4 oz./125 g) sugar
2 tablespoons butter, melted and cooled
⅓ cup (80 ml) oil
1 tablespoon (11 g) baking powder
4 cups (1 lb. 2 oz./500 g) all-purpose flour
   (you may not require the entire quantity)

FOR THE COATING
1 13-oz. (370-g) jar smooth apricot jelly,
   divided in half
6–8 tablespoons (90–110 ml) orange flower
   water, divided
½ cup (3 ½ oz./100 g) sugar, divided
3 ⅓ cups (9 oz./250 g) unsweetened
   shredded coconut

For this recipe, I'd like to thank Myriam, a Moroccan friend who was generous enough to share her family recipe with me. I first tasted these astonishing little treats at her home in Casablanca and fell in love with them. Though to be quite honest (and this seems to happen to many people when they try them for the first time), at first bite, I wasn't quite sure what to make of them. I guess my brain first had to come to grips with what I was eating, because the flavor combination is rather unusual. So I had a second bite—and then I couldn't stop. My neurons were firing on all cylinders, sending out the following information: 1) these little balls are just the right size for one mouthful; 2) the combination of apricots, orange flower water, and coconut is nothing short of perfection. Trust me, when you try them, you'll find yourself saying the same thing Moroccans do when devouring a plate of them, "How about just one more?"

Preheat the oven to 320°F (160°C). Line a baking sheet with parchment paper.

Place all the ingredients for the dough except the flour in a large mixing bowl and combine thoroughly. The mixture should be creamy. Gradually add the flour, stirring constantly until the mixture is perfectly smooth. If it reaches this consistency before all the flour is added, stop immediately! Shape the dough into small balls weighing about ¼ oz. (7 g). Bake for 10 to 12 minutes, until nicely golden on top. Transfer to a rack and allow to cool.

Set aside 1 tablespoon plus 2 teaspoons (20 g) of the sugar. Pour half of the apricot jelly into a small saucepan with 2 tablespoons of the orange flower water and the remaining sugar. Cook over low heat to reduce, stirring with a wooden spoon, until you have a fairly thick sauce to use to sandwich two small cakes together.

Spoon a small quantity of the sauce on to the bottom of a cake and sandwich another one to it. Repeat with the remaining cakes.

Pour the other half of the apricot jelly into another small saucepan over low heat with 4 tablespoons orange flower water and the remaining sugar. Cook, stirring constantly, until the sauce is fairly liquid but thick enough to coat the cakes. If necessary, add a little orange flower water.

Dip each round cake into the apricot sauce and roll them in the shredded coconut. Serve or place them carefully in an airtight container, where they will keep for a few days.

Algerian Nut Cookies
Montecaos

DAIRY AND EGG FREE
Makes about 15 cookies
Preparation time: 20 minutes
Cooking time: 30 minutes

INGREDIENTS
¾ cup (2 ¼ oz./65 g) ground almonds
1 ¼ teaspoons (5.5 g) baking powder
1 ¼ cups (5 ¾ oz./160 g) confectioners' sugar
4 cups (1 lb. 2 oz./500 g) cake flour
1 cup (250 ml) neutrally flavored vegetable oil (you may need a little more or less)
½ teaspoon vanilla extract
A little ground cinnamon for dusting

Montecaos are large and very crumbly almond cookies. Because they contain neither eggs nor butter, they keep well. They are readily available across North Africa, particularly in Algeria, but their origins can be traced back to Andalusia, where they were traditionally made with lard. In Spain, a similar cookie called *mantecado* is still available today. I learned to make *montecaos* when I was kindly invited to a workshop in an Algerian pastry shop for a few days to learn the secrets of the trade. It was an ideal way to gain a deeper understanding of the techniques and aesthetics of such a rich and varied pastry tradition.

Preheat the oven to 340°F (170°C). Line a baking sheet with parchment paper.

Sift together the ground almonds, baking powder, confectioners' sugar, and flour into a large bowl and combine. Begin drizzling in the oil, stirring constantly. Depending on the flour and the almonds used, you may need more or less oil than the quantity I've given.

Stop drizzling in the oil as soon as you can clump the dough together; it's easy to see when this occurs. At first, the texture will be powdery, but as you add more oil, you'll see that you can start to shape it together using some pressure. When you can press it into one piece, well, that's when you have to stop adding oil. Add the vanilla extract and knead a little to incorporate it.

Take a small ball of dough in the palm of your hands and close your hands around it as if you had caught an insect in them. Keeping your hands in this position, use your upper hand to roll the dough into a ball. Flatten one side.

Place the *montecaos* on a baking sheet and dust lightly with cinnamon.

Bake for about 30 minutes, until lightly colored and cracks form on the surface.

Transfer carefully to cool on a rack and then serve or store in an airtight container for up to a month.

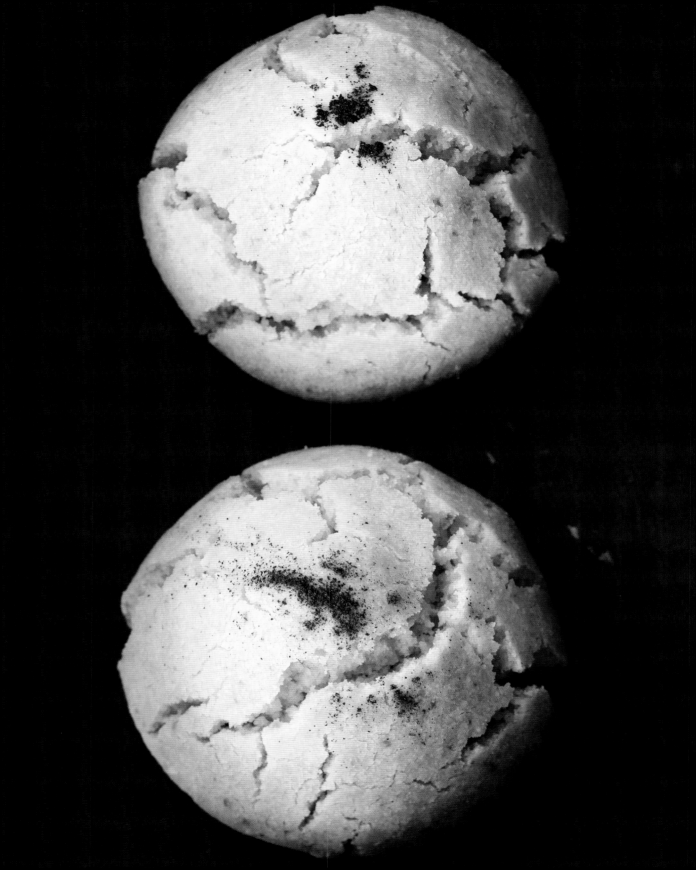

Yeasted Fritters in Honey Syrup

Zalabia

DAIRY AND EGG FREE
Makes about 40 fritters
Preparation of the dough: 5 days ahead
Preparation time: 35 minutes
Cooking time: 7 to 8 minutes per batch

INGREDIENTS

FOR THE DOUGH
⅔ oz. (20 g) fresh (compressed) yeast
4 cups (1 liter) lukewarm water, divided
8 cups (2 ¼ lb./1 kg) all-purpose flour
Powdered yellow or orange food coloring

FOR THE HONEY SYRUP
6 ½ lb. (3 kg) sugar
6 cups (1.5 liters) water
Juice of 2 lemons
1–2 tablespoons honey
3–4 tablespoons (45–60 ml) orange
  flower water

The recipe for *zalabia* fritters posed quite a challenge for me. It's relatively simple, but I was missing one key ingredient: patience. *Zalabia* dough needs a long time to rise, five whole days, in fact! This lengthy proofing period is the only way to produce the characteristic little spikes around the edges of the fritters. I turned the problem of these spikes over in my mind obsessively, wondering how they were formed. It takes a lot of practice to get the sleight of hand and the shape just right. And I'd be misleading you if I told you that in just one try, you'll succeed. Far from it. Practice makes perfect. But what's reassuring is that even if you don't get the shape right at first, the taste will still be excellent. I'd been dreaming about *zalabia* for a long time and it took me several months to be able to make them properly. I'm very grateful to the professional pastry chefs who answered my questions. It's also thanks to them that I can give you the recipe now. This recipe makes a large quantity, but that's what you need to practice!

Begin by preparing the dough. In the bowl of a stand mixer or large mixing bowl, stir the yeast in a scant ¼ cup (50 ml) of the water until completely dissolved. Using the dough hook of a stand mixer or a hand whisk, add the flour and the remaining water until combined. The dough may seem lumpy initially, but it will gradually liquefy thanks to the action of the yeast.

Cover the dough with a clean cloth and allow to rise for no less than five days at room temperature. Therein lies the secret to making *zalabia* successfully. The dough must be allowed to rise several times, and in fact it will rise and deflate two or three times. Depending on the weather conditions, this takes between 3 and 5 days, because *zalabia* dough is actually a pre-ferment—or fermentation starter—that is fried. This is a traditional bread-making method that involves using half flour, half water, with a little yeast. The pre-ferment is left to rise and then the baker continues the recipe with additional flour and water to make the bread.

After 3 to 5 days, the dough begins to smell like sour yogurt. If you taste it, it will tingle in your mouth, a sure sign that it's ready.

(continued on page 218)

At this stage, when a portion of dough is placed in hot oil, the famous little spikes on the outside rim of the *zalabia* will develop. *Zalabia* still taste good if fried at an earlier stage, but if you want those little spikes, you'll have to wait.

The day you want to serve the *zalabia*, prepare the honey syrup (following the method on page 227).

Whip the dough with a hand whisk. It should have the consistency of a thick crêpe or pancake batter. Add just a little food coloring, no more than a knife's-tip worth.

Prepare all the equipment: the bowl of dough, a ladle, and a funnel big enough to pour the quantity of dough for 4 fritters in one batch. Make sure, too, that you have the saucepan containing the honey syrup close at hand. I use a paella pan. Use a funnel whose nozzle you can cut off if you need to widen it. All you need is about ¾ inch (1.5 cm) of oil in the pan.

When the oil is nice and hot (but not too hot, otherwise the fritters will be too dark), fill the funnel with dough, blocking the nozzle with your finger. It takes quite a long time to get the knack of making pretty *zalabia* fritters. You have to draw out spirals, working from the outside to the center in one movement, and make 4, one after another, or even more, if your funnel is bigger.

Fry them for 7 to 8 minutes, until their texture is firm and their color a light gold. Remove them from the oil and immediately dip into the honey syrup. This is when the magic happens. The fried cake absorbs all the honey it requires.

Place them on a rack to drain. After a few hours, they will be less shiny than they were initially, the excess honey syrup will have dripped off, and the balance of flavors will be perfect. The *zalabia* are best eaten the day they are made.

Moroccan Doughnuts
Sfenj

DAIRY AND EGG FREE
Makes 40 doughnuts
Preparation time: 45 minutes
Resting time: 25 minutes to 2 hours
Cooking time: 5 to 7 minutes per batch

INGREDIENTS

3 ½ cups (15 oz./420 g) all-purpose flour
⅓ oz. (10 g) fresh (compressed) yeast, divided
About 1 ½ cups (350 ml) water, depending
  on the flour
1 teaspoon (5 g) salt
1 generous pinch baking powder
1 generous pinch vanilla sugar, or 2 teaspoons
  sugar plus ½ teaspoon vanilla extract,
  optional
Oil for frying

Sfenj are doughnuts that are made all across northern Africa. Eating *sfenj* for breakfast or in the afternoon takes me back to when I was a young child. Savoring a nice crisp *sfenja* in the morning, a glass of hot mint tea in my hand, sitting under the palm trees and enjoying the sun, reminds me of the Morocco I visited several times when I was young. It's a country that holds a special place in my heart.

I learned to make *sfenj* in Morocco with my dear friends Touria and Myriam, and Taoufik, a professional *sfenji* (or *sfenaj*, a maker of *sfenj*) who was kind enough to share his know-how with me. Taoufik has a difficult job: from 4 a.m. to 6 a.m. every day he prepares his dough, and from 10 to noon he fries the *sfenj*. He makes more dough in the afternoon, working until 8 p.m., and he does this seven days a week. The *sfenj* sell for 1 *dirham* each and are made only of flour, water, and yeast. I add a pinch of baking powder to speed up the rising of the dough, so you won't necessarily need to let it rest for 2 hours. Taoufik proved to me that *sfenj* can be prepared quite quickly.

Note that a gas burner is essential! Use the largest pan you have. I use a paella pan, just as I do for the *zalabia*.

Make sure that your work surface is solid and robust. Place all the flour in a large bowl or clean plastic tub. Make a well in the center and crumble half the yeast into it. Pour in a little of the water to dilute the yeast. Using your fingertips, gradually work the surrounding flour into the liquid. Add the salt. Knead the dough that forms in the center, gradually incorporating more flour. If necessary, add a little water so that the dough is not too firm. Now knead for 5 minutes until the dough is smooth, gradually adding water. At this stage, you should have added about two-thirds of the total quantity of water.

The dough will become increasingly soft. To knead it, make fists and crush it as though you are punching it. When your knuckles reach the bottom of the basin, make a 90° turn with your wrists to crush the dough well. From time to time, pull the dough from the side and fold it over before you continue punching energetically. Continue for 15 minutes.

Cover with a clean cloth and allow to rest for 15 minutes. Then pour some more of the remaining water around the dough and add the remaining yeast to the water. Dilute the yeast in the water and knead again, using the same punching movement and folding the dough over on itself from time to time.

(continued on page 220)

It should be easy to knead the dough at this stage: because only half of the yeast was added at the start, the dough won't have risen too much.

Gradually pour in the remaining water until the dough is very soft, elastic, and fairly sticky. Knead for an additional 10 to 15 minutes.

Sprinkle the baking powder and vanilla sugar, if using, over the dough and knead for an additional 3 to 4 minutes to work it in. Cover the dough with a cloth and leave in a warm place to rise.

After all the work you've done on it, the dough should be quite warm and so it will be ready in a short time. It's quite possible to fry the *sfenj* even after just 25 minutes of rising, but you can let it rise for up to 2 hours. Taoufik explained that he leaves it for even longer because he prepares vast quantities, but using the recipe I give you here, we fried the *sfenj* after 25 minutes and they were perfect.

The dough is ready for frying when it's fairly elastic and large bubbles form on the surface. Place the largest frying pan you have on the gas burner. To fry my *sfenj*, I use a paella pan, just as I do for the *zalabia*. Underneath one of the sides of the pan, place a small metal rack to tilt the pan slightly. One of the secrets to successfully making *sfenj* lies in the inclination of the pan. Any means you find to tilt the pan is fine. At home, I used an adjustable wrench in addition to the small rack!

Pour the oil into the pan and turn the gas to medium-high. When you pour the oil in, only a small part of the pan should be covered. And by placing the dough on the part where there is the least oil, you'll ensure that the *sfenj* will have one flat side. Once this side is cooked, place it in the part where the oil is deeper, turn it over and allow it to swell freely.

Shaping the *sfenj* is the most difficult part, technically speaking, of the recipe. Place a small bowl of water near the pan and the bowl of dough. Lightly wet your hands and take a piece of dough the size of a large egg. With a slightly wet finger, make a hole in the middle and keep widening it until it measures 3 to 4 inches (8 to 10 cm), taking care not to break the ring of dough. Do be careful not to wet your hands too much, because this adds uncalled-for water to the dough when you break off the pieces, and it will be harder to work with.

Place the ring in the part of the pan where there is the least oil. It will swell and shrink in the middle. Fry for 3 minutes, then transfer it to the part where the oil is deepest. There, turn it over so that it can swell; it will be floating this time. Of course, you can fry several *sfenj* at once.

Turn the *sfenj* over several times while they are frying. After 5 to 7 minutes, they should have a lovely golden color, which means they are done. If they brown too quickly, this means your oil is too hot.

Making attractive *sfenj* requires patience and practice. When they are ready, you can roll them in sugar or crush them lightly, break an egg over them, and return them to the oil to fry.

Egyptian Bread Pudding
Oum Ali

• • • • • • • • • • • • • • •

Serves 6 to 8
Preparation time: 20 minutes
Cooking time: 15 to 20 minutes

INGREDIENTS
4 stale croissants
¼ cup (2 oz./50 g) pistachios
⅓ cup (2 oz./50 g) raisins
⅔ cup (2 oz./50 g) sliced (flaked) almonds,
 plus more for the garnish
Scant ½ cup (2 oz./50 g) whole walnuts
⅔ cup (2 oz./50 g) shredded coconut
¾ cup (5 ¼ oz./150 g) sugar
½ teaspoon cinnamon
Scant ½ cup (2 oz./50 g) powdered milk
3 cups (750 ml) whole milk
1 cup (250 ml) heavy cream
1 tablespoon rose water

• • • • • • • • • • • • • • •

A few years ago, I spent some months in Cairo. I have fond memories of my time there.

It was on a cold winter's evening at a café in the heart of the city, in the Zamalek quarter, where I first tasted *oum ali*, a classic Egyptian bread pudding. It was love at first bite: warm, sweet, and comforting. The dessert was a revelation. Its name was also one of the few words in Egyptian Arabic that I could pronounce perfectly, which turned out to be quite useful for ordering it in all the restaurants I subsequently frequented. *Oum ali* is made with stale croissants, lots of crunchy nuts and dried fruit, and the haunting flavors of the Middle East. You can vary the nuts or dried fruit according to taste and sweeten it as much or as little as you like. If you don't have day-old croissants, you can bake ready-made puff pastry until it's golden brown and then use that. But I prefer the version with croissants: they absorb more liquid and make for an even creamier dessert.

Preheat the oven to 400°F (200°C).

Tear the croissants into large pieces and place them in an ovenproof dish or ramekins. Add the dried fruit and nuts. Combine these ingredients by hand.

Combine the sugar, cinnamon, and powdered milk in a saucepan and set over medium heat. Gradually pour in the milk, stirring constantly. Then pour in the cream and rose water. If you wish, you can add extra rose water, or replace it with vanilla extract. Bring to a boil and pour evenly over the croissant pieces and dried fruit and nuts.

Allow to stand for 10 minutes so the croissants can absorb the liquid. If you like, sprinkle the top with extra sliced almonds.

Bake for 15 to 20 minutes, until the top begins to turn golden brown. Serve warm.

Lebanese Cashew Baklava Rolls

For one 8-inch (21-cm) square pan,
  or about 40 pastries
Preparation time: 45 minutes
Cooking time: 30 minutes

INGREDIENTS

4 ½ cups (1 lb./500 g) raw cashew nuts
Scant ½ cup (3 ¼ oz./90 g) sugar
7 oz. (200 g) ghee
20 sheets 8 x 12 inches (21 x 30 cm) phyllo
  pastry (trim with scissors if necessary)
1 cup (250 ml) honey syrup (page 227)

For as long as I can remember, I've been fascinated by baklava. It combines everything I love: nuts, unbelievably thin sheets of pastry, and of course, honeyed syrup. Baklava is found in all North African countries as well as Turkey, Greece, and Lebanon. I like them all, but the Lebanese version, filled with cashews and ground pistachios, is particularly special. I've never been able to resist these delicate pastries. To make them at home, I actually dissected some I bought, layer by layer, with a pair of tweezers, to count the number of layers of phyllo. This was at a time when I hoped to make the phyllo pastry myself, but you have to come down to earth sometimes, don't you? Phyllo pastry must be so thin that it can only be either machine-made or pulled by hand over an incredibly large surface (bigger than a ping-pong table). The unique flavor of this rolled baklava comes from using ghee, lightly fermented clarified butter that you can find in Indian, North African, and Lebanese grocery stores. Don't hesitate to use the quantities I indicate below. The combination of butter, honey, and nuts creates something magical.

First, place the raw cashew nuts and sugar in the bowl of a food processor. Process to a fine powder, but do be careful not to overdo it, because you'll end up with a paste.

Melt the ghee in a small bowl over a hot water bath or in the microwave oven.

Preheat the oven to 340°F (170°C).

Place a sheet of phyllo pastry on your work surface, with the shorter side facing you. Brush the entire surface with ghee. Set another sheet of phyllo over the first and brush it with ghee. Sprinkle three-quarters of the phyllo sheet with the ground cashew-sugar mixture to make a fine, even layer. Leave the farthest quarter without any topping.

Starting from the base nearest you, roll the pastry up tightly lengthwise. Place the roll in the pan and immediately brush it with melted ghee. Repeat the procedure with 2 sheets of phyllo pastry, brushed with ghee and sprinkled three-quarters of the length with the ground cashew-sugar mixture.

Continue until you have used up all the filling and phyllo sheets to fill the pan with 10 rolls.

(continued on page 226)

1 Brush the phyllo sheets with ghee.

2 Sprinkle three-quarters of the sheet with ground cashew nuts and sugar.

3 Roll up tightly toward the far end.

4 Cut 20 sheets, placed one on top of the other, into several squares or rectangles.

5 Fold the corners of the sheets toward the center.

6 Drizzle with honey syrup as soon as you remove the pastries from the oven.

Brush the rolls with ghee and bake for about 30 minutes, until golden. Just before the baking time is up, heat the honey syrup to liquefy it.

As soon as you remove the dish from the oven, drizzle it evenly with the warm syrup. Allow to cool completely and cut into 1 ½-inch (4-cm) pieces.

You can also make square pastries, using more sheets of phyllo pastry at once. To make this shape, place 20 sheets one on top of the other, brushing each one with melted ghee.

Cut into 2 x 3 inch (5 x 8 cm) rectangles. Pour a little melted ghee into the cashew-sugar mixture, just enough to enable you to shape it into a ball. Place a small ball of filling in the center of each rectangle and fold the edges of the phyllo sheets toward the center.

Pack all the rectangles tightly into a pan. Bake as above and drizzle evenly with honey syrup as soon as you remove the pan from the oven.

These rectangles are even crisper than the rolls, and surprisingly enough their taste is very different, even though the ingredients are identical.

All these pastries will keep for 3 to 4 weeks if stored in an airtight container.

Honey Syrup

DAIRY, EGG, AND GLUTEN FREE
Makes 3 ⅓ lb. (1.5 kg) honey syrup
Preparation time: 5 minutes
Cooking time: 20 minutes

INGREDIENTS
2 ¼ lb. (1 kg) sugar
2 cups (500 ml) water
1 small piece alum stone, or 4 slices lemon
2 tablespoons honey
1 tablespoon orange flower water

North African, Turkish, and Lebanese pastry chefs use the word "honey" for what is actually a sugar syrup. When it's sold in large 2-pound pots, it's actually corn syrup. You can make this honey syrup at home using a small piece of alum stone, a water-soluble mineral that gives acidity to the syrup and prevents it from crystallizing. Alum stone can be found at North African grocery stores. But if you can't find any, you can use lemon slices, which bring a slightly tangier note to the syrup. In my homemade honey syrup, I add some real honey and orange flower water, but you could opt for rose water instead.

Place the sugar in a heavy saucepan over medium heat and pour in the water. Bring to a boil. When the syrup begins to boil, add the alum stone or lemon slices. There's no need to stir, neither at this stage nor later.

Let the mixture boil over medium heat for about 20 minutes. At first, the mixture will be light and clear, but it will soon darken. When the syrup turns amber, just like the color of natural honey, remove the saucepan from the heat. Add the honey and orange flower water and allow to cool.

Transfer the honey syrup to an airtight jar until you need it. It keeps for several months.

Before using it, heat it gently to liquefy it. You can dip pastries in the syrup or heat it and pour over baklava.

Sesame Nougatines with Hazelnut Paste

This is not a typically Moroccan recipe, but during a vacation in Morocco I was visiting friends in Rabat who asked me to taste these delicious little cookies. My friends had found them at a nearby pastry shop and hoped that I could duplicate the recipe at home. The cookies looked simple enough, but I had to make three batches before I got the texture of the crisp sesame nougatines just right. At first I hesitated between a nougatine prepared using the traditional method, cooked in a saucepan, spread over a marble slab, and cut up with a cookie cutter, or a caramel cooked in the oven in small molds. It also took a good while before I found the right percentage of chocolate to incorporate into the hazelnut paste to give the *gianduja* the perfect consistency. But the wait was more than worth it.

EGG AND GLUTEN FREE
Makes about 50 sandwich cookies
Preparation time: 20 minutes
Cooking time: 15 to 17 minutes per batch

Special equipment: a candy thermometer and 1 ½-inch (3-cm) diameter silicone molds

INGREDIENTS
½ cup (3 ½ oz./100 g) sugar
Scant ⅓ cup (3 ½ oz./100 g) corn syrup
1 tablespoon plus 2 teaspoons (25 ml) water
1 tablespoon plus 1 teaspoon (¾ oz./20 g) salted butter
⅔ cup (4 oz./110 g) white sesame seeds
2 oz. (55 g) bittersweet chocolate
5 ½ oz. (160 g) hazelnut paste (page 20)

Preheat the oven to 350°F (180°C).

Place the sugar, corn syrup, and water in a heavy saucepan over medium heat and cook to 234°F (112°C), checking with a candy thermometer.

Remove from the heat and add the butter and all the sesame seeds at once. Mix well, until completely incorporated.

Drop ½ teaspoon of the mixture into each of the silicone molds. This should only cover half the surface of the molds, because the caramel spreads when baked.

Bake for 15 to 17 minutes, until a nice amber color, but not burned.

Allow to cool for a few minutes before turning out of the molds.

While the nougatines are baking, melt the chocolate and stir the hazelnut paste into it. Stir well and let cool. You've now made a *gianduja*. When it has the consistency of a paste and is malleable, spoon it into a piping bag fitted with a plain ½-inch (14-mm) tip.

Pipe a little of the *gianduja* onto the smooth side of a nougatine and sandwich another nougatine, smooth side inward, onto it. Press very lightly so you don't break them.

Store carefully in an airtight box—they are very fragile! They keep for about a week.

Enjoy them with coffee.

Algerian Gazelle Horns

EGG FREE
Makes 25 cookies
Preparation time: 2 hours plus 12 hours
    (or overnight) in the confectioners' sugar
Chilling time: 1 hour
Cooking time: 15 minutes

Special equipment: disposable (latex) gloves
    and an oval cookie cutter about 5 inches
    (12 cm) long

INGREDIENTS

1 cup (250 ml) orange flower water, for both
    parts of the recipe (you may not need it all)

FOR THE DOUGH

1 ¾ sticks (7 oz./200 g) butter, chilled
4 cups (1 lb. 2 oz./500 g) pastry flour
Orange flower water as needed

FOR THE FILLING

4 ½ cups (13 oz./375 g) ground almonds
1 teaspoon cinnamon
½ cup (3 ½ oz./100 g) sugar
1 teaspoon vanilla extract
Orange flower water as needed

FOR THE SOAKING SYRUP

3 cups (1 lb. 5 oz./600 g) sugar
1 ¼ cups (300 ml) water

TO COAT THE GAZELLE HORNS

3 ⅓ lb. (1.5 kg) confectioners' sugar

These delicate little gazelle horns are nothing short of tantalizing. Beneath a thick cloak of confectioners' sugar lie all the flavors of North Africa: almonds, orange flower water, a hint of cinnamon, and butter. These are the first gazelle horns I learned to make when I was in training at an Algerian pastry shop. They have to be shaped with great precision, but if you take your time, maybe even working with friends, they should be within everyone's reach. I've always loved handling ingredients and during my training period I did so to my heart's content. I had to stir pounds and pounds of ground almonds and sugar by hand. While I was there, I also learned an ingenious technique to get the confectioners' sugar to adhere to the cookies. With the same ingredients used for the gazelle horns, I give you another, quick technique to make small, cork-shaped molded pastries to dip in honey. With both techniques, you'll be able to fill a lovely dessert tray to serve with tea.

First prepare the dough. Dice the butter and place it in a large mixing bowl with the flour. Rub it in with your fingertips. You can also use a stand mixer fitted with the flat beater attachment. Continue until the texture is sandy. Gradually add the orange flower water, pouring very slowly to see how the flour absorbs it. The dough must be fairly soft but not sticky.

Wrap the dough in plastic wrap and chill for 1 hour.

Meanwhile, prepare the filling. Place the ground almonds, cinnamon, and sugar in a large mixing bowl and stir with your hands to combine. Make a well in the center and pour in a little orange flower water and the vanilla extract.

Knead the mixture by hand, very slowly adding orange flower water as needed. If you don't add enough, the filling makes your fingers shiny because of the oil contained in the almonds. So the trick is to keep adding a little until the mixture is slightly sticky and your fingers stop shining.

Weigh ⅔ oz. (20 g) balls and shape them into oblong logs about 4 inches (9 to 10 cm) long.

Preheat the oven to 350°F (180°C). Line a baking sheet with parchment paper.

Roll the dough out extremely thinly, to less than ⅛ inch (2 mm). Cut out shapes with the cookie cutter. (Mine is oval, but pointed at each end, like an eye.) Use the excess dough between the cut-out shapes to roll out again and use.

(continued on page 232)

Place a log of filling along the center of each oval. Carefully fold the dough over it, sealing it like a little pouch or turnover. This is a very tricky procedure but after about 3 or 4 gazelle horns, you'll get the hang of it. Pinch the join of the dough firmly to seal. You should now have a little log that tapers off at each end.

Transfer to a clean work surface (I find that a wooden surface is best for this) and roll the logs under the palms of your hands to make the tips even finer; however, try to keep the oblong shape. Then shape it into a horseshoe. Repeat to make the other gazelle horns.

Transfer to the prepared baking sheet and bake for 15 minutes.

Meanwhile, make the syrup. Place the sugar and water in a saucepan. Bring to a boil and remove from the heat. Sift the confectioners' sugar into a large plastic resealable bag. As soon as you remove the gazelle horns from the oven, dip them for 20 seconds into the syrup and drain well. Then place them in the plastic bag. When you have the first batch in the bag, seal it and shake gently to distribute the confectioners' sugar evenly. Continue, using other plastic bags as required.

Allow to rest for 12 hours or overnight, the time it takes for the gazelle horns to exude their moisture, which sets the confectioners' sugar in a fine layer that sticks to the surface.

The next day, don disposable gloves: this ensures that your fingers don't stick to the cookies or leave behind fingerprints.

Carefully take each gazelle horn and smooth it with your hands to remove any surplus confectioners' sugar. If any of the sweet coating falls off, take some of the sugar from the bag and gently press it on to repair the damage. The confectioners' sugar in the bag no longer has its usual texture because it's absorbed moisture. This means it will stick better to any pastries that have lost some of their coating.

You can store these fragile gazelle horns in an airtight container for a week, carefully protected from moisture—and hungry eyes!

Algerian Rolls

In the photo on page 231, you'll see a round pastry that I made using the same ingredients as in the Algerian gazelle horns. They couldn't be simpler to make. Shape the filling into a long log with a diameter of 3 inches (8 cm). Roll the dough out thinly, to less than ⅛ inch (2 mm).

Wrap the dough around the filling and trim off the excess so that there is no overlap.

Roll the filled log until its diameter is reduced to 1 ½ to 2 inches (4 to 5 cm).

Chill for 1 hour and cut into slices about 1 ½ inches (3 to 4 cm) long.

Using a flat, serrated *nakash* clamp (you'll find them in Middle Eastern stores or online), pinch the dough on each slice to make angled lines. You can also use a pastry tong (or tweezers) or the type of lemon zester that has a wavy steel head.

Bake at 350°F (180°C) for 20 minutes.

Meanwhile, heat some honey syrup (see page 227). As soon as the cookies come out of the oven, immerse the slices in the hot syrup for 1 to 2 minutes. Drain and store in an airtight container for up to a couple of weeks.

The almond heart
of gazelle horns,
my heart in disarray
as I sip my mint tea
steeped in memories of us.
Camila Nicácio

Almond Baklava

A few years ago, I was lucky enough to spend an entire week in an Algerian pastry shop, where I was shown many of the secrets of their craft. Baklava isn't originally from Algeria (opinions differ on whether it comes from Greece or Turkey), but it was in Algeria that I learned to make phyllo pastry by hand, a lifelong dream of mine. This recipe makes enough phyllo for four sheets at the base of the baklava and four as the topping. You can use more—up to seven on each side—but of course this will involve more time. The sheets of pastry aren't quite as thin as store-bought phyllo, but that's what gives these almond baklava their textural charm. Naturally, you can use store-bought phyllo pastry to assemble the baklava I show here, but if you do, use between 15 and 20 sheets in total. Instead of almonds, you can use either pistachios or walnuts.

For one 11-inch (28-cm) diameter cake pan, or 30 to 35 pieces
Preparation time: 1 hour 45 minutes
Chilling time: 1 hour
Cooking time: 1 hour
Resting time: 12 hours or overnight

INGREDIENTS
1 cup (250 ml) orange flower water, for both parts of the recipe (you may not need it all)

FOR THE FILLING
1 ¾ lb. (800 g) chopped almonds
1 teaspoon cinnamon
1 cup (7 oz./200 g) sugar
Orange flower water as needed
10 ½ oz. (300 g) ghee, melted, or clarified butter
1 egg and 2 yolks for the egg wash
Whole blanched almonds for decoration

FOR THE PASTRY SHEETS
6 cups (1 lb. 10 oz./750 g) all-purpose flour
3 ⅓ sticks (13 oz./375 g) butter
⅓ cup (2 ½ oz./75 g) eggs
Orange flower water as needed

2 cups (500 ml) honey syrup (page 227)

Begin by preparing the filling. Place the chopped almonds in the food processor and process for 20 seconds, then check the progress: the almonds should be ground coarsely. Transfer to a large mixing bowl, incorporate the cinnamon and sugar, and then add a little orange flower water. The filling should be just a little bit sticky, enough to clump if you grasp some in the palm of your hand, but not more; it should have the texture of coarse, damp sand.

Now prepare the pastry sheets. Combine all the ingredients in a bowl or in the mixer. Either rub with your fingertips or process briefly. Add a little orange flower water so that the dough can come together. If necessary, add more orange flower water.

Shape into a ball, cover with plastic wrap, and chill for 1 hour.

Brush the cake pan well with the ghee. Dust a work surface with flour.

Divide the dough into 8 equal balls.

Roll 1 ball out very thinly to make a disc slightly larger than the cake pan. Brush off the excess flour on both sides of the disc (you can dust the bottom as you drape it around the rolling pin to transfer to the pan) and set it in the cake pan. Using a pastry brush, brush it with ghee.

Roll out another ball of dough and place it over the first one. Brush it with ghee. Repeat the procedure with 2 more balls of dough. Don't worry if at this stage the sheets of pastry don't look very pretty: things will improve with the following stages.

1 With a rolling pin, roll out each ball of dough very thinly.

2 Add the almond filling and press in carefully with a spoon.

3 Trim the excess pastry.

4 Run the knife around the inside rim of the pan.

5 Cut the baklava into diamond shapes.

6 Pour the honey syrup over as soon as the baklava are removed from the oven.

Spread all of the almond filling evenly over the pastry sheets. Press downward carefully so that it is densely distributed; be careful not to tear the pastry, though. Even it out with the back of a tablespoon or an offset spatula.

Now you can preheat your oven to 350°F (180°C).

Trim the pastry a little above the level of the filling and fold it back over the edge of the filling.

Roll out the remaining 4 balls of dough and place the layers of pastry carefully over the almond filling, brushing the first 3 layers with ghee and leaving the last one unbrushed.

Trim the pastry sheets around the rim of the cake pan and then run the knife around the inside of the pan to cut off the layers of pastry from the outside of the filling.

Using a knife and making sure to cut to the base, cut 1 ½-inch (4-cm) strips in one direction and then another to make the typical diamond shapes.

(continued on page 236)

Combine the egg and egg yolks to make the egg wash. Brush the entire surface of the baklava with the mixture. Place 1 blanched almond in the center of each diamond shape and press it in lightly.

Bake for 1 hour, keeping a careful eye on the color, particularly toward the end. The baklava should be a lovely golden color.

Heat the honey syrup and pour it all over the baklava as soon as you remove the pan from the oven. The pastries absorb the honey as they cool and rest. Allow to rest for 12 hours before carefully removing them from the pan.

You might want to use a small spatula to remove the pastries from the pan. Cut the baklava well again and insert the spatula below each pastry to transfer carefully to a serving dish.

The baklava soaks up the honey
that on your lips
is sweeter still.
From the crossroads of the world
comes a twofold marvel:
the scent of rose water
the cunning of the hummingbird.
Camila Nicácio

Sweet *B'stilla*

This irresistible Moroccan dessert is made of layers of crisp brick pastry filled with an unctuous orange flower cream. It can be prepared very quickly. The only risk is a bit of a mess when it comes time to eat! I didn't realize how much I'd like *b'stilla* the first time I tried it. But the balance between the textures and flavors is just perfect. This is a dessert not to be missed if you're in Morocco—and now you can make it at home, too. My heartfelt thanks go to my dear friend Myriam for her advice and tips.

EGG FREE
Serves 4 to 5
Preparation time: 35 minutes
Cooking time: 10 minutes
Chilling time: 1 hour minimum

INGREDIENTS
FOR THE CREAM
2 cups (500 ml) low-fat milk, divided
⅓ cup (2 ½ oz./70 g) sugar
1 stick cinnamon
¼ cup (2 oz./50 g) rice flour
¼ cup (60 ml) orange flower water

Oil for frying
5 oz. (150 g) blanched almonds
4 sheets brick pastry (often sold as *feuilles de brick*), diameter approx. 12 inches (30 cm)
Confectioners' sugar and ground cinnamon for sprinkling

Pour three-quarters of the milk into a heavy saucepan over medium heat. Immediately add the sugar and cinnamon stick.

In a mixing bowl, combine the rice flour and the remaining milk. When the milk comes to a boil, reduce the heat to low and whisk in the milk–rice flour mixture. Bring to a simmer, whisking continuously until large bubbles appear and the mixture thickens.

Remove from the heat and allow to cool completely. Stir in the orange flower water and remove the cinnamon stick. Process with an immersion blender to ensure that the cream is perfectly smooth, cool to room temperature, and chill for at least 1 hour, but preferably overnight.

Preheat the oven to 375°F (190°C).

Toast the almonds for 10 minutes. In Morocco, almonds are fried in oil until well colored; this is a method you can also try. When cool enough to handle, chop the nuts roughly with a knife.

Cut each sheet of brick pastry into 6 equal triangles. Pour a little oil into a frying pan and set over medium heat. Test the heat with a piece of pastry: it should color in 1 minute. Fry the pieces of brick, turning them over halfway through. When they are done, place on paper towel to drain. For a lighter version, brush them with oil and bake them in the oven until crisp.

To assemble (you can do this directly on individual plates or a large serving dish), place 4 pieces of brick pastry on a plate and spoon a little cream in the center. Sprinkle with chopped almonds and, if you wish, a little ground cinnamon. Set a second piece of pastry over the cream, spoon some cream over and sprinkle with a few chopped almonds. Repeat the procedure 4 or 5 times, finishing with some almonds and a little confectioners' sugar.

Serve immediately.

Turkish Delight

Rahat Lokum

When I was thinking ahead about the recipes to include in this book, the recipe for *lokum*, a Turkish specialty par excellence, seemed an obvious choice. When I was younger, I wasn't exactly wild about Turkish delight. I thought they were awful, pastel-colored cubes with an insipid taste. How wrong I was. In 2001, I traveled to Istanbul several times and discovered the very best of Turkish delight. I have a clear memory of tiny pistachio-scented *lokum*, just enough for one mouthful. They were mouthwatering. After this discovery, I tried other flavors. New horizons opened up for me, a million miles away from what I remembered tasting as a child.

Authentic Turkish delight doesn't contain any gelatin. No agar-agar or gum arabic, either. The special texture of Turkish delight comes from a precise dose of cornstarch and sugar. First, you must make a sugar syrup and then incorporate it into a starchy jelly. Then this mixture has to cook slowly for one hour. This is what guarantees that the texture of your Turkish delight will be perfect, its colors iridescent, and the flavors delicate. When all's said and done, the recipe is actually simple. The recipe I've given you here uses rose water and toasted pistachios as flavoring, but you can play around with lemon, orange flower water, apple, pear, and even mastic resin flavorings. Almonds and hazelnuts are also delicious.

Since cornstarch and sugar are staples in our kitchens, we can potentially make many varieties of Turkish delight. To bring you this recipe, I shut myself in my kitchen for several days to experiment until I got the proportions just right and found a foolproof method. When I finally succeeded, I tasted the exact flavors I'd enjoyed in the Grand Bazaar in Istanbul.

To make this recipe, I use a 6-inch (16-cm) square metal confectionery frame, but you can certainly use a square baking pan instead. The pistachio Turkish delights are just under ½ inch (1 cm) thick and the rose-scented ones just under 1 inch (2 cm). If you're buying a mold, make sure that the rim is deep enough to make both of them. When you choose the flavors, go for concentrated extracts (always buy them in specialized grocery stores or online), not flavored waters, which could well spoil the texture you're aiming to achieve.

And just like for *macarons*, because it's so important to get the proportions right here, I'd strongly advise weighing the ingredients, using the metric system if you have a digital scale that indicates both metric and imperial weights.

Turkish Delight
Rahat Lokum

· · · · · · · · · · · · · · ·

DAIRY AND EGG FREE
Makes 16 *lokum* pieces
Preparation time: 1 hour
Cooking time: 1 hour
Cooling time: 8 hours minimum

Special equipment: a candy thermometer
and a 6-inch (16-cm) square metal
confectionery frame (optional)

INGREDIENTS
FOR THE ROSE- AND LEMON-SCENTED
TURKISH DELIGHT
4 cups (1 ¾ lb./800 g) granulated sugar with
1 cup plus 2 tablespoons (270 ml) water
2 small pieces of alum stone, each about the
size of a small marble, or 3 tablespoons
(45 ml) lemon juice
1 scant cup (4 ¾ oz./135 g) cornstarch
2 cups (500 ml) water
4 drops red food coloring for the rose
and 4 drops yellow for the lemon
5 drops concentrated rose or lemon flavoring

FOR THE PISTACHIO TURKISH DELIGHT
2 ½ cups (1 lb./480 g) sugar with ⅔ cup
(160 ml) water
1 small piece of alum stone the size of
a small marble, or 2 tablespoons (30 ml)
lemon juice
½ cup plus 1 teaspoon (2 ¾ oz./80 g)
cornstarch
1 ¼ cups (300 ml) water
1 drop concentrated rose flavoring
5 oz. (140 g) unpeeled pistachios

TO DUST THE TURKISH DELIGHT
⅓ cup (1 ½ oz./40 g) confectioners' sugar
1 cup (5 ½ oz./160 g) cornstarch

· · · · · · · · · · · · · · ·

Put the sugar and water in a heavy saucepan over medium heat. Add the alum stone or lemon juice. I have a preference for alum stone, which you can find in North African grocery stores or online. It's an excellent acid that prevents sugar from crystallizing.

Be careful that no grains of sugar stick to the inside of the saucepan. If you see any, dip a pastry brush in water and brush these offending grains down to melt them.

Heat the sugar syrup to 240°F–243°F (116°C–117°C).

While the syrup is cooking, pour the second measure of water into a large pot. Whisk in the cornstarch. The liquid should look something like milk.

Place the pot over medium heat and, whisking constantly and very briskly, bring to a boil. The liquid should have the consistency of thick béchamel sauce. It's important to keep whisking so that no lumps form.

Drizzle in the hot syrup in several batches, whisking each time with a hand whisk. When it has all been added, reduce the heat to low and, using a wooden spoon or heat-resistant silicone spatula, begin stirring, including the bottom and sides of the pot.

Now is the time you've been awaiting expectantly: one whole hour of constant stirring. A long time, I agree, but when everyone wolfs down your Turkish delight, think of the kudos you'll get.

Meanwhile, preheat the oven to 350°F (180°C). Put the pistachios on a baking sheet and roast for 10 to 12 minutes.

Initially, the cornstarch mixture will be soft and barely translucent. As it cooks, it becomes increasingly transparent. After 50 minutes, the paste should be easy to detach from the bottom of the pot and become harder to stir. After 1 hour, the paste will stick to the wooden spoon. If you lift it up, the paste will take quite a while to fall back into the pot.

By this time, the consistency will have changed entirely and the color will be yellow. Remove from the heat.

Now add the coloring, the flavoring, and/or the roasted nuts and stir well for 1 minute.

Prepare the frame or pan. If you're using a frame, place it on a silicone baking mat or parchment paper dusted with cornstarch. The cornstarch will adhere better to the silicone mat, but will slip more on the paper. With your fingers, spread the starch on the inside of the frame. If you're using a pan, line it with parchment paper and proceed in the same way. Traditionally,

(continued on page 244)

Turkish delight is molded in wooden frames, to which the starch sticks very well. It's the starch that will prevent the Turkish delight from sticking to the frame or pan.

Pour in the mixture, using a silicone scraper or spatula to get it all out of the pot. Smooth the top. Or you can dip your hands in the cornstarch (it will protect them to a certain extent from the heat) and use your palms to smooth the top.

Allow to cool for at least 8 hours at room temperature.

To prepare the Turkish delight powder, combine the confectioners' sugar and cornstarch. Sift them together and pour most of the mixture onto a work surface.

Remove the frame or take the square of set paste from the pan. Place it on the dusted work surface. Dust the top too so it doesn't stick to your fingers.

With a knife, cut strips of the paste and then cut the strips into cubes. Roll the cubes in the powder to coat them well.

Place in an airtight container. The *lokum* will keep for several months.

Moroccan Semolina Cake

For one 10-inch (24-cm) ring cake pan
Preparation time: 5 minutes
Cooking time: 40 minutes

INGREDIENTS

1 cup plus 2 tablespoons (5 ¼ oz./150 g)
   flour
1 ¼ cups (8 oz./230 g) medium ground
   durum wheat semolina (*not* couscous)
1 scant cup (6 oz./170 g) sugar
2 eggs
Generous ¾ cup (185 ml) buttermilk
2 ½ tablespoons (2 oz./55 g) honey
1 tablespoon (15 ml) orange flower water
5 tablespoons (2 ½ oz./70 g) butter
5 tablespoons (2 ½ oz./70 g) ghee
   (if unavailable, use butter)
1 teaspoon (5 g) baking powder

Here's a cake you can make in just five minutes.

A trip to Morocco inspired me to make a loaf cake with flavors and textures that evoke the country so strongly: honey, orange flower water, durum wheat semolina, and ghee (clarified butter). So I came up with this recipe—delicious with a small glass of traditional Moroccan mint tea.

The semolina gives an extra dimension to this cake. I made my version in a ring pan, but you can use any shape of pan you wish.

My recipe uses ghee, available at Indian groceries, but if you can't get hold of this, you can simply use the same quantity of butter.

Preheat the oven to 350°F (180°C). Butter the cake pan or spray it with non-stick spray.

Combine the flour, semolina, and sugar. Stir in the eggs and buttermilk and mix well. Add the honey and orange flower water.

Melt the butter and ghee together (or all of the butter, if you're not using ghee).

Stir the melted ingredients into the mixture, mix well, and then add the baking powder. Stir until thoroughly incorporated.

Pour the batter into the cake pan. You should fill it no more than three-quarters full.

Bake for about 40 minutes, until a cake tester inserted into the center comes out dry.

Allow the cake to cool for 5 minutes in the pan, turn it out, and cool completely on a rack.

Asia and Oceania

Japanese Rice Balls

Mochi

Have you ever tasted *mochi*, those tender and delicious Japanese confections? Their texture is soft and chewy, but they don't taste like much until you add a flavoring, because their main ingredient is sticky rice flour. From Tokyo to Osaka, from Los Angeles to Sao Paulo, where the world's largest Japanese diaspora lives, I spent a great deal of time analyzing these little delights. I tried every single possible method (or almost every method, because there's always another one to learn), without achieving a result that satisfied me. I boiled the *mochi*, I steamed them, I cooked the dough in dumpling shapes, I rolled it, crushed it, and chucked it away. But I simply couldn't get the texture right, even though the method is actually simple. And it was the same for the proportions of the ingredients. I carried out any number of experiments before finding the ingredients that seemed just right.

For stuffed *mochi* (*daifuku mochi*), I tried out several methods before finding the one that I give you here. In my opinion, it's the simplest. The traditional method involves cooking sticky rice, then calling on your friends to help you hit the rice with wooden hammers in a special bowl until a soft paste forms. Yet another method requires you to steam the sticky rice flour batter for a lengthy period. The problem is that most people won't have the right size of bowl to use in the steamer. If you do have one, go ahead and try it. Here the dough is prepared in the microwave in a matter of minutes. Also, the stuffing is frozen—making it easier to handle—and can be inserted directly into the basic dough.

Note Sticky rice flour is also known as sweet rice flour, though it is not sweet, and glutinous rice flour, in reference to its high starch content (it contains no gluten).

Plain *Mochi*

DAIRY, EGG, AND GLUTEN FREE
Makes 12 *mochi*
Preparation time: 5 minutes
Cooking time: 4 minutes

INGREDIENTS
5 oz. (150 g) sticky rice flour
3 ½ tablespoons (1 ½ oz./40 g) sugar
1 cup minus 2 tablespoons (230 ml) water
Potato starch for rolling and dusting

Place the rice flour, sugar, and water in a microwave safe bowl and mix until smooth. The batter will be quite loose.

Place the bowl in the microwave and heat on high for 30 seconds at a time, stirring well after each time. Depending on your oven, it should take 3 to 4 minutes (but it's essential to work in 30-second bursts) for the batter to fill with air and swell and then deflate immediately. It will look a bit like chewing gum.

Generously dust a work surface or large plate with potato starch sifted through a small sieve. Transfer the dough to the surface and sprinkle it with potato starch. You're going to be handling the dough while it is still hot and the potato starch protects your hands.

Break off a piece of dough—enough to make a ball the size of a ping-pong ball—with one hand and press it down on your palm. Then squeeze it between your thumb and index finger and roll it into the shape of a ping-pong ball. Work fast, even though the dough is hot, as the balls have to be formed quickly.

If the dough is too hot for you, dust your hands with a little more potato starch. It provides insulation (see page 254, photos 1 to 4). Roll the balls in the potato starch. If there is too much potato starch on the *mochi*, brush it off gently with a soft pastry brush.

Flatten the balls slightly between the palms of your hands.

Serve the same day, or store in an airtight container, tightly wrapped with plastic wrap, for an additional day.

The mochi spread out
as tender as a kiss
on a woman's cheek
caresses a cherry blossom.
Camila Nicácio

From top to bottom:
Peanut Butter Daifuku Mochi,
Adzuki Bean Daifuku Mochi,
Sesame Daifuku Mochi, *and Plain* Mochi

Peanut Butter
Daifuku Mochi

EGG AND GLUTEN FREE
Makes 12 *mochi*
Preparation time: 35 minutes
Freezing time: 2 hours
Cooking time: 4 minutes

INGREDIENTS

1 medium jar crunchy peanut butter,
   chilled for at least 12 hours
1 batch plain *mochi* (page 250)
4 drops red food coloring
Potato starch for rolling and dusting

Begin by preparing the peanut butter balls. Line a baking sheet with plastic wrap or parchment paper. Using a melon scoop, scoop out 12 balls of peanut butter. If they are not nicely shaped, roll them lightly between your hands. Freeze for at least 2 hours, or until very firm.

Prepare the plain *mochi* and incorporate the food coloring just before you cook the dough.

Break off enough dough to make a ping-pong sized ball and use your other hand to insert the ball of frozen peanut butter in the center of the *mochi* dough through the tear at the point where you broke it off. Close up the *mochi* by joining the dough around the peanut butter, and ensure that it is sealed.

Roll the ball between your palms, adding a little potato starch if necessary, to make a nice shape (see step-by-step instructions on page 254). Repeat with the remaining dough.

Dust a baking sheet with potato starch and place the *mochi* on it. If there is too much potato starch on them, brush it off gently with a soft pastry brush. Flatten the balls slightly between the palms of your hands.

Serve the same day, or store in an airtight container, tightly wrapped with plastic wrap, for an additional day.

Adzuki Bean
Daifuku Mochi

DAIRY, EGG, AND GLUTEN FREE
Makes 24 *mochi*
Soaking time: 12 hours
Preparation time: 20 minutes
Cooking time: 1 hour 30 minutes

INGREDIENTS
8 oz. (250 g) adzuki beans
¾ cup (5 oz./150 g) sugar
2 batches plain *mochi* (page 250)
A few drops of food coloring, optional

TO FINISH
Kinako (grilled soy flour), optional

Prepare the adzuki bean paste. Soak the beans in water to cover for at least 12 hours. Drain and place in a large pot, with water to cover. Bring to a boil and cook for 10 minutes. Drain well in a colander and return to the pot. Cover again with water and bring to a boil. Boil for 45 minutes to 1 hour, until the beans are very soft—you should be able to crush them easily between your fingers (but rinse first to cool them down!).

Place a colander over a large bowl to catch the water (set it aside, as you might need it for the next step) and drain the adzuki beans. Return the beans to the pot and mash them with a fork to get a coarse texture. You can also use a potato masher or push them through a sieve to remove the skins, which gives a more delicate texture—it's your choice. What I've done here is to use a fork, which leaves fairly large pieces of the beans.

Add the sugar to the beans and cook over low heat, stirring frequently with a wooden spoon, for about 30 minutes. The sugar brings out the water still remaining in the beans. If the paste dries out too much as it cooks, add a little of the cooking water you have set aside. Continue until the paste is fairly thick but can be rolled into balls with your hands.

Allow the paste to cool. Place in an airtight container, press a piece of plastic wrap directly on the surface, and chill.

Prepare the plain *mochi*. If you wish, add a few drops of food coloring—but go lightly!

Scoop out walnut-sized balls of adzuki bean paste.

You can insert the paste into the *mochi* in one of two ways: either insert it at the tear of the dough as explained in the peanut butter *daifuku mochi* recipe on page 252, or gently roll the pieces of *mochi* dough out into discs (see photos 4 and 5 overleaf). Place the ball of adzuki paste in the center and pinch the dough together to seal completely at the top. Roll the balls in the potato starch.

If you've opted to use *kinako*, briefly dip the sealed *mochi* balls in water, gently wipe or shake off any excess, and then dip them into a bowl of *kinako*.

Serve the same day, or store in an airtight container, tightly wrapped with plastic wrap, for an additional day.

(continued on page 254)

1 Transfer the hot dough to a work surface covered with potato starch.

2 Press the dough between your hands and squeeze a small ball out between thumb and index finger.

3 Insert a ball of stuffing at the tear and close the dough around it.

4 & 5 For the folding method, roll out the dough, place the stuffing in the center, and pinch the dough to seal at the top.

6 Dip the *mochi* very briefly in water, remove any excess, and roll in the *kinako*.

Sesame *Daifuku Mochi*

DAIRY, EGG, AND GLUTEN FREE
Makes 12 *mochi*
Preparation time: 45 minutes
Cooking time: 15 minutes

Special equipment: a candy thermometer

INGREDIENTS
FOR THE SESAME PASTE
1 cup (6 oz./170 g) black sesame seeds
½ cup (3 ½ oz./100 g) sugar
2 tablespoons plus 2 teaspoons (40 ml) water
1 tablespoon (20 g) corn syrup

1 batch plain *mochi* (page 250)
Potato starch for rolling and dusting

TO FINISH
A mixture of black and white sesame seeds

Prepare the sesame paste. Place the sesame seeds in a food processor and grind to a coarse powder.

Place the sugar, water, and corn syrup in a small heavy saucepan.

Cook to 240°F (116°C). Remove from the heat and stir in the ground black sesame seeds until well combined.

Pour the sesame mixture onto a sheet of parchment paper or a silicone mat and let it cool completely. It should be hard and grainy.

With a rolling pin, gently crush the paste. Continue rolling until the paste has softened and sticks to the rolling pin. It's preferable to use a rolling pin for this procedure: if you soften the paste in a food processor, this would separate the oil from the seeds.

With your hands, remove the paste from the rolling pin and knead it like bread dough for 2 minutes.

The sesame paste is now ready. Shape it into small balls and cover them in plastic wrap.

Prepare the plain *mochi* dough. Break off enough *mochi* dough to make a ping-pong sized ball. Use your other hand to insert the ball of sesame paste into the center of the *mochi* dough through the tear at the point where you broke it off. Close up the *mochi* by joining the dough around the sesame paste and ensure that it is sealed.

Roll the ball between your palms, adding a little potato starch if necessary, to make a nice shape (see step-by-step instructions on page 254). Repeat with the remaining dough.

Dust a baking sheet with potato starch and place the *mochi* on it. If there is too much potato starch on them, brush it off gently with a soft pastry brush. Flatten the balls slightly between the palms of your hands.

Dip the *mochi* very briefly in water, remove any excess, and roll in a bowl of mixed black and white sesame seeds.

Serve the same day, or store in an airtight container, tightly wrapped with plastic wrap, for an additional day.

Indian Semolina-Carrot Cake

EGG FREE
Serves 8
Preparation time: 20 minutes
Cooking time: about 30 minutes

INGREDIENTS
5 cardamom pods
2 cups plus scant ½ cup (600 ml) low-fat milk
1 ¼ cups (8 ½ oz./240 g) sugar
6 saffron threads
3–4 drops orange or yellow food coloring
1 ½ cups (5 oz./150 g) tightly packed, finely grated carrots
3 tablespoons (2 oz./50 g) butter
3 tablespoons (2 oz./50 g) ghee
1 tablespoon (15 ml) oil
8 oz. (230 g) fine semolina (about 1 ⅓ cups)
Any (or a combination) of the following:
⅓ cup (2 oz./50 g) cashew nuts
⅓ cup (2 oz./50 g) pistachios
⅔ cup (2 oz./50 g) sliced (flaked) almonds
⅓ cup (2 oz./50 g) raisins

This fragrant and delicious cake is sometimes seen on menus in Indian restaurants. It's incredibly simple to prepare and wonderful served either warm or still quite hot from the pan and topped with chopped nuts. You don't even need to turn on your oven to make it: just cook the batter in a saucepan and then pour it into a cake pan. Preparing this cake is like taking a trip down the ancient spice route, with the scent of cardamom and saffron wafting from the kitchen. You'll find ghee, also known as clarified butter, at Indian and specialty grocery stores. The food coloring is not essential, but its orangey-yellow hue gives the dessert a special touch—the colors and flavors of India on your plate.

Line an 8-inch (20-cm) square cake pan with parchment paper.

Shell the cardamom pods and grind the seeds using a pestle and mortar.

Pour the milk into a pot and add the sugar, coloring if using, saffron threads, ground cardamom, and grated carrots. Bring to a boil and simmer for 20 minutes over low heat, stirring frequently. The carrots should be very soft—they should melt in your mouth.

Place the butter, ghee, and oil in a large saucepan over medium heat. When hot, pour in the semolina. Cook for 5 minutes, stirring constantly with a wooden spoon.

Pour the hot milk-carrot mixture over the semolina. Reduce the heat to low and continue cooking for 5 to 7 minutes, stirring constantly, until the mixture pulls away from the sides of the saucepan.

If you wish, stir in the nuts and/or raisins. Personally, I prefer to add them afterward so guests can select what they like best.

Pour the mixture into the prepared cake pan and smooth the top with the back of a large spoon or offset spatula. Allow to cool to room temperature.

If you're not planning on serving the cake immediately, place it in the refrigerator. Cut portions that you can heat in the microwave to serve either warm or hot.

Thai Pralines

DAIRY, EGG, AND GLUTEN FREE
Makes 1 lb. (500 g) pralines
Preparation time: 5 minutes
Cooking time: 15 minutes

INGREDIENTS
1 ¼ cups (8 oz./250 g) sugar
½ teaspoon fine sea salt
1 ½ cups (8 oz./250 g) raw cashew nuts
1 tablespoon untoasted sesame seeds

Whenever I travel to Bangkok, I always treat myself to these lightly caramelized, fantastically crunchy sugar-coated cashews with sesame. On every trip I make sure to buy some at the street markets. It's the hint of salt and crunchy sesame seeds that make the pralines particularly addictive. For years, I would bring packets home with me only to finish them within five minutes of arriving. I swore that one day I'd learn to make them myself so that I'd no longer have to travel halfway around the globe to buy them. Luckily, they're very easy to make.

Place a sheet of parchment paper or a silicone mat on a work surface.

Place the sugar and salt in a large frying pan and pour in enough water to soak the sugar completely. Bring to a boil and let boil until the sugar begins to form large, thick bubbles. Add the cashew nuts to the pan, stirring constantly with a wooden spoon. The sugar will begin to turn grainy (see step-by-step instructions for praline paste on page 19). Keep stirring to coat the cashews, and try to keep them separate. Continue until the surface of the nuts is lightly caramelized, without allowing all the sugar to melt.

Stop when the cashews are covered in a light coating. Pour in the sesame seeds and stir until they stick to the caramel.

Pour the mixture onto the prepared surface and let cool.

Separate any cashews that are stuck together. Store in an airtight container—these candies don't like any moisture at all. If well protected, they keep for a few weeks.

Wrap them attractively for an unusual homemade gift.

Crunchy Caramel-Coated Apple Fritters

DAIRY FREE
Makes 16 fritters
Preparation time: 30 minutes
Cooking time: 25 minutes

INGREDIENTS
4 firm apples
4 cups (1 liter) peanut oil for frying
¾ cup plus 2 tablespoons (3 ½ oz./100 g)
   flour
⅔ cup (3 ½ oz./100 g) cornstarch or rice flour
Scant ½ cup (100 ml) ice water
1 egg
1 tablespoon (11 g) baking powder

FOR THE CARAMEL
Scant ⅓ cup (3 ½ oz./100 g) corn syrup
1 ½ cups (10 oz./300 g) sugar
Scant ½ cup (100 ml) water
3 tablespoons oil
2 tablespoons untoasted sesame seeds
A large bowl of ice water

You may well have enjoyed these fritters, coated in a crunchy caramel with sesame seeds, at a Chinese restaurant. Here I show you how to make them at home. And if you make them while your guests watch, I guarantee that it will be quite a show! You'll have to work quickly to prepare this recipe. The apple fritters must be fried while the caramel is cooking. Prepare the fritters and caramel in the kitchen, then bring them to the dining room table with the bowl of ice water. If you dip the fritters in the caramel and then into the ice water, you'll bring your meal to a spectacular climax.

Peel and core the apples and cut them into quarters.

Pour the peanut oil into a pot and put on the stove to heat.

Meanwhile, prepare the fritter batter. Combine the flour and cornstarch and stir in the water and egg. When combined, add the baking powder and mix well. What's important is to add the raising agent just before you cook the batter so that it doesn't begin acting before it comes into contact with the heat.

When the oil is hot, dip the apple quarters into the batter and then slip them into the pot of hot oil. Cook until the fritters are golden on all sides.

Meanwhile, prepare the caramel. Place the corn syrup, sugar, and water in a heavy saucepan and bring to a boil over medium heat. Add the oil. Continue cooking the syrup until it becomes a nice caramel color. Stir in the sesame seeds. If the fritters are not yet cooked, reduce the heat to minimum to keep the syrup warm.

Remove the fritters from the oil, place them on a paper towel to drain, and then drop them into the caramel syrup.

With a slotted spoon, immediately transfer them briefly into the bowl of ice water. This will set the caramel instantly.

Arrange the fritters on dessert plates and sprinkle with extra sesame seeds. Serve immediately.

Chinese Moon Cakes

These moon cakes are traditionally served in China during the annual Mid-Autumn Festival, which is celebrated between early September and early October, depending on when the moon is full. I learned how to make them in China, and it was in Guangzhou that I bought the molds I used to make the cakes in the photo opposite. In the Shaxi area, there are literally hundreds of kitchen equipment stores—a paradise for foodies. But back in the West, you can buy them in most well-stocked Asian supermarkets or online. The same goes for dried lotus seeds. Wooden molds are nice, but I prefer the plastic ones with a spring-operated plunger, as they make the task considerably easier—and result in very pretty motifs. The most time-consuming part of this recipe is preparing the lotus seed paste. The batter for the cakes themselves takes practically no time at all. The cakes are baked in two stages. The special ingredient required for the batter is light corn syrup, but you can also use honey syrup (see page 227).

Make the lotus seed paste. Of course, you can buy ready-made paste, but it's far better if you make it at home. Place the seeds in a large bowl of cold water and soak for 12 hours. Drain them and cook in a pot, well covered with water. Boil for 40 minutes and drain, keeping some of the cooking liquid.

Place the beans in a food processor or blender with a little of the liquid and process to a smooth purée. The amount of water you use actually isn't very important, because it will evaporate when cooked at the next stage.

Push the purée through a fine-mesh sieve into a bowl.

In a saucepan (use one large enough to stir the purée in) over low heat, place ¼ cup (2 oz./50 g) sugar and 3 tablespoons plus 1 teaspoon (50 ml) of the oil. Cook until the sugar caramelizes, taking care that it doesn't burn. Add the lotus bean purée and mix well until it takes on the color of caramel. Bring to a boil, stirring constantly. Gradually add the remaining oil. When all of the oil has been absorbed, continue to cook for about 30 minutes, still stirring constantly. The paste will now begin to dry out. Now, add the remaining sugar. The paste will render a little liquid. Keep cooking for another 30 to 45 minutes, until the paste pulls away easily from the sides of the saucepan (just as choux pastry does).

Remove the saucepan from the heat and transfer the paste to a bowl. Press a piece of plastic wrap on the surface. When the paste has cooled, you should be able to shape it into a ball. This means that it is ready! You can freeze it, or store it in the refrigerator for up to 3 days.

(continued on page 264)

Makes about 20 cakes
Soaking time: 12 hours or overnight
Preparation time: 2 hours
Chilling time: 1 hour
Cooking time: 1 hour 30 minutes for the lotus bean paste and 25 minutes total for the cakes

INGREDIENTS
FOR THE LOTUS SEED PASTE
7 oz. (200 g) lotus seeds
1 scant cup (6 oz./180 g) sugar, divided
Scant ¾ cup (170 ml) neutral vegetable oil, divided

FOR THE DOUGH
2 cups (9 oz./250 g) flour
⅔ cup (150 ml) light corn syrup or honey syrup (page 277)
¼ cup (65 ml) oil, such as canola
1 teaspoon water

FOR THE EGG WASH
1 egg yolk
1 tablespoon milk

Now you can make the moon cake dough. This stage is quick and fun. You'll need to have a baking sheet lined with parchment paper ready for the last stage. Place all the ingredients in a mixing bowl and beat with a metal or wooden spoon until the batter is smooth and has a shiny surface (the shine is due to the oil). No need to chill at this stage.

Take your moon cake mold. I have quite a few at home, and on each one, the weight it contains is indicated—in grams. When the mold holds 100 g (3 ½ oz.) I subtract one-third of the weight, and that gives me just over 2 oz. (66 g). This corresponds to the amount of filling—here, the lotus bean paste—required. So for my three molds, I subtracted one-third of the weight stamped to calculate how much I would need for the filling. Weigh out the filling for each of your molds and shape it into balls.

On a piece of parchment paper, place a ball of dough the same size as the ball of filling. Cover it with another piece of parchment paper so that it doesn't stick to the rolling pin. Roll it out very thinly, to under ⅛ inch (3 mm). Place the ball of lotus bean paste in the middle and cut the dough into a square twice the size of the ball of filling. For example, if the ball is 1 ½ inches (4 cm) in diameter, cut a square measuring 3 inches (8 cm).

Remove the excess dough and carefully fold the corners of the square over the filling to enclose it. The 4 corners should be neatly placed on top of the ball. Carefully pick it up and, using a knife, trim off any excess dough around the 4 folds. Make sure that the ball of filling is completely wrapped in the dough. Now roll it between your hands to make a perfectly shaped ball. Place the ball in the moon cake mold.

Turn the mold onto the prepared baking sheet and press the mold several times over the dough. Carefully turn the cake out of the mold by lifting the mold up and pressing down on the plunger. Repeat with the remaining moon cakes.

Place the baking sheet in the refrigerator for at least 1 hour.

Preheat the oven to 350°F (180°C).

Bake the cakes for 10 minutes. At this stage, they are half-baked. Remove from the oven and let cool for 20 minutes.

Combine the egg yolk with the milk and brush the tops of the cakes. Don't let any of the egg wash run down the sides. It's important to apply the egg wash at this stage, because if you do it before the cakes are baked, the egg yolk will cause the wash to crack and create pressure on the surface of the dough. And because the lotus bean paste tends to swell slightly, it's important to let the cakes cool halfway through the baking process.

When all the cakes have been brushed with the egg wash, return them to the oven (at the same temperature) and bake for 10 to 15 minutes, until the egg wash is a lovely golden color.

Allow the cakes to cool before serving. They keep well in an airtight container for up to 2 weeks.

Three Thai Desserts with Coconut Milk

Here are three Thai desserts that use coconut milk as their main ingredient. It's hard to decide which is the most delicious!

The flavors of these desserts are exotic yet soothing—perfect for resting the palate after a hot, spicy meal. You shouldn't have any problem finding an ingredient like tapioca starch: it's readily available in Asian grocery stores and online. In the recipes for Water Chestnuts with Tapioca and Pandanus Leaves, and Mango Sticky Rice, it's tapioca starch that's called for. Don't confuse this with real tapioca flour, which looks like coarse semolina. Tapioca starch is visually very much like cornstarch, but doesn't give the same result at all.

Water chestnuts are generally available in cans, which is perfect for the recipe I give you here. What I'm looking for is their crisp texture rather than their flavor.

In the recipe that calls for water chestnuts, the main flavor is imparted by the pandanus leaves. Pandanus leaves? A strange name for one of the most surprising plants I've come across. Its flavor is quite unique and worth getting to know. You can find the leaves either fresh or in extracts and flavorings. It's sometimes labeled as "pandan leaves."

As for coconut milk, you've certainly seen both coconut milk and coconut cream in stores, and the difference between the two is not always clear. Coconut water, increasingly popular, makes matters even more complicated. Coconut water is the liquid contained within coconuts; I don't use it for my recipes here. Coconut milk is made from the flesh of the coconut. It is grated and then water is added to it; it is pressed and filtered through cheesecloth to drain it completely. The resulting liquid is left to rest. A fine layer of cream rises to the top; below that remains the more liquid coconut milk. You'll find all kinds of coconut milk and you should be aware that the milk is supposed to be very fluid, while the cream is, as is to be expected, creamier, just like whipping cream. You're sure to see creamy milk and fluid cream—confusion guaranteed. But the bottom line is that these labels are not particularly important as long as you find what suits your recipes best.

Bananas with Coconut Milk and Coconut Palm Sugar

DAIRY, EGG, AND GLUTEN FREE
Serves 4
Preparation time: 10 minutes
Cooking time: 15 minutes

INGREDIENTS
3 ⅓ cups (800 ml) coconut milk
1 good pinch salt
Generous ⅓–½ cup (3–4 oz./80–100 g)
   coconut palm sugar, depending
   on the sweetness of the bananas
4 baby bananas
4 tablespoons thick coconut cream, optional

Pour the coconut milk into a saucepan over low heat and add the salt and coconut palm sugar. Start with the smaller quantity of sugar listed.

Peel and cut the bananas, either in slices or lengthwise. When the milk is simmering and the sugar is completely dissolved, add the sliced bananas. Cook until they are softened. The cooking time will depend on the size of the bananas and how you've cut them. This generally goes very quickly, not more than 5 minutes.

Remove the saucepan from the heat, check the sweetness, and add extra sugar if necessary.

Divide the dessert between 4 dessert bowls. If you're using cream, pour 1 tablespoon of coconut cream over each bowl and serve very hot.

Clockwise, from top left:
Bananas with Coconut Milk and Coconut Palm Sugar;
Mango Sticky Rice; and
Water Chestnuts with Tapioca and Pandanus Leaves

Water Chestnuts with Tapioca and Pandanus Leaves

DAIRY, EGG, AND GLUTEN FREE
Serves 4
Preparation time: 30 minutes
Resting time: 1 hour
Cooking time: 10 minutes

INGREDIENTS
3 ½ oz. (100 g) drained water chestnuts
6 drops red food coloring
3 ½ oz. (100 g) tapioca starch (see
    explanation page 265)
Scant ⅔ cup (4 oz./120 g) granulated sugar
¼ cup (60 ml) water
1 pandanus leaf or 8 drops pandanus
    flavoring
2 ¾ cups (600 ml) coconut milk, well chilled
¾ cup (200 ml) coconut cream, well chilled
A few ice cubes for serving

Cut the water chestnuts into small pieces and place them in a small mixing bowl. Add the food coloring. Pour in enough water to cover the chestnuts and leave for 1 hour while the color takes effect.

Place the tapioca starch in a bowl. When the pieces of water chestnut are pink, drain them. Transfer to the bowl with the tapioca starch and shake to coat them. They should be well coated, but without any excess starch.

Bring a small saucepan of water to a boil and drop the water chestnuts in. When they are cooked, they come to the surface. At this stage, remove and drain them, and let cool on a plate, well separated. If they come into contact with one another, they stick together.

Place the sugar and water in a saucepan. If you're using a fresh pandanus leaf, cut it into pieces. Bring to a boil, remove from the heat, and infuse for 5 to 10 minutes. If you're using flavoring, make the syrup and add the drops.

Stir the coconut milk and cream together in a mixing bowl and divide between 4 dessert bowls.

Divide the pieces of water chestnut between the bowls. Remove any pandanus leaf pieces and pour the syrup over the bowl. Stir to combine, add a few ice cubes, and serve immediately.

Mango Sticky Rice

DAIRY, EGG, AND GLUTEN FREE
Serves 4
Soaking time: 12 hours or overnight
Preparation time: 40 minutes
Cooking time: 30 to 40 minutes

INGREDIENTS
14 oz. (400 g) sticky rice
Generous ⅓–½ cup (3–4 oz./80–100 g)
  coconut palm sugar
¼ teaspoon salt
1 cup (250 ml) coconut milk
3–4 drops pandanus flavoring

FOR THE CREAMY TOPPING
4 teaspoons tapioca starch (see explanation
  page 265)
¾ cup (200 ml) coconut milk
⅓ cup (2 oz./60 g) coconut palm sugar
  (or granulated sugar)
¼ teaspoon salt
3–4 drops pandanus flavoring
2 ripe mangoes
Toasted sesame seeds or mung beans (lightly
  toasted) for sprinkling, optional

Rinse the sticky rice under running water for 2 minutes. Place it in a large pot, well covered with cold water, and leave for 12 hours (or overnight) to swell.

When you're ready to cook, bring a large pot of water to boil and steam the rice over it for 30 to 40 minutes, shaking the steam basket halfway through the cooking process.

Place the coconut palm sugar (begin with the smaller quantity), salt, coconut milk, and flavoring in a saucepan over medium heat and cook until the sugar has dissolved.

Place the hot cooked rice in a mixing bowl and pour in the sweetened coconut milk in several additions, stirring well each time. When the rice can no longer absorb any milk, stop pouring—but in any case you should have used it all up. Allow to rest for 20 minutes. Taste and, if necessary, add the remaining coconut palm sugar.

Meanwhile, prepare the creamy topping. Place the tapioca starch in a small saucepan. Pour in a little of the coconut milk and stir to combine. The starch should dissolve easily.

Add the remaining coconut milk, coconut palm sugar, and salt. Cook over low heat, stirring constantly, until the cream thickens and comes to a simmer. Remove from the heat.

Peel the mangoes and slice or dice them.

Divide the sticky rice between 4 small bowls. Pour over a little of the creamy topping, add the mango pieces, and serve immediately. If you wish, you can sprinkle the bowls with toasted sesame seeds or mung beans.

Steamed Coconut Balls

DAIRY AND GLUTEN FREE
Makes 15 to 20 coconut balls
Preparation time: 45 minutes
Cooking time: 15 to 20 minutes

INGREDIENTS
Filling of your choice: coconut-peanut or
    egg custard (pages 273–74)

FOR THE DOUGH
7 oz. (200 g) sticky rice flour
¼ cup (2 oz./55 g) sugar
½ cup (130 ml) boiling water
Unsweetened dried shredded coconut
    for the coating

Here are two Chinese desserts I'm particularly fond of. Coconut balls are soft like *mochi* (see page 250) and come with one of two fillings: an egg custard (my favorite) or a filling made of coconut, peanuts, and sesame seeds. *Maqiu* are fried to give them a crisp surface, made even better by a delicious sesame seed coating. I learned how to make these two desserts in Shanghai on one of my trips to China. I'd wanted to learn how to make them for years. In restaurants, you often see them at morning and afternoon tea time, served alongside dim sum like shrimp ravioli, *siu mai*, and chicken feet!

Place the sticky rice flour and sugar in a mixing bowl (or the bowl of a food processor) and stir in the boiling water. When combined, pour the mixture onto a clean work surface or a marble pastry slab if you have one.

Begin kneading, folding over and pushing away with the palms of your hands. Continue for 5 to 10 minutes, until the dough is very soft to the touch and satiny. Cut it into 3 equal pieces and roll each one into an even log shape. Cut the logs into 6 pieces. Roll each piece between your hands to form balls.

To prepare the egg custard filling, roll it into small balls about half the size of the sticky rice balls.

Insert a finger into the ball of dough and place the ball of egg custard or coconut-peanut filling in the cavity. Close the dough over the filling and roll between your hands to shape into a smooth ball. Make sure that the seam is invisible, even though this is less important for this recipe, which is steamed, than it is for the fried *maqiu*—but they should look attractive! Repeat with the remaining pieces of dough.

Dip the balls for a few seconds into a bowl of cold water and then roll them in the coconut. To do this, take a small handful of coconut in your hand and roll the balls between your palms to push the coconut into the surface of the dough. The coconut balls are ready to be steamed.

Line a bamboo steamer basket with parchment paper and pierce a few holes in it. Steam over a pot of boiling water for 15 to 20 minutes, depending on the size you've made. They will be completely soft when done.

Serve while still hot. If you like, you can store them in the refrigerator, covered with plastic wrap, and reheat them for 1 minute in the microwave or 5 minutes in a steamer basket.

Steamed Coconut Balls (left) and
Sesame Fritters (right)

Sesame Fritters
Maqiu

· · · · · · · · · · · · · · · · · ·

Makes about 16 fritters
Preparation time: 45 minutes
Resting time: 20 to 25 minutes
Cooking time: 20 minutes

Special equipment: metal tongs

INGREDIENTS
FOR THE FILLING
Egg custard (page 273)

FOR THE DOUGH
7 oz. (200 g) sticky rice flour, plus a little more
   if necessary
¼ cup (2 oz./55 g) sugar
½ cup (130 ml) cold water, plus a little more
   if necessary
Untoasted sesame seeds for coating
Oil for frying

· · · · · · · · · · · · · · · · · ·

Place the sticky rice flour in a mixing bowl or the bowl of a food processor and make a well in the center. Pour in the sugar and water and beat for about 10 minutes, adding a little rice flour or water, depending on the consistency, until the dough forms a ball.

Cover with plastic wrap and let the dough rest at room temperature for 20 to 25 minutes, until all the sugar crystals have dissolved.

Knead again on a work surface, rolling the dough up into a log, folding it over, and pushing away with the palms of your hands, just like kneading bread.

Roll the dough into a log shape with a diameter of about 1 ½ inches (2 to 3 cm) and cut it into 16 slices. Take a slice between your hands and roll it into a ball. Insert a finger into the ball to make a cavity. Place a ball of egg custard the size of the cavity in the sticky rice dough. Fold the sides of the dough upward to enclose the egg custard. Roll again between your hands to close the seams and ensure that the ball is smooth. Repeat with the remaining dough.

Place them, one by one, in a bowl filled with sesame seeds. Take a small handful of sesame seeds and roll the balls between your hands to push the seeds into the surface of the dough.

Heat a large amount of oil in a wok. When it begins to heat but is not yet boiling, carefully place the *maqiu* in it. As the oil heats, it will begin cooking them gently. It's said to be difficult to cook *maqiu*, but I really don't see why! The trick lies in using the tongs to gently crush them to remove the air that makes them swell. It's also very important to keep turning them, pinching them as you do so.

When the *maqiu* are a nice golden color, remove them and drain. Let them cool slightly on paper towel and serve still hot and crisp. *Maqiu* are best eaten the day they are made.

Egg Custard

Preparation time: 25 minutes
Cooking time: 10 minutes

INGREDIENTS

1 egg
½ cup plus 1 tablespoon (4 oz./110 g) sugar
3 tablespoons (2 oz./30 g) flour
1 oz. (25 g) wheat starch (available in Asian
   supermarkets and online)
4 tablespoons (2 oz./30 g) powdered whole
   milk
2 ½ tablespoons (1 oz./25 g) custard powder,
   or 2 ½ tablespoons (1 oz./25 g) cornstarch
   plus 1 teaspoon vanilla extract
2 tablespoons (1 oz./30 g) melted butter
Scant ½ cup (100 ml) water

Place the egg and the sugar in a mixing bowl and whisk just to combine the ingredients—no need for the mixture to become thick and pale.

Whisk in the flour, wheat starch, powdered milk, and custard powder. Stir in the melted butter and then gradually pour in the water, whisking constantly (but lightly). The batter will be very fluid, much like a crêpe or pancake batter.

The traditional Chinese method involves steaming the batter for about 30 minutes, stirring every 10 minutes. However, if you're like me and don't have a bowl that fits in a bamboo steam basket or other steamer, you can cook it in the microwave in 30 second bursts (or even 20 seconds if your oven is powerful), stirring each time. It'll take just a few minutes to cook, between 3 and 6. To check for doneness, see if the dough has firmed up and is forming small bubbles on the surface. It looks like pancake or crêpe batter that is cooking.

As soon as it reaches this stage, stop the cooking process by transferring the dough to another bowl. Let it cool briefly and then knead it for a few minutes with your hands, just like bread dough. Shape it into a ball and cover with plastic wrap. Chill until you need it to make the *maqiu* or coconut balls.

Peanut and Coconut Filling

DAIRY, EGG, AND GLUTEN FREE

INGREDIENTS
⅔ cup (3 ½ oz./100 g) peanuts
1 ⅓ cups (3 ½ oz./100 g) unsweetened
   shredded coconut
⅔ cup (3 ½ oz./100 g) toasted sesame seeds
½ cup (3 ½ oz./100 g) sugar

Place the peanuts in the small bowl of a food processor and grind to a fine powder. Add the remaining ingredients and process until they form a powdery mixture.

All you have to do now is fill the coconut balls with this mixture.

I wouldn't recommend using the peanut and coconut filling for the *maqiu* because when they're fried, they might explode because of the air in the mixture. (The egg custard, however, is very compact and perfect for *maqiu*.) So use this delicious filling for your steamed coconut balls.

Crunchy Peanut Bars

DAIRY, EGG, AND GLUTEN FREE
Makes 8 bars
Preparation time: 5 minutes
Cooking time: 20 minutes

Special equipment: a candy thermometer and
a metal confectionery frame

INGREDIENTS

2 tablespoons (20 g) white sesame seeds,
plus extra for the frame
3 ½ oz. (100 g) maltose syrup or honey
Scant ½ cup (100 ml) water
¼ teaspoon salt
Scant ¾ cup (4 ¾ oz./135 g) sugar
1 tablespoon oil, plus extra for the frame
1 ¾ cups (10 oz./270 g) unsalted roasted
peanuts

You'll often see these sweet and crunchy peanut or sesame seed bars in Asian stores. The only problem with them is that once you start eating them, you can't stop. In Beijing, I saw them being made in the street in large woks—a snack to be sold alongside skewers of scorpions.

On my return home, I tried to make the bars myself. After three attempts, I found the right proportions for the ingredients and the right quantities for the confectionery frame I use. Of course, you can simply use a well-oiled, lined brownie pan or pour the caramel onto a silicone mat or onto parchment paper. The essential ingredient is maltose syrup, available in Asian markets. It's this syrup that makes the authentic recipe. But if you can't find any, simply use honey.

Preheat the oven to 300°F (150°C). Set a confectionery frame on a silicone mat or parchment paper and oil the inside rim. (Or line and oil a brownie pan.) Sprinkle the silicone mat with sesame seeds.

Place the maltose syrup, water, salt, and sugar in a heavy saucepan. Bring to a boil and stir in the oil. Stirring frequently with a wooden spoon, bring the mixture to 300°F (150°C) Check with a candy thermometer.

Meanwhile, spread the roasted peanuts and sesame seeds on a baking sheet and place in the oven to warm them up, ready to incorporate into the caramel without hardening it. When they are hot, pour them all at once into the hot caramel so that the mixture doesn't harden before it should. Mix well to combine.

Pour into the prepared frame and spread out evenly, using a rolling pin or offset spatula. The best way to avoid burning yourself and ensure that the mixture doesn't stick to the utensil is to place a sheet of parchment paper on the top.

When the mixture is smoothly spread out, remove the parchment paper and sprinkle the top with a few sesame seeds. To press them in, roll the rolling pin over.

Allow the caramel to cool. When it is completely firm, remove the frame and cut out bars using a bread knife. Store in an airtight container to avoid all contact with any humidity in the air.

Crunchy Sesame Bars

DAIRY, EGG, AND GLUTEN FREE
Makes 1 ¼ lb. (600 g)
Preparation time: 5 minutes
Cooking time: 20 minutes

Special equipment: a candy thermometer

INGREDIENTS
¾ cup (6 oz./150 g) sugar
Scant ½ cup (100 ml) water
¼ teaspoon salt
3 ½ oz. (100 g) maltose syrup or honey
1 tablespoon oil, plus oil for the work surface
1 cup plus 1 scant cup (10 ½ oz./300 g)
   untoasted sesame seeds

Preheat the oven to 300°F (150°C). Oil a smooth work surface and rolling pin. If you have a marble pastry slab and rolling pin, this is ideal.

In a heavy saucepan, place the sugar, water, salt, and maltose syrup and bring to a boil. Stir in the oil. Stirring frequently with a wooden spoon, bring the mixture to 300°F (150°C). Check with a candy thermometer.

Meanwhile, spread the sesame seeds on a baking sheet and roast for about 10 minutes.

When the caramel registers 300°F (150°C), pour in the hot sesame seeds and stir quickly to combine.

Pour the mixture onto the prepared surface and using the rolling pin, spread it out to the desired thickness. The thinner it is, the crisper it will be.

Allow to cool completely and cut into pieces with a bread knife. Immediately store in an airtight container to prevent contact with any humidity in the air.

Crunchy Sesame Bars (top) and
Crunchy Peanut Bars (bottom)

Pavlova

Serves 6 to 8
Preparation time: 20 minutes
Cooking time: 1 hour 15 minutes to
   1 hour 30 minutes

Special equipment (optional): a 7-inch
   (16 to 18 cm) diameter dessert ring or
   rim of a springform pan

INGREDIENTS
FOR THE MERINGUE
4 egg whites, room temperature
1 cup plus 2 tablespoons (8 oz./220 g) sugar
2 teaspoons (10 ml) white vinegar
1 tablespoon (10 g) cornstarch

FOR THE WHIPPED CREAM
1 vanilla bean
¾ cup (190 ml) whipping (heavy) cream,
   well chilled
⅔ cup (5 ½ oz./160 g) mascarpone, well
   chilled
⅓ cup (2 oz./50 g) confectioners' sugar
Assorted berries for the topping (strawberries,
   raspberries, blueberries, blackberries,
   redcurrants, etc.)

This famous Australian dessert is multitextured: a crisp and chewy meringue shell topped with softly whipped cream. When it is topped with berries, it makes a refreshing and light dessert. The first time I ever tasted pavlova, at a potluck dinner party a long time ago, I didn't fall head over heels in love with it. The cook had filled the pavlova with whipped cream out of a can and topped it with apples and grapes, hardly the best choice. When it was time for dessert, she brought her pavlova into the dining room in her hands. It broke in half and fell on the floor. I was secretly delighted not to have to eat her creation, but no luck, she was determined to serve it and gathered up whatever had not directly touched the ground. Witnessing (and sampling) this failure did, however, pique my curiosity and I decided to try the dessert out myself. With a nice, crisp meringue, homemade, lightly sweetened whipped cream with vanilla and mascarpone, and ripe, fresh berries, pavlova is not only an attractive dessert, but also pleases the most refined palates.

First make the meringue. Place the egg whites in a mixing bowl and whip them. When they begin to hold soft peaks, gradually pour in the sugar. Continue to whip until they hold firm peaks. Take a little between your fingers: you should not be able to feel any grains of sugar.

In a small bowl, combine the white vinegar and cornstarch. Pour the liquid into the whipped meringue and whip for another 2 to 3 minutes.

Preheat the oven to 320°F (160°C). Line a baking sheet with parchment paper and set a dessert ring on it. Pour the meringue into the ring, spooning it against the rim. Using a spatula, draw waves in an irregular pattern. Remove the dessert ring—your meringue will be perfectly round. If you don't have a dessert ring, use a pencil to trace a circle on one side of the parchment paper. Then turn the paper over, spread the meringue, and make patterns with the spatula.

Place in the oven and immediately lower the temperature to 230°F–250°F (110°C–120°C). Bake for 1 hour 15 minutes to 1 hour 30 minutes, checking that it barely colors. It should be hard on the surface. Allow to cool and cover until needed, up to a day before serving.

For the whipped cream, place the cream and mascarpone in the mixing bowl in the refrigerator for 1 hour. A chilled bowl helps the cream whip up nicely. Slit the vanilla bean with a small knife and scrape the seeds into the cream. Add the confectioners' sugar. Whip until you can see the marks of the whisks in the cream. Place the meringue on a serving dish and, using a spatula, decorate it with the whipped cream, spreading it unevenly to follow the outlines of the pavlova. Scatter with berries and serve immediately.

Notes and General Advice

Butter: If possible, I recommend using European-style butter with a high butterfat content (a minimum of 82%), which gives superior results in baked goods. High-fat European-style and American premium butters are increasingly available. In the US, regular butter has a lower butterfat content (around 80%), but will still give excellent results in all of my recipes.

In some recipes, I call for butter at room temperature. In those cases, be sure to take the butter out of the refrigerator and leave it out long enough for it to soften. You should easily be able to make an indentation in the butter with your finger.

Salted butter is a staple in Breton cuisine and cakes, and the offerings I have available to me in France range from *demi-sel* (lightly salted) to *salé* (salted), or even *beurre aux cristaux de sel* (butter speckled with salt crystals, which add a delightful crunch). However, all of my recipes will work well with standard salted butter. Should you be able to find butter with salt crystals, it is delicious on bread, but I would advise against using it in pastry making, because the crystals may tear the dough.

Eggs: Unless otherwise specified, the eggs I use in my recipes are chicken eggs with an average weight of 2 oz. (55 to 57 g). These are "large" eggs in the US and Canada and "medium" eggs in the UK. The egg yolk weighs about 0.63 oz. (18 to 20 g) and the white, about 1 oz. (30 g). But in many of my recipes, I give specific egg weights, because the outcome of the recipe depends on it.

To weigh the eggs (whole, whites, or yolks), first place them in a small bowl and lightly beat them with a fork. Don't incorporate any air or whip them up; simply beat them just enough to break up their jelly-like texture. Then set a second bowl on your scale, turn the scale to zero, and pour in exactly the quantity of egg called for. The advantage of beating eggs lightly before weighing them is that you can drizzle them evenly into the measuring cup or bowl.

Gelatin sheets: Gelatin sheets give better, more delicate results to finished products than powdered gelatin. Most professional bakers only use gelatin sheets, but they can be difficult to find in certain countries. Amazon.com and kingarthurflour.com are good sources for them. Gelatin sheets are classified according to their gel grade (gold, silver, platinum, and bronze): I recommend using the silver grade, which is a reliable intermediate grade. To use gelatin sheets, you must first soften them in water and then squeeze out the excess water before adding the sheets to the mixture you plan to gel. The mixture to which the gelatin is added should be warm or hot, and stirred until the gelatin dissolves completely.

Ground almonds: For the most delicate texture, make sure your almonds are finely ground (and ideally sifted). If you're not sure of the degree of fineness, it's advisable to process them with a blade knife before incorporating them into the recipe; this is particularly important for *macarons*.

Oven temperature: I use convection heat when baking and the recipes in this book reflect that. If your oven does not include this option, increase the oven heat by 25°F (14°C) in each recipe and keep an eye on the baking time. Bear in mind that ovens are quirky by nature. You'll need to observe how yours behaves and possibly make minor adjustments to the baking times given.

Preparation of baking pans: Correct preparation of your baking pans can be a make-or-break step, so don't skimp on the time you spend on this. Make sure your pans are ready and waiting to have the batter poured into them. When you butter a pan, don't leave any spots or corners untended. Then lightly dust the pan with flour, turn it upside down, and tap it gently to remove any excess. Parchment paper on the bottom of the pan will greatly facilitate your task; all you'll have to do when your cake is out of the pan is peel off the parchment paper carefully. I'm also a great fan of non-stick baking spray as a failsafe alternative. If you use it, there is no need to dust the sprayed pans with flour, but do make sure to wipe off any excess spray with paper towel. (It's only for the Bordeaux Tea Cakes on page 29 that you need to turn the molds upside down to let the excess drip off.)

Scales: Though I have given cup, tablespoon, and teaspoon measures throughout this book, I highly recommend weighing ingredients using a scale—preferably a digital scale—when baking, as it allows you to be far more accurate and precise with your ingredient measurements. Digital scales are affordable and available all over the world. I actually bought mine on a visit to the US!

Vegetable oil: Always use a neutral-flavored vegetable oil that won't impart any taste to the baked goods. I much prefer canola oil, but you can also use sunflower seed oil or grapeseed oil.

Whipping cream stabilizer: To make a long-lasting whipped cream, I use a gelatin-based stabilizer in certain recipes like my Vanilla Mille-Feuille (see page 126). The stabilizer does not change the texture or flavor of the whipped cream, but helps it keep its shape much longer. It can be purchased online in the US at kingarthurflour.com. You can also use a cornstarch-based stabilizer, such as Dr. Oetker Whip It (available in Canada). To get your whipped cream to last longer without additives, use an immersion blender instead of electric beaters to whip the cream. It won't hold its shape as long as the stabilized whipped creams, but it's a good alternative.

Index

Sources

Here's a list of stores worldwide where I often source ingredients and equipment for my recipes. As I live in Paris, I regularly visit the boutiques listed in the France section, but I also love popping into the stores in the other sections when I'm in town. Of course, much is now available on the Internet; I've included my favorite online sources at the end.

FRANCE

A. Simon
52 rue Montmartre, 75002 Paris
For baking equipment, such as disposable piping bags, tips, and molds.

Déco Relief
deco-relief.fr
6 rue Montmartre, 75001 Paris
For concentrated flavors (orange flower water, jasmine, and violet, among many others) and for silicone baking molds.

Les Délices d'Orient
52 avenue Emile-Zola, 75015 Paris
For alum stones, a wide variety of whole nuts, phyllo pastry, and raw pistachios.

G. Detou
58 rue Tiquetonne, 75002 Paris
For a wide range of baking supplies that includes couverture chocolate in bulk, concentrated vanilla extract, vanilla beans, ground almonds, whole nuts, powdered food coloring, and *poudre à crème*.

Tang Frères
48 avenue d'Ivry, 75013 Paris
An Asian supermarket that stocks sticky rice flour, custard powder, sesame seeds, adzuki beans, spices, pandanus leaf flavoring, and more.

UNITED KINGDOM

Cake Craft Shop
cakecraftshop.co.uk
Unit 8, North Downs Business Park, Lime Pit Lane, Sevenoaks, Kent TN13 2TL
7 Chatterton Road, Bromley, Kent BR2 9QW
For every cake-decorating tool under the sun, as well as baking supplies like rice paper, gold leaf, and gum arabic.

Creative Cookware
creativecookware.co.uk
89 Rose Street, Edinburgh EH2 3DT
For high-quality baking equipment and kitchen utensils.

Divertimenti
divertimenti.co.uk
227–229 Brompton Road, London, SW3 2EP
74–75 Marylebone High Street, London, W1U 5JW
For a wide range of high-quality bakeware and cookware.

Kitchens Cookshop
kitchenscookshop.co.uk
4&5 Quiet Street, Bath BA1 2JS
167 Whiteladies Road, Bristol BS8 2SQ
14 High Street, Cardiff CF10 1AX
For baking equipment and supplies, as well as a high-quality assortment of food processors and other kitchen machines.

Livsstil
livsstil.co.uk
4 The Minories, Temple Court, Birmingham B4 6AG
48 Chapel Walk, Sheffield S1 2PD
20 High Street, Burton Upon Trent, Staffs DE14 1HU
Unit SU152 (Ground Floor), North Mall, The Westfield Centre, Derby DE1 2PQ
For basic bakeware and some specialty items.

Squires Kitchen Shop
squires-shop.com/uk
3 Waverley Lane, Farnham, Surrey, GU9 8BB
For baking equipment as well as a large assortment of cake decorating items, and ingredients like gelatin, flavor extracts, and couverture chocolate.

Sugarshack
sugarshack.co.uk
Unit 12, Bowmans Trading Estate, Westmoreland Road, London NW9 9RL
For baking supplies, including molds and specialty pastry tools.

Surbiton Sugarcraft
surbitonart.co.uk
140 Hook Road, Surbiton, London KT6 5BZ
For good-quality baking equipment as well as specialized sugarcraft utensils and ingredients.

UNITED STATES

Broadway Panhandler
broadwaypanhandler.com
65 East 8th Street
New York, NY 10003
A New York institution. Good-quality baking equipment and tools.

Gloria's Cake & Candy Supply
gloriascakecandysuplys.com/store
12453 Washington Boulevard, Los Angeles, CA 90066
From cake pans to flavorings, pastry bags to kitchen torches, this well-stocked store has it all. It also offers classes and has a good book and DVD department.

Local Root
localroot.com
221 Concord Avenue, Cambridge, MA, 02138
2284 Washington Street, Newton Lower Falls, MA 02462
High-quality cookware and bakeware with an eye for good design. Additionally, a nice assortment of knives and cookbooks.

New York Cake
nycake.com
56 West 22nd Street
NY, NY 10010
A fabulously well-stocked emporium of baking and decorating equipment. Also offers international shipping.

Rainbow Grocery
rainbow.coop
1745 Folsom Street, San Francisco, CA 94103
A well-known emporium for nuts, spices, and baking chocolates in bulk, as well as a well-chosen selection of baking pans and other basic baking equipment.

Le Sanctuaire
le-sanctuaire.com
315 Sutter Street, San Francisco, CA 94108
This high-end store is known for selling equipment for molecular gastronomy, but also happens to have a good selection of kitchen scales, pastry tools, and food processors.

Spun Sugar
spunsugar.com
1611 University Avenue, Berkeley, CA 94703
A baker's dream, selling decorating supplies, well-priced bulk chocolate, and tools for sugarcraft and confectionery.

Surfas
surfasonline.com
8777 West Washington Boulevard, Culver City, CA 90232
An eclectic selection of specialty ingredients like tapioca pearls and high-quality cocoa and couverture chocolates, as well as kitchen equipment. Classes are also offered.

Zabar's
zabars.com
2245 Broadway, New York, NY 10024
The second floor of this iconic New York delicatessen offers a well-chosen selection of professional bakeware, appliances, and kitchen gadgets.

ONLINE

For baking tools and specialty items, including ingredients:
UK
bakingdeco.co.uk
cakecraftshop.co.uk
cake-stuff.com
meilleurduchef.com (an English/French website)
US
confectioneryhouse.com
kitchenkrafts.com
pastrychef.com
thebakerskitchen.net

For a wide range of cooking equipment and accessories:
UK
johnlewis.com
lakeland.co.uk
US
surlatable.com
williams-sonoma.com

Acknowledgments

I am fortunate to have among my family and friends many people who encouraged me to fulfill my dream,
first of creating a blog and then a book. I am extremely grateful to you all:

First of all, my parents, especially my mother, from whom I have inherited a love of cooking and good food
Leandro, who pressed me to start writing my blog and who tasted so many of the dishes I made
Nicolas, my brother, for submitting my blog for the Golden Blog Awards,
the positive outcome of which attracted so many new readers
Sébastien, for his unshakeable confidence in me
Ryma, who believed in my project and suggested I write this book
Kate and Helen, for making this English-language edition possible
Carmella, who translated my recipes and text as faithfully as possible and with immense meticulousness
Camila Nicácio, the author of *Courts métrages, poèmes visuels*,
for the culinary haikus that are dotted so poetically throughout this book
Touria, Lalla Myriam, and Lalla Fatima, for their friendship and their boundless love for the cuisine of their country,
and also for teaching me so many wonderful Moroccan recipes. We still have a great deal ahead of us, I'm certain
Stéphanie, for our unfailing friendship, despite the distance and borders that separate us
Ariane, who graciously ate so many meals at my home and willingly tried so many of my experiments
Yves and Claudine, with whose kind help I baked numerous cakes when my oven gave up on me
Peter and Peggy, for their delicious dinners that prove that cooking only strengthens friendships
Nadine, for all the delicious Swiss specialties she introduced to me
Jean-Philippe, for all the PR work and for his comments
Monique and Marie—perched on high heels, champagne glasses in hand—for opening their kitchen to me
and for the uncontrollable fits of giggles. Thanks to them, I was able to begin my cooking workshops
Christelle, who has kept me at the professional kitchen and enabled me to continue the workshops I so enjoy
Monica, who organized my course in Algerian pastry-making,
for the shared delight in cooking and for our excursions to professional equipment stores
Valérie, for her chocolate cream, which is just out of this world
Moh Saïd and Hakim, for the time spent at the Délice de la Casbah
Hassen, for teaching me how to make *zalabia*, and Taoufik, for the *sfenj*
Audrey and Amélie, who transposed my ideas with such precision into magnificent photos
Arthur, who patiently waited in his mum's belly while we finished the photos before emerging into the world
Bruno, the pastry chef of Valentin, for sharing so many professional secrets
Monique Vaugeois of the G. Detou boutique, for her kindness and practical help
And of course all the regular readers of my blog, who, sometimes unknowingly, encouraged me
to share all the delicious dishes I've tasted, and who, in ever-growing numbers, made this book possible.
Heartfelt thanks to you all!